03/04/09

OHIYESA

OHIYESA

Charles Eastman, Santee Sioux

o3|0 4 |o9

RAYMOND WILSON

UNIVERSITY OF ILLINOIS PRESS   Urbana   Chicago   London

This book is printed on acid-free paper.

Library of Congress Cataloging in Publication Data

Wilson, Raymond, 1945-
  Ohiyesa (The Winner)

  Bibliography: p.
  Includes index.
  1. Eastman, Charles Alexander, 1858-1939.
2. Santee Indians—Biography.   I. Title.
E99.S22E188   970.004'97 [B]   82-4937
ISBN 0-252-00978-9   AACR2

To William T., Frances A., Sharon K., and Raymond N. Wilson

CONTENTS

PREFACE

While preparing for a doctoral degree in Native American history, I read for the first time Robert M. Utley's *The Last Days of the Sioux Nation*. In that unsurpassed study of the Ghost Dance among the Sioux, I came upon the name of Dr. Charles Alexander Eastman (Ohiyesa), a Santee Sioux who served as government physician at Pine Ridge Agency, South Dakota, from 1890 to 1893. The fact that he was both a Sioux and a physician, and that he had attended to the wounded after the tragedy at Wounded Knee, intrigued me. I began to study this man whose life, I quickly surmised, was dramatic enough to be made into a film or to serve as the basis for a good historical novel.

Charles Eastman spent much of his childhood within the traditional society of the Eastern Sioux. He received training that would prepare him for a life as a skillful hunter and brave warrior. And at the very time that his people faced the destruction of their traditional culture by an alien society, Eastman at the age of fifteen was abruptly introduced into white civilization. His responses to this complete change in his life, and his successes and failures as an Indian operating in white society, are worthy of study.

Eastman attended such prestigious schools as Dartmouth College and the Boston University School of Medicine. His career, in and out of government service, was varied. He served within the Indian service as government physician, clerk of the revision of the Sioux allotment roll, and finally Indian inspector. His life independent of the Bureau of Indian Affairs included such work as traveling Indian secretary for the Young Men's Christian Association and helping to found the Boy Scouts of America. He was a charter member and later

president of the Society of American Indians, a reform organization
dedicated to the advancement of Indians and the interests of Indians.
In addition to his life as an Indian ombudsman, he won renown as
an author and gifted lecturer. It is perhaps in these latter roles that
Eastman distinguished himself. Through his writings, which include
such books as *Indian Boyhood, From the Deep Woods to Civilization, The Soul of the Indian: An Interpretation, The Indian Today:
The Past and Future of the First American, Indian Heroes and Great
Chieftains,* and *Old Indian Days,* plus numerous articles, he hoped to
make non-Indians aware of the Indians' contributions to American
civilization and thereby reduce the chasm between two seemingly in-
compatible cultures.

The years which encompass Eastman's adult life were important
ones for Native Americans, and several significant studies have been
written which chronicle the reform of federal Indian policy during
the last three decades of the nineteenth century and the first four
decades of the twentieth century. Eastman frequently spoke out on
important issues affecting Indians, especially in the case of the General Allotment Act or Dawes Severalty Act of 1887, which attempted
to solve the "Indian problem" by recreating the American Indian as
an independent yeoman farmer. He also worked closely with the two
most important reform organizations founded in the 1880s to protect
Indians from injustice and to influence legislation on their behalf:
the Indian Rights Association, established in 1882 by Herbert Welsh
of Philadelphia, who served for several decades as its leader, and the
Lake Mohonk Conference of Friends of the Indian, created in 1883
in New York by the Smiley brothers. Members of these organizations, while championing Indian rights, often admired Indian values
but thought them inappropriate to the present age. Eastman and a
few other acculturated Indians became for the white reformers living
exhibits of what Indians could achieve in a lifetime. But Eastman
never entirely rejected his Indian heritage. He took pride in his
Indianness as well as pride in his accomplishments within the dominant society. A person could function within both worlds by adopting the best attributes from each according to Eastman, who would
spend much of his life in an attempt to prove such a contention. At
the end of his life, unlike other ostensibly acculturated Indians, he
could not return to the reservation to die; nor could he remain in a

society in which he was forever unique, the exception to the rule that proved Indian inferiority. He chose instead to end his life in a world of his own making never totally absorbed in or free from the influences of either the deep woods or civilization.

During his adult years he became, in the minds of his non-Indian colleagues in the reform organizations, the quintessential, modern Indian spokesman. He was, however, never a systematic thinker when it came to reform of federal Indian policy. The problems proved to be more complex than his proposed solutions would have otherwise indicated. His personal experiences in both worlds no doubt contributed to his facile conclusions and the conclusions of others, that since he had achieved fame (if not fortune) in an alien culture, other Indians could also progress and learn to survive and prosper in a modern world. For many years, Eastman allowed himself to be exhibited as living proof of the reformers' faith in progress.

Unlike so many other self-made men in the late nineteenth century who glorified their success as if it were a metaphor for Gilded Age America, Eastman never so much praised his creator as he praised the gifts that he believed all Indians possessed. Chance, he would maintain for many years, was all that separated him from his people confined to the reservations. Chance alone, however, could not explain his success, nor were other Indians as inherently gifted as Eastman claimed, but to his honor he never became embittered towards his people who failed to equal his accomplishments.

When one considers Eastman's rise to prominence from such humble beginnings, his story is even more remarkable. He lived a long life (1858–1939) and was involved in a myriad of activities, yet there has not been a full-scale published study of him.

A full-scale study is made difficult by the lack of a depository containing a major collection entitled the Charles A. Eastman Papers. Information about Eastman was obtained by searching through collections of persons with whom he was associated to obtain letters and other materials, but very little of this primary material can be described as personal. Much of the information available concerning his work for the government can be found in the National Archives, Washington, D.C., and the Federal Records Center in Kansas City, Missouri. Other constraints were that correspondence and interviews with his relatives are limited, and because Eastman was involved in

[handwritten margin note: some of my informal notes]

several controversies and his marriage was considerably less than successful, some informants I contacted have wished to remain anonymous. I have had to rely upon Eastman's books and articles combined
with a varied and disparate documentary record to recreate his life.
This then is his story.

ACKNOWLEDGMENTS

In the process of collecting material and information on Charles A. Eastman, I became indebted to numerous archivists, librarians, and other individuals throughout the United States. In particular, I would like to thank Richard Crawford, Ed Barrese, and Jerry Clark, Natural Resources Branch of the National Archives, Washington, D.C.; R. Reed Whitaker and Bob Knecht, Federal Archives and Records Center, Kansas City, Missouri; Tina Ashton, Baker Library, Dartmouth College; Susan Rockwood, Johnson Reprint Corporation; Charles Gillette, New York State Museum; Ellen Sowchek, YMCA Historical Library; Marilyn Hamilton, BSA Historical Library; Susan L. Boone, Smith College; Robert H. Irrmann, Beloit College; Mrs. Philip S. Haring, Knox College; William E. Wallace, College of Idaho; and F. W. Hyde, Jr., Grace Hospital, Detroit, Michigan. In addition, Herbert B. Fowler, Hazel W. Hertzberg, Robert M. Utley, Frederick W. Turner III, James D. Ewing, Grace Moore, Bessie Jones, and Donald Jackson provided valuable assistance.

I would also like to acknowledge Richard N. Ellis, Donald C. Cutter, William M. Dabney, Richmond L. Clow, and L. G. Moses—scholars whom I have worked with and learned from. Nancy Krueger, Assistant Editor of the University of Illinois Press, provided valuable manuscript editing. Portions of this book have previously appeared in *South Dakota History* and *Minnesota History*. Financial assistance from the Student Research Allocations Committee at the University of New Mexico helped defray expenses of my research. Finally, I would like to thank my wife Sharon, who spent many tedious hours helping me complete this study.

CHAPTER 1

FROM THE DEEP WOODS

N EW YEAR'S DAY 1891 dawned clear and cold at Pine Ridge Reservation. The search party had left the agency an hour after sunrise and arrived at the battle site, eighteen miles away, a little after noon. Just north of the creek called Wounded Knee some in the party turned their wagons onto a side road that climbed a gentle slope to the cemetery while the rest halted along the agency road. West of the latter road and along the creek bed lay evidence of the battle. Except for the scorched and bare lodgepoles and a few abandoned wagons, the snow which had fallen during the previous two days and nights had softened and rounded some of the wreckage. Here and there an arm or leg emerged from the snow-draped landscape to reveal the awful secrets of the whitened mounds.

It had been three days since the battle and two days since the blizzard had forced the relief parties to abandon their search for survivors and seek shelter themselves at the agency. The wounded who had managed to reach the agency on their own, and the rest who were brought in by units of the Seventh Cavalry the night of December 29, were treated in the Episcopal chapel which, stripped of its pews, became an emergency hospital. The agency physician, a Santee Sioux, had worked himself to emotional and physical exhaustion. His understanding had been equally taxed, as much by his strained loyalties as by the human misery that surrounded him on the chapel's straw-covered floor.

But on that clear winter morning when in command of the search party that had reached the scene of the battle, Dr. Charles Eastman became momentarily a man lost between two worlds. One was the world of the grandfathers and his youth that had perished at

Wounded Knee; and the other was the world of his white bene-factors with its confusion of religions, its rigid interpretation of what was truly civilized, and its disinclination to tolerate any threat to progress. He could at that moment no more join those Sioux who defied the government and its programs of civilization in their long-ing after a messiah, the promise of the Ghost Dance Religion, than he could embrace a civilization that now defied his comprehension. The slaughter raised troubling questions in the doctor's mind. Rapid-fire Hotchkiss guns had also made a mockery of the proclamations of peace and good will that normally attended the season.

He climbed down from his horse and began to search frantically for survivors while those Sioux in his charge began crying their an-guish and singing their death songs. He dug into the mounds of bodies and looked under every abandoned wagon. Incredibly, some of the Sioux had survived both the storm of shells the morning of the battle and the blizzard that followed. The Whites in the party grew increasingly nervous as they searched the debris. They feared that the Sioux in the search party and those Sioux who watched from horse-back on nearby hills would seek vengeance for the slaughter of their kin. Someone, the white teamsters insisted, should return to the agency to fetch a cavalry escort. Because the doctor rode the swiftest horse, the mission fell to him. It was just as well. The few survivors had been found and put into wagons which were then on their way to the agency. The dead would be gathered from the battlefield by the teamsters, who had agreed to bury the grim harvest at two dollars a body.

As Eastman left behind the field of death, his thoughts returned to the living at the agency, where his services were needed far more just then. Despite his outrage at what had happened, he avoided making quick judgments about Christian love and the lofty ideals of the white man in which, up until then, he had placed such trust. He had been taken from his Indian world when still a youth and trained in the civilized world for a life of service. He had returned to his people. Indeed, what else could he have done but return? Who among the Whites would trust their lives to a doctor, however well educated, who had once been trained in the warrior's craft and whose color re-vealed his heritage? And what better way to foster civilization of the savage than to show what the savage could accomplish given the chance? Treating the sick was only one of the important functions that he could perform on the reservation.

An educated Indian such as Eastman could help to ease in the transition of other Indians from savagery to civilization. The old ways of Indians were dying, and Indians who defiantly refused to make the transition might very well suffer the same fate as the Sioux ghost dancers. Civilized society could be as vicious and dangerous as uncivilized society, as Wounded Knee had made abundantly clear. Civilized society, however, had the numbers, the advanced technology, and the spirit of the age on its side. The time for unfettered Plains Indian cultures, for unfettered Indian cultures in general, had passed, giving Indians no other choice but to walk the white man's road.

Charles Eastman had traveled that road and could serve as a guidepost to other Indians. Those who could not or would not follow would perish at the reservation. Only one road led from the reservation, though few Indians had traveled it. What remained unclear to Eastman that New Year's Day as he rode his horse toward Pine Ridge Agency was whether he should remain at the reservation to serve as a model to other Indians, or whether he should seek his own destiny in the white world.

Before the arrival of Europeans in the New World, the inhabitants of what would become the United States had their own distinct names for themselves. Eventually they would be known collectively as Indians. Some were food gatherers, others food producers. Some were aggressive, others docile. Although these aboriginal societies shared many similar attitudes regarding social organization and religious ceremonies, at the same time, they were a diverse people.

One method of categorizing and studying Indians is by the language they spoke. Siouan, one of the major language families, is spoken by Dakotas, or Sioux, as they are more widely known. It was the French who ultimately shortened and distorted the Ojibway (Chippewa) word "Naduesiu" to "Sioux." Since these people officially call themselves the Sioux today, that name will be used in this study.

The Sioux are divided into the Eastern Sioux, the Middle Sioux, and the Western Sioux, which are in turn separated into seven tribes. Among the Eastern or Santee Sioux are the Mdewakantons, the

Wahpekutes, the Sissetons, and the Wahpetons, who all spoke the "D" or Dakota dialect. The Yanktons and Yanktonais made up the Middle division and spoke the "N" or Nakota dialect, while the Western division was composed of the Teton Sioux, who spoke the "L" or Lakota dialect. The latter were by far the most numerous, the most warlike, and indeed the most renowned of the three main divisions.

It was not until the seventeenth century that Europeans established contact with the Eastern division or Santee Sioux. The Santees were then primarily an agricultural people. At the time of initial contact they were living near Mille Lacs Lake in what is now central Minnesota. The Santees had migrated over the centuries to that region perhaps from the Ohio Valley. The Santees supplemented their production of crops with hunting deer and buffalo, fishing, and harvesting wild rice. Toward the end of the eighteenth century, they began to make the transition to a plains culture which had already been developing among the Middle and Western Sioux.[1]

Much has been written about the persons who made the earliest contacts with the Santees. Such French explorers as Pierre Esprit Radisson, Medard Chouart, Sieur des Groseilliers, and Father Louis Hennepin, a Recollet missionary, provided valuable reports on the culture of the Santees, though such pieces were often laden with ethnocentric observations.

Toward the middle of the eighteenth century, the Santees were driven southward from their home around Mille Lacs Lake by the Ojibways. This forced migration helped accelerate their transition to a plains culture. With the expulsion of the French from America in 1763, English explorers appeared among the Santees. Again, observations regarding their customs and manners were provided by such persons as Captain Jonathan Carver, who visited the Santees in 1766, and Peter Pond, a trader among the Sioux from 1773 to 1775.

During the American Revolution the Sioux sided with the British. Many saw limited action in several battles along the central Mississippi River. U.S. independence in 1783 became the next major influence on the lives of the Santees. The results of U.S. Indian policy upon the Santee Sioux remain to this day a matter of intense controversy.[2]

Lieutenant Zebulon M. Pike in 1805 and in 1806 negotiated the first treaties between the United States and the Santees. As with most treaties made with Indians, the methods employed by the government representatives are often points of extreme contention. The Santees relinquished about 100,000 acres of land through the Pike treaties. Pike also tried to gain their allegiance to the United States and at the same time to cease their hostilities with the Ojibways, their traditional enemies. The Santees received in return for their land and their solemn pledges presents valued at $200, some whiskey, and $2000. Pike expressed great pride in his accomplishments; he estimated that the land cession alone was worth over $200,000.

Pike's efforts to obtain the loyalty of the Santees proved ineffective. When the United States and England went to war once again in 1812, most of the Santees sided with the British due to the effective diplomacy of the British traders and the quality of the gifts they distributed. Some Santee bands switched sides as the war progressed, lured away from the British by Americans who had come to appreciate the advantages gained through largesse. When the Treaty of Ghent in 1814 ended the War of 1812, tribes who had allied themselves with the British signed new treaties with the United States, reaffirming their pledges of peace and friendship. Several Santee bands signed such treaties during the summer of 1815.

Wars and treaties created an intense factionalism in Indian societies. Until the War of 1812, tribes in the eastern United States could adopt a playoff policy between the young republic and England, its major adversary. Once the war was concluded, Indian relations became primarily domestic relations for the United States. Indians no longer figured prominently in the clash of imperial interests. They now represented simply impediments to progress and to the peaceful occupation of the nation's interior. The government adopted various policies that would in time bring civilization to the Indians, policies whose goals remained constant, but whose means were ever-changing.

The most important revision in early nineteenth century federal Indian policy was the concept of removal of all the eastern tribes to the "Great American Desert" which, it was believed, would prove undesirable to white settlers. This policy, conceived during the Jeffersonian era, further included the ultimate assimilation of Indian people into the mainstream of the dominant society after they had acquired "civilization." Lands were granted in perpetuity to the Indians when they signed treaties, and legislation in Congress defined the limits of a permanent Indian Territory and the restrictions placed upon unauthorized Whites in the region. Indian tribes were regarded as domestic, dependent nations, and Indian agents as surrogate ambassadors. Tribes were given limited prerogatives of self-government, and their agreements with the United States were ratified in the Senate. By persuasion and force the bulk of the eastern tribes were removed beyond the Mississippi and established on the fringes of the Great Plains within the bounds of what eventually became the states of Oklahoma and Kansas.[3]

The Indian service, which provided the official contact between Indians and the government, also underwent a substantial change in the years after the War of 1812. In 1822 the government discontinued the factory system regulating Indian trade. Independent traders had long chafed at the government's monopoly. Principles of free enterprise were again recognized after a vigorous lobbying campaign led by John Jacob Astor and Thomas Hart Benton.

In 1824 a Bureau of Indian Affairs was created within the War Department with the intention of relieving the Secretary of War of so many tedious details. John C. Calhoun established the bureau on his own authority, appointing Thomas L. McKenney as its head. McKenney had served the War Department previously as Superintendent of Indian Trade from 1816 until its abolition in 1822. Finally, in 1832 Congress established the office of Commissioner of Indian Affairs. The commissioner was to be appointed by the President and to serve under the Secretary of War. As a part of the larger Indian Reorganization Act of 1832, this was an attempt to satisfy some of the critics of the Indian service. Many positions were abolished while others, such as that of the commissioner, were altered and clarified.[4]

Administrators of the Indian bureau were to be upstanding Christians of unimpeachable character. Although most commissioners proved to be men of this type, numbers of their subalterns were less than inspirational in their devotion to their wards. One interesting provision of the act was that tribal annuities were to be paid to the chiefs rather than the individual members of the tribes. The practice of paying annuities to individuals had proved a lever for removal.

Paying the chiefs, however, served to reestablish their position within the tribe, a development which would subsequently exasperate the assimilationists in and out of government who regarded destruction of tribalism as the first step toward civilization.

Opinion was virtually unanimous among the leaders of the Indian service that agriculture was superior to hunting as a way of life and was a necessary step in the "Americanization" of the Indian. Arguments about how this process could be accomplished were numerous and not always equal in their persuasiveness to the commissioner. Most agreed that the best way to deal with the Indians was to either remove them beyond the borders of civilization or confine them to reservations. Progress was equated with the white way of life and too often the Indian stood in the way of that progress. To protect the Indian from the worst attributes of civilization until such time that he could be absorbed peacefully within the larger society was the mission of the reformers. Yet even a cursory examination of the history of the Indian tribes during the period of Indian removal leads one to the conjecture that they could hardly have been worse off if they had remained subjects of the Whites in their ancestral homes.

The transformation of the Indian from savage to citizen through education was founded upon the Civilization Fund. Starting in 1819, Congress authorized $10,000 to be spent annually to complete the task. As no administrative machinery existed, the government invited churches and benevolent societies to request money from the fund for establishing schools. In the 1840s the government was still expending only its original contribution but by this time private groups and many of the tribes themselves were providing upwards of $150,000 annually to the fund. The House committee which had created the program in 1819 had neatly summarized the philosophy underlying assimilation: "Put into the hands of [Indian] children the primer and the hoe, and they will naturally, in time, take hold of the plough . . . and they will grow up in habits of morality and industry."[5]

For most of the nineteenth century down to the 1880s most of the proposals for advancing Indian civilization so as to foster assimilation were Christianization, education, and the appreciation of private property through farming. The variable factor remained the consistency with which these policies were applied. The 1850s, the decade of Eastman's birth, witnessed the notion of a permanent Indian country shattered by the rapidly advancing white population and the proposed railroad network devised to serve it. That this concept became obsolete was not specifically the fault of either the Indian bureau or of the Department of the Interior which, by an act of Congress in 1849, took over tribal management from the War Department. The nation's attention was diverted by more pressing matters.

In his 1856 report, Commissioner George Manypenny expressed concern for the welfare of the Indians when he advised the adoption of new codes and regulations governing Indian affairs. Because "the existing laws for the protection of the persons and property of the Indian wards . . . [were] sadly defective . . . ," new and more stringent statutes were required. In all the clamour between the antislavery and proslavery parties in the Kansas Territory, the rights and interests of the Indians had been completely overlooked. In many ways the good conduct and patience of the Indians contrasted favorably with the disorderly and lawless conduct of many of their white antagonists. "While they [Whites] have quarrelled about the African," Manypenny wrote, these same white men "have united upon the soil of Kansas in wrong doing toward the Indian!"[6] It was evident to the commissioner that there was no place in the West where Indians could be placed with a reasonable assurance that they would escape molestation or inundation by the Whites. This was true for Indians who had been resettled in the West as well as for Indians who had been placed upon reservations near their homelands and who were now surrounded by Whites.

Succeeding commissioners also recognized the inadequacies of the removal philosophy as well as the limitations of a reservation policy. A need existed to create a new policy for the domestic, dependent nations. Commissioner Charles Mix in 1858 emphasized that removal from place to place had prevented Indians from acquiring settled habits and a taste for civilized pursuits; that assignment of large areas to the tribes had postponed any increased appreciation for private property; and that the payment of annuities tended to promote habits of indolence and profligacy while constantly subjecting Indians to victimization by the unscrupulous and unsympathetic businessmen and land speculators. In 1862 Secretary of the Interior Caleb Smith questioned the wisdom of treating the tribes as "quasiindependent nations," suggesting instead that it would be more realistic to regard them strictly as wards of the government, however unpleasant-sounding that word might be.[7]

It was obvious to these observers that the only practical and humane answer to the "Indian problem" was to assimilate the Native American into the dominant society. The central question was how best to accomplish this task. Here, according to the prevailing wisdom, were comparatively a Stone Age people, culturally separated from their white neighbors by more than three thousand years of accomplishment, who were to be transformed within the space of a few decades. Could the Indians be forced to give up their cultures without any struggle?

The Santees were only one of many tribes to rebel against federal Indian policy. The record of federal relations with the Santees between the War of 1812 and the great uprising of 1862 is only a small part of a larger tragedy affecting U.S. Indians.

During the War of 1812 no serious efforts had been made to occupy the Santee land purchased by Pike. In 1817, however, Major Stephen H. Long headed an expedition to inspect the area Pike had obtained. Long's report, as well as the ones submitted earlier by Pike, did not contain a great deal of information on the customs and traditions of the Santees, but Long did indicate the location of several Santee villages. From the geographical data provided by Pike and Long, a site was selected to build a military post.

Major Thomas Forsyth, an experienced Indian agent, left St. Louis in 1819 and headed northward with provisions for the soon-to-be-constructed fort. He held several councils with the Indians where he distributed belatedly those gifts earlier promised by Pike. Forsyth emphasized the benefits of having a military post close by. From the records Forsyth kept, it was apparent that many of the Santees, like so many other Indian tribes after initial contact with a culture possessing superior technology, had not only become dependent on such technology, but had also acquired some of the bad habits of the alien culture, especially the consumption of liquor. Forsyth's suggestion of applying the golden rule while negotiating treaties with Indians was indeed noble, but it had already been violated by Pike.[8]

Fort St. Anthony was completed by late summer 1819. Six years later it was renamed Fort Snelling after its commander, Colonel

Josiah Snelling. The fort also became the headquarters for the Indian agent, a position held by Major Lawrence Taliaferro for nearly twenty years (1820–39).

Although Taliaferro often displayed a conventional ethnocentrism in his relations with Indians, he was nevertheless far from the stereotypical corrupt Indian agent. He frequently attacked the unscrupulous actions of Whites, including both military personnel and civilians, which he believed were attempts to defraud the Indians and the government. At St. Peter's Agency, located at the confluence of the Mississippi and Minnesota rivers, Taliaferro attempted to make his wards truly civilized, meaning that his charges had to relinquish their customs and culture.[9]

Civilization programs resulted often in the growing dependency of Indians on annuity payments, the increased distribution of liquor by traders, the constant pressure to acquire more Indian land, the attempts by missionaries to convert Indians to Christianity, and the feeble and unrealistic efforts to make Indians white farmers. The Santees faced these and other assaults upon their traditional way of life.

When Minnesota became a territory in 1849, Alexander Ramsey, the newly appointed governor, advocated the liquidation of Santee land claims. Through deception, intimidation, and liberal use of whiskey, two treaties were negotiated with the Santees in 1851. In the Treaty of Traverse des Sioux and the Treaty of Mendota, the Santees ceded virtually all of their remaining lands. They became squatters on their traditional homeland once the Senate ratified the treaties, and were allowed to remain on certain sections until relocated. In return for the cession, they were to receive from both treaties $3,075,000. From this sum held in trust and its accrued interest over the next fifty years, the government would pay for programs taht would help to make the Santees civilized. As happened with nearly all treaties that stressed civilization programs supposedly in the Indians' best interests, those who actually benefited most were traders, government officials, and settlers who coveted Indian lands.[10]

From the white perspective, no civilization program would be complete without missionaries. The Santees received several sincere and dedicated men. Among the first to come were Gideon H. and Samuel W. Pond, Dr. Thomas S. Williamson, and Stephen R. Riggs. The Ponds had been fired with religious enthusiasm during the years of

revivalism known as the Second Great Awakening that especially
affected residents of New York and the Connecticut Valley. Armed
with nothing more than their fervor and their Bibles, and without
either training or support from the burgeoning domestic home mission societies, the Ponds set out to convert the heathen Santees in
1834. In succeeding years, besides establishing missions, they translated religious and educational tracts into a written form of the Sioux
language. Samuel Pond, the more prolific of the two, outlived Gideon
by thirteen years, dying in 1891.

Williamson and Riggs, on the other hand, were ordained Presby-
terians sent by the American Board of Commissioners for Foreign
Missions. Williamson, who earned a medical degree at Yale and
served as a missionary among the Sioux for forty-five years, dying in
1879, established one of the more successful missions among the
Santees at Lac qui Parle near the upper Minnesota River in 1835.
Riggs, who died in 1883, became one of the foremost authorities on
Siouan languages, ultimately publishing his *Grammar and Diction-
ary of the Dakota Language* in 1852. The sons of Williamson and
Riggs, John P. Williamson and Alfred L. Riggs, continued the work
of their fathers.

Although these missionaries and others frequently became spokes-
men against the wanton injustices inflicted upon the Santees, their
main goal was to eradicate what they considered the Indians' pagan
beliefs. The schism that missionaries created between Christianized
Indians and those who tenaciously clung to their traditional beliefs
caused much resentment and turmoil. And despite the work of missionaries, it was not until after the Santee Sioux Uprising of 1862,
when tribal morale was at its lowest, that they succeeded in winning
many converts.[11]

One of the earliest converts to the civilization programs among the
Santees was Charles Eastman's great grandfather, Mahpiya Wichasta
(Cloud Man), born about 1780. His adoption of civilization according to the white man can be directly linked to a dreadful experience
he had while hunting buffalo during the winter of 1828–29. Caught
in a ravaging blizzard, he almost died. In desperation, finding little
succor from his gods, he turned to the Christian God for help and
vowed upon deliverance to walk the white man's road. Several followers of Cloud Man also decided to join him when he determined

to renounce hunting in favor of farming. Agent Taliaferro enthusiastically supported such a resolution, and with his help, Cloud Man
and his followers established the village of Eatonville near Lake Calhoun six miles from Fort Snelling. This venture appeared to the agent
and missionaries as the first fruits of civilization among the Santees,
with a great harvest sure to follow. What followed, however, was disappointment. Although the farming experiment at Eatonville had to
be abandoned in 1839 because of its vulnerability to Ojibway attacks,
and despite repeated crop failures, Cloud Man clung to his faith in
the superiority of white civilization and continued to support the
programs of the government and the missionaries until he died in
1863.[12]

Most other Santees were less sanguine than Cloud Man. By the
late 1850s, they were a homeless people, riddled by factionalism. Into
this world of turmoil a baby was born on February 19, 1858, near
Redwood Falls, Minnesota, to one of Cloud Man's granddaughters.
The child's father was Ite Wakanhdi Ota (Many Lightnings), a
Wahpeton Sioux. Both parents were descendants from a long line of
Santee leaders. Many Lightnings' father and grandfather were chiefs,
and his mixed-blood wife, Wakantankanwin (Goddess), whose En-
glish name was Mary Nancy Eastman, was the granddaughter of
Chief Cloud Man. Mary Nancy's mother, Wakan inajin win (Stands
Sacred), had married Captain Seth Eastman, the noted artist.

Seth Eastman, born in Maine in 1808, was graduated from West
Point as a topographical engineer in 1829. The captain met Stands
Sacred while stationed at Fort Snelling in 1830. That same year,
Stands Sacred gave birth to Mary Nancy. Eastman left his wife and
child when he was reassigned by the War Department to conduct a
railroad survey in Louisiana in 1833. He did, however, establish credit
for them at Henry Hastings Sibley's store at the fort. Sibley, an early
fur trader in the region and the first state governor of Minnesota,
would later lead the militia against the Santees in 1862. Eastman
returned to Fort Snelling in 1841 and served as its commander until
1848. Accompanying the captain was his white wife, Mary Hender-
son Eastman, born in Virginia in 1818. The second Mrs. Eastman
later wrote several books on the Sioux, most notably, *Dahcotah: Or,
Life and Legends of the Sioux around Fort Snelling*, published in
1849. No extant material has been located regarding the relationship

of the captain or his Virginia-born wife to his former Indian wife and child. During the 1850s the Bureau of Indian Affairs employed Eastman to illustrate the Indian tribes of the United States. Eastman retired from the service in 1863 and died twelve years later in Washington, D.C.

The marriage of Many Lightnings to Mary Nancy Eastman in 1847 was accomplished in a rather dubious manner. Mary Nancy, renowned for her beauty, had many Indian suitors. Because her favorite did not have the needed possessions to bestow on her family as a bride-price, they planned instead to elope. Many Lightnings secretly desired Mary Nancy. He learned about the planned elopement and its prearranged signal from the Indian suitor. Many Lightnings arrived ahead of his unsuspecting friend, and with a blanket over his head, sneaked off with her. When she discovered that she had eloped with the wrong man, Mary Nancy decided that Wakan Tanka (The Great Mystery or The Great Spirit), the Sioux chief deity, had punished her for disobedience to her parents. She vowed that she would accept such providence and remain Many Lightnings' wife. Her affection for Many Lightnings grew in time.[13]

From the union of Many Lightnings and Mary Nancy came four sons and one daughter. Mary Nancy died at about age twenty-eight from lingering complications resulting from the difficult birth of her son in February, 1858, and also from a severe throat infection. The infant, because of his mother's death, was given the humiliating name of Hakadah (The Pitiful Last). He was taken to be raised by his paternal grandmother, Uncheedah, who would become the one most responsible for his early education. Uncheedah was a traditionalist. Despite the influences and dramatic changes introduced into the Santees by the technologically superior white culture, she raised her grandson to become a warrior and hunter. She taught Hakadah about the pervading presence of the Spirit and Giver of Life in all things. The young boy was taught to adapt himself perfectly to nature by building his strength in body and spirit.

When still an infant he began to eat soup his grandmother made from pounded maize, strained wild rice, and venison broth. He grew strong. He learned early never to cry at night. Such self-control promoted both fearlessness and a sense of responsibility to his tribe, for his crying, if unchecked, might reveal the presence of the Indian camp to marauding bands of the Santees' enemies. Whenever he awoke at night, frightened and disoriented, Uncheedah quietly sang him a lullaby relating the deeds of brave young warriors.

The Santees, like all the Sioux, placed great importance upon bravery, instilled through example on the battlefield and on the hunt, but also through the games they devised. Some games, like the pony races, involved a strong spirit of competitiveness. If a boy declined to race for any reason, he was considered weak and was chided unmercifully. Another game which aroused the valour of young warriors through example was the lacrosse contest, which climaxed the events of the Midsummer's Feast, an annual gathering of many bands to celebrate a productive year. The competing bands selected young warriors to represent them in the contest. In 1862, Hakadah's band chose him. Being victorious in the game, his band bestowed upon the four-year-old boy the new name of Ohiyesa (The Winner), the name he retained even after he adopted an English one.

The first major test of a young Sioux's courage occurred when he was initiated into manhood. As part of the ritual of passage, a boy proved his courage by sacrificing a prized possession to Wakan Tanka. By performing such a personal sacrifice, he could then ask The Great Mystery to make him a great warrior and hunter. Although shaken by the request to sacrifice his dog, Ohiyesa, as he later remembered, "swallowed two or three big mouthfuls of heartache and the little warrior was master of the situation."

In spite of the emphasis placed on nurturing the virtue of bravery, Sioux children had many opportunities to pursue more pleasant tasks. One such activity was the annual sugar-making. Every spring, while the warriors hunted for game, the old men, the women, and the children made sugar. After obtaining brass and iron kettles in which to boil the sap, the women, Uncheedah among them, hollowed out birch trees in the shape of canoes to catch the sap. Ohiyesa and the young children were given the responsibility of gathering fuel for the fires, bringing it to the sugarhouse, and then watching the boiling pots of sap until it was ready to be poured. Once the sap was poured, the young boys protected the valuable cache from intruding animals. The sugar products gleaned from sugar-making lasted the tribe throughout the year. Activities such as sugar-making provided the children with a brief respite from the harsh realities of survival.[14]

By 1862, the Santees had been located along the southern side of the upper Minnesota River, living on a strip of land 150 miles long and 10 miles wide. They had sold the 150-mile-long, 10-mile-wide strip on the north side of the river in 1858 for $266,880, most of which went to pay debts that Indians owed to traders. The Wahpeton and Sisseton tribes were settled on the Upper or Yellow Medicine Agency, while the Medwakantons and Wahpekutes were placed on the Lower or Redwood Agency. Conditions on the reservation and events leading to the Sioux Uprising of 1862 have been subjects of considerable scholarly inquiry. Suffice to say, the reservation was a powder keg filled with depressed, bitter, and debt-ridden Indians having to deal with tribal factionalism, mismanaged government programs, inept and corrupt Whites, and late annuity payments. All that was needed was a spark, and that came on August 17, 1862, when four Indian youths murdered five white settlers. The Indians had been on a hunt near Acton, north of Redwood Agency. The deaths of the settlers resulted from foolish dares the young Indians made to one another. This incident, known as the "Acton Massacre," coupled with past injustices caused the Sioux Uprising of 1862.

Published accounts on the actual fighting are vast and need not be retold here. Several points should be noted, nevertheless. Most of the principal Santee leaders either refused to participate or gave limited support. The Santees at the Lower Agency were in the vanguard of the uprising. Yet because of the hundreds of Whites killed and mutilated, all the Santees were blamed. Listed among the leaders were Little Crow, Young Shakopee, and Red Middle Voice. Dissension regarding the proper strategy to employ spelled their doom. Attacks against the town of New Ulm and Fort Ridgely failed. By the end of September the Sioux Uprising was over, largely because of Colonel Henry Hastings Sibley's decisive victory over Little Crow at the Battle of Wood Lake.

The white citizens of Minnesota screamed for revenge. An extralegal court was established to try Indians for the atrocities they committed. Evidence presented was often circumstantial, and in one case the wrong Indian was executed. A total of 303 Indians received the death sentence by hanging. Fortunately, the matter was brought to the attention of President Abraham Lincoln, and he reduced the number to forty. Of this number, thirty-eight were ultimately exe-

cuted in a mass hanging held at Mankato on December 26, 1862.
The bodies were all buried in a common grave. Moreover, nearly all
the Santee Sioux were removed from Minnesota to Dakota Territory.
All treaties with them were abrogated, and the remaining annuity
payments went to victims of the uprising.[15] The Santees would later
contest the loss of annuity payments in a long, tedious claims case
(discussed in Chapter 6), in which Charles A. Eastman would play
a major role.

Separated from his father and two brothers after the 1862 Sioux
Uprising, Ohiyesa was among the fleeing Indians who escaped to
Canada. There, he received word that his father, Many Lightnings,
was among the thirty-eight "hostiles" hanged in the mass execution.
Ohiyesa was then adopted by his father's brother, Mysterious Medi-
cine, who was also called White Foot Print, Big Hunter, and Long
Rifle.

Groomed to become a successful warrior to avenge his father's
death, Ohiyesa learned well. Early in the morning he would be
awakened by a war whoop from his uncle, and he was expected to
jump to his feet, weapon in hand, and answer with a whoop of his
own. By the time he was nearly fifteen years old he had acquired such
traits as courage, patience, self-control, and generosity; and he was
eager to go to war.[16]

Ohiyesa's life suddenly changed with the appearance of his father.
Instead of being hanged, he was one of the fortunate "hostiles" whose
execution sentence was changed by President Lincoln to three years'
imprisonment at the federal penitentiary in Davenport, Iowa. While
in confinement, Many Lightnings fell under the influence and teachings of Dr. Thomas S. Williamson and Stephen R. Riggs. They converted Many Lightnings to the Christian religion, and he took the
Christian name of Jacob and the surname of his dead wife, Eastman.
In addition, Jacob's eldest son was Christianized and renamed John
Eastman. John later served as a Presbyterian minister for many years
at Flandreau, South Dakota.

After his release from prison in 1866, Jacob was placed on the
Santee Reservation, near the mouth of the Niobrara River, in north-
eastern Nebraska. Unhappy with conditions on the reservation, he
and several other Indian families left in 1869. They settled along the
Big Sioux River about forty miles from Sioux Falls, South Dakota.

Aided by the Reverend John P. Williamson, the group filed for and received homesteads in accordance with the Homestead Act of 1862 and the Sioux Treaty of 1868, which contained a provision allowing Indians to do so. This was the beginning of the Sioux community of Flandreau. After he had established himself there, Jacob started searching for his lost son.[17]

Locating his former tribe camped in the province of Manitoba, Canada, Jacob was reunited with his son after a ten-year separation. Ohiyesa, who had just returned from a hunt, reluctantly decided to go with his father back to Flandreau. He later recalled, "I little dreamed of anything unusual to happen on my return. As I approached our camp with my game on my shoulder, I had not the slightest premonition that I was suddenly to be hauled from my savage life into a life unknown to me hitherto."[18] Abruptly introduced to a new, alien existence in the world of white men, Ohiyesa arose to the challenge and, at the request of his father, started upon his quest to obtain the education that was to influence his bicultural future.

NOTES

1. See Roy W. Meyer, *History of the Santee Sioux: United States Indian Policy on Trial* (Lincoln: University of Nebraska Press, 1967), pp. viii–ix, 5, 13–14, 21–23; Royal B. Hassrick, *The Sioux: Life and Customs of a Warrior Society* (Norman: University of Oklahoma Press, 1964), pp. ix, 3–8; Stephen E. Feraca and James H. Howard, "The Identity and Demography of the Dakota or Sioux Tribe," *Plains Anthropologist* 8 (May, 1963) : 80–84.
2. Meyer, *History of the Santee Sioux*, Chapter 1. In fact, much of the information regarding European and American contacts with the Santees is based on Meyer's excellent book.
3. See "House Debate on the Indian Removal Question (1830)," in Wilcomb E. Washburn, ed., *The American Indian and the United States*, 4 vols. (New York: Random House, 1973), vol. 2, pp. 1017–23; "The Removal Act," in ibid., vol. 3, pp. 2169–71; and the government treaties with the Choctaws, Creeks, Seminoles, Chickasaws, and Cherokees, in ibid., vol. 4, pp. 2423–61. See also Bernard W. Sheehan, *Seeds of Extinction: Jeffersonian Philanthropy and the American Indian* (New York: W. W. Norton, 1974).
4. Washburn, *The American Indian and the United States*, vol. 1, p. 3.

5. As quoted in William T. Hagan, *American Indians* (Chicago: University of Chicago Press, 1961), p. 87.

6. U.S. Department of the Interior, *Annual Report of the Commissioner of Indian Affairs to the Secretary of the Interior for the Fiscal Year Ending June 30, 1856* (Washington: Government Printing Office, 1856), p. 572. All reports of the Commissioner of Indian Affairs hereafter cited as CIA, *Annual Report,* followed by the year of the report.

7. Henry E. Fritz, *The Movement for Indian Assimilation* (Philadelphia: University of Pennsylvania Press, 1963), pp. 18–19; see also Commissioner Dole's report for 1862 in Washburn, *The American Indian and the United States,* vol. 1, pp. 80–101. At one point in the perennial argument over relocating Indians, Spotted Tail, a famous chief of the Brule Sioux, is supposed to have quipped, "Why does not the Great Father put his red children on wheels, so he can move them as he will?" Quoted in Hagan, *American Indians,* p. 121.

8. Meyer, *History of the Santee Sioux,* pp. 24–35.

9. Ibid., pp. 35–38; See also Lawrence Taliaferro, "Auto-biography of Major Lawrence Taliaferro, Written in 1864," *Collections of the Minnesota Historical Society* 6 (1887–94), 189–225; Willoughby M. Babcock, Jr., "Major Lawrence Taliaferro, Indian Agent," *Mississippi Valley Historical Review* 11 (Dec., 1924): 358–75.

10. Meyer, *History of the Santee Sioux,* pp. 56–58, 70, 75, 78–84; William Watts Folwell, *A History of Minnesota,* 4 vols. (St. Paul: Minnesota Historical Society, 1961), vol. 2, pp. 216–17.

11. Meyer, *History of the Santee Sioux.* pp. 52–53; Theodore C. Blegen, "The Pond Brothers," *Minnesota History* 15 (Sept., 1934): 273–81; Stephen R. Riggs, *Mary and I: Forty Years with the Sioux* (Chicago: W. G. Holmes, 1880); Winifred W. Barton, *John P. Williamson: A Brother to the Sioux* (New York: Fleming H. Revell, 1919).

12. Charles A. Eastman to H. M. Hitchcock, Sept. 8, 1927, H. M. Hitchcock Papers, Ayer Collection, The Newberry Library, Chicago, Ill.; Meyer, *History of the Santee Sioux,* pp. 49–50, 63–64; Thomas Hughes, *Indian Chiefs of Southern Minnesota* (Mankato: Free Press, 1927), pp. 19–23.

13. Eastman to Hitchcock, Sept. 8, 1927, Hitchcock Papers; Ernst Jerome Mensel, "John, Charles, and Elaine Goodale Eastman: Their Story— A Contribution to the American Indian" (B.A. thesis, Dartmouth College, 1954), pp. 6–8, 10 (Mr. Mensel is Dr. Eastman's grandson); Mary Nancy Eastman Biography, Minneapolis Collection, Minneapolis Public Library, Minneapolis, Minn.; Hughes, *Indian Chiefs of*

Southern Minnesota, pp. 25–27. See also John Francis McDermott, *Seth Eastman: Pictorial Historian of the Indian* (Norman: University of Oklahoma Press, 1961).

14. Eastman to Hitchcock, Sept. 8, 1927, Hitchcock Papers; Mensel, "John, Charles, and Elaine Goodale Eastman," p. 9; Charles A. Eastman, *Indian Boyhood* (1902; reprint ed., New York: Dover Publications, 1971), pp. 6–10, 19, 24–28, 32–37, 54–55, 92.
15. Meyer, *History of the Santee Sioux,* pp. 109–32; Folwell, *A History of Minnesota,* 2, 109–301; Charles A. Eastman, *From the Deep Woods to Civilization: Chapters in the Autobiography of an Indian* (Boston: Little, Brown, 1916), p. 3; Mensel, "John, Charles, and Elaine Goodale Eastman," pp. 10–13.
16. Eastman, *Indian Boyhood,* pp. 9, 44–48; Eastman, *From the Deep Woods,* pp. 1, 6.
17. Charles A. Eastman, *The Indian Today: The Past and Future of the First American* (Garden City: Doubleday, Page, 1915), pp. 97–99; Eastman, *Indian Boyhood,* pp. 244–45; Eastman, *From the Deep Woods,* pp. 14–15; Elaine Goodale Eastman, *Pratt, The Red Man's Moses* (Norman: University of Oklahoma Press, 1935), pp. 129–31. See also Meyer, *History of the Santee Sioux,* pp. 242–57 for information on the Flandreau settlement.
18. Eastman, *Indian Boyhood,* p. 245; Eastman, *From the Deep Woods,* pp. 6, 9, 14.

CHAPTER 2

TO CIVILIZATION

THE ABRUPTNESS with which Jacob Eastman reentered Ohiyesa's life left him bewildered. The life Jacob offered his son seemed the antithesis of the life to which he had been bred. For fifteen years Ohiyesa trained to be a skillful hunter and warrior, to be unconcerned with material possessions, and to revere Wakan Tanka, the brotherhood of man and nature. He listened as his father told him how he had been converted by Protestant missionaries and how he and all Indians must put aside the old ways and accept the type of life offered by the white man. "Our own life, I will admit, is the best in a world of our own, such as we have enjoyed for ages," the son remembered his father saying, but "the sooner we accept their mode of life and follow their teaching, the better it will be for us all."[1]

Although filled with doubts, Ohiyesa nevertheless agreed to accompany his father, whom he loved and feared a little, into an alien world. The knowledge that Uncheedah would remain with them made his initial adjustment a little easier.

Throughout their journey to his 160-acre farm on the north bank of the Big Sioux River, Jacob sang hymns and read from his Bible. "It was his Christian faith and devotion," the son later wrote, "which was perhaps the strongest influence toward my change of heart and complete change of my purpose in life." He gradually accepted his father's wish that he adopt Christianity and was baptized Charles Alexander Eastman, selecting the first and middle names from a book of names loaned to him by a minister from the river settlement.[2]

Christianity was only one of the many blessings white civilization had to offer. Jacob wanted his son to read and write English, so he enrolled Charles in the mission school at Flandreau about two miles from his farm. The boy felt uneasy around the other Indian pupils, who wore white men's clothing and their hair cut short. "I was something like a wild cub caught overnight, and appearing in the corral next morning with the lambs," he recalled. With no knowledge of English, Charles was unable to follow his teacher's instructions, a predicament which his classmates, most of them younger than he, found amusing. Their laughter seared him. When he could stand their taunts no longer, he ran from the schoolroom fighting back his tears of rage.[3]

On his way back to his father's log cabin hours before afternoon dismissal, he considered fleeing to Canada. He felt that classroom was hardly the proper domain for a warrior and hunter. His father had asked too much of him. Let *him* reside among the blackrobes and teachers, the boy thought. Uncheedah, sensing what was in her grandson's heart, especially resented Jacob's attempt to Christianize Ohiyesa. Did Jacob think that he could transform her creation through will alone? Jacob, reading the pain on his son's face and the resentment in Uncheedah's eyes, tried to comfort the boy. He understood his son's shame. No one enjoyed ridicule, he told him, but there could be no going back: the old ways were dead, and they could never be brought back to life. If Indians chose to survive in the dominant white world, they would have to change. Ohiyesa's future was to be found in the classroom, not on the prairies of Canada. The young man acquiesced and returned to school the following day. He even had his hair cut.

Submission to his father's will did not derogate from his internal struggle. As the dissension between his father and grandmother became more vocal, Charles's conflict intensified. "The subject occupied my thoughts more and more, doubtless owing to my father's decided position on the matter; while, on the other hand, my grandmother's view of this new life was not encouraging." He was caught between the two people he most loved; caught between their contrary visions of what his future should hold. Tormented by indecisiveness, he sought solace in the silence of the deep woods where, after much rumination, he attained a renewed strength and belief in himself. His father was probably right: he, and Indians everywhere, must adapt to the white man's world to survive.[4]

Charles had begun a journey into his own spiritual labyrinth. By using nature as a means of attaining inner peace and strength, he re-affirmed his identity with the past. His decision to adapt his life to the white man's world revealed a need to conform to those goals his father had established for him, goals which in time might be his own also. His decision to become educated represented an immediate need to bring into balance the forces that pulled him back into the deep woods, and those that pushed him forward into a life whose benefits he could only imagine.

He endured his education at Flandreau for two more years. During this time, Jacob impressed upon his son the need to continue his education, comparing the pursuit of education to attaining status as a successful hunter and warrior and hoping his son would appreciate the comparison. Whether Charles thought it an apt comparison is unknown. He did, however, enroll at Santee Normal Training School in Nebraska where his brother John, acculturated as was his father, worked as an assistant teacher under Alfred L. Riggs, the school's superintendent and the son of the Presbyterian missionary, Stephen R. Riggs. The younger Riggs devoted most of his seventy-eight years to the Sioux.[5]

Stephen R. Riggs originally conceived the idea for Santee Normal when he first toured the reservation with Thomas S. Williamson in the late 1830s. Graduates of the school would serve as the teachers of their people. Funds for such an enterprise were unavailable either from the government or private charities until after the Santee Sioux Uprising of 1862. As a result of the investigations that followed the rebellion and a renewed sense of urgency among reformers that only civilization and assimilation would eliminate the causes of any future rebellion, Riggs received $28,000 from the American Board of Commissioners for Foreign Missions to establish a training school at Santee. He also recommended, and it was decided to his satisfaction that Alfred, his eldest son, be placed in charge of the school.

In 1870, the Santee Normal Training School opened its doors. The Siouan language newspaper, *Iapi Oave*, edited by John P. Williamson, carried the news of the opening. Williamson, formerly a missionary at the Santee Reservation, was the son of Thomas S. Williamson. John spent many years among the Sioux. Because of the growing controversy over government financial support for sectarian schools, Congress in 1901 withdrew subsidies. Until then Santee Normal maintained an enrollment much higher than any other school operated by the Board. In fact, Santee Normal was considered by many people in the Indian service the educational center for all Sioux students.[6]

The school expanded its mission beyond the training of teachers, to produce preachers, businessmen, and interpreters, who would then return to their people and become useful, responsible citizens. The school offered a varied curriculum, the core of which was religious, with mandatory attendance at church and Sunday school. Students also learned the more prosaic subjects of arithmetic, geography, music, reading, and writing.

Although considered by many people at the time to be one of the best schools of Indian education, the institution received criticism for teaching Indians to read and write in their own language. Objections to this method were based on the belief that there was little, if any, opportunity for educational advancement through the Sioux language. Riggs defended the practice, maintaining that it was easier to educate Indians in a language they understood. The dispute lasted until 1901, or as long as the school remained opened.[7]

During Charles's 150-mile walk to Santee Normal, he gained his first favorable impressions of the white man when he was befriended by a white farmer and his family, who welcomed him into their home and gave him food and lodging, refusing to take the money he offered. He would always remember their kindness. Perhaps there was much good, he thought at the time, in the white world.[8]

When Charles arrived at the school, he was warmly greeted by his brother and Riggs. His adjustment to the new environment proved somewhat difficult, but his father's letters did much to reassure him. He overcame, with some gentle prodding by his brother, a punishing shyness that sent him running into the woods and its solitude whenever he felt himself lost in a world of polite conversation and proper manners. He soon hid himself in his studies. In his two years at Santee Normal, he improved his English and learned to read and translate his native tongue. He began also to study elementary algebra and geometry. Riggs, sensing his latent abilities, encouraged him to work hard because achievement was its own reward. "Next to my own father," Eastman wrote, "this man did more than perhaps any other to make it possible for me to grasp the principles of true civilization." Because he did so well in his studies, Riggs was able to gain him admission to the preparatory department at Beloit College, a state-supported institution in Beloit, Wisconsin. Riggs also obtained government aid for him amounting to $25 per quarter or $100 a year maximum.[9]

But before leaving for Beloit in September, 1876, Eastman received word from Flandreau that his father had died. This was a tremendous blow to him; yet he pledged himself to his father's dream of a well-educated son. John Eastman comforted his younger brother and became a substitute father to Charles, insisting, as had Jacob, that he continue to pursue his education.[10]

Charles's two-day train trip to Beloit provided his first real contact with white civilization. Everywhere he fixed his gaze, some new wonder enthralled him: the crowds of white people in the streets, the wealth of goods in the window displays of stores. If the townspeople stared at him, he took no notice, until, that is, he arrived in Beloit and a rumor quickly spread that he was the nephew of Sitting Bull, the great Hunkpapa Sioux leader. The year was 1876 and there was, of course, deep resentment against the Sioux, especially since the Custer debacle three months earlier. Charles later wrote that "when I went into the town, I was followed on the streets by gangs of little white savages, giving imitation war whoops."[11] From his brother and Alfred Riggs he had learned that survival demanded his turning the other cheek. Though injustice abounded, he felt that he could only live righteously and that others might learn from his example.

He buried himself in his school work. While he polished his English, he expanded his knowledge of geography, history, and mathematics. He ranked at the top of his class in his grammar and bookkeeping courses. He also attended to his physical training, exercising daily, a regimen he continued throughout his student years. During the summer months he obtained work at local farms and felt on occasion the sting of racial prejudice. For many people he was *only* an Indian.[12]

Eastman's three years at Beloit College hardened his commitment to acculturation. He fully realized that he must adopt the positive aspects of white civilization if he wanted to become successful in an alien culture. Furthermore, Christianity no longer threatened the religion his grandmother taught him. He had developed a type of syncretism. For the remainder of his life, and especially during his involvement with the Young Men's Christian Association among Indians, he professed there was no difference between the worship of the Christian God and Wakan Tanka. His signature also demonstrates a compatibility or reconciliation; he used both his Christian and Indian names interchangeably.

Soon after he left Beloit in 1879 and returned to South Dakota, he learned that Riggs had made arrangements, under the same government aid program, for him to attend the preparatory department of Knox College, in Galesburg, Illinois, from which Riggs had graduated.[13]

At Knox College, a co-educational institution, he had his first significant and prolonged contact with white women. "I mingled for the first time with the paleface maidens," he observed, "and as soon as I could shake off my Indian shyness, I found them very winning and companionable." Indeed, he later chose a white wife. In observation of the "pale-face maidens," he became more acquainted with the restricted roles women played in white society. To supplement his government money, he taught an exercise class to a group of coeds, whom he found charmed by his handsomeness as well as his uniqueness. He still looked like the erstwhile warrior he was, stood two inches under six feet, and carried not an ounce of fat on his body. He grew more self-confident around the admiring women and throughout his life would remain more comfortable in the presence of women.[14]

Eastman attended Knox College from the fall session of 1879 through the spring session of 1881, though he is listed in the class of 1884 as a nongraduating member.[15] It was in these years that he grappled with the timeless problem of what his future occupation would be. He had advanced well beyond the level of education he received at Santee Normal. He was not yet ready to return to the reservation and a job, such as teacher, that required few of his skills. And what were those skills? He had shown himself to be gifted academically yet he had been trained for no specific job. In the white world he was still only a curiosity, an articulate Indian. What he needed was a career, useful and meaningful in either world. He narrowed his choices of a career to two: he would be either a lawyer or a physician, and in contemplation of his obligations to his people, he decided that medicine represented a greater level of service.[16]

Eastman returned to South Dakota in 1881 and worked for a while as a clerk in the store of his brother-in-law at Flandreau. His brother John was then in charge of the mission school which Charles first attended. John offered him a temporary teaching position at the school for one term.[17]

During his stay that summer and fall in South Dakota, his old friend and mentor, Alfred Riggs, enticed him with stories about a prestigious college in the East that had been originally founded as a school for Indians: Dartmouth College in Hanover, New Hampshire. Riggs was influential in obtaining a scholarship for his young Indian protege, and Eastman left South Dakota in January, 1882, for college and New England.[18]

His trip by train, as his earlier one to Beloit, was filled with new and interesting experiences. In Chicago where he changed trains, he observed masses of humanity rushing madly along, many with unhappy looking faces. Having been warned before leaving his brother and friends not to trust strangers and to guard against pickpockets, he experienced a few anxious moments alone in the train station and was relieved when he saw several burly Chicago policemen walking their beats. But when he boarded the eastbound train from Chicago and was soon accosted by a white man who asked him a number of embarrassing questions about his Indian heritage, he learned that thieves and scoundrels were not the only dangers for the traveling Indian.[19]

He was met in Boston by Mr. and Mrs. Frank Wood, friends and associates of Riggs who were also deeply involved in Native American reform. Eastman later referred to the Woods as his white parents. Frank Wood was active in the Lake Mohonk Conference of Friends of the Indian, the Indian Rights Association, and the Boston Indian Citizenship Committee—organizations that came to prominence around the time that Charles went East and addressed themselves to the cause of federal Indian policy reform and the assimilation of the Indian into white, middle-class society.

Federal Indian policy had become well enough publicized by 1865 to prompt a congressional investigation. From Texas in the south to the Dakotas in the north, the Indians of the plains were at war with the Whites. After two years of work a report, authored by Senator James Doolittle of Wisconsin, was submitted to the President and Congress for consideration. Doolittle's committee in the Senate found Indian population decreasing everywhere except in Indian Territory. The committee attributed the decline to disease, alcoholism, war, and starvation. The onslaught of white settlement from both east and west crushed the Indians' cultures, while a class of adventurers who recognized no laws other than necessity and self-defense overran the middle regions of the nation. In their eager search for gold and fertile tracts of land, Whites consistently disregarded the boundaries of Indian reservations. Wars often followed Indian reprisals against the interlopers. The construction of two railroads across the plains—the Union Pacific along the valley of the Platte River and the Kansas Pacific by way of the Smoky Hill—would soon reach the Rocky Mountains and sever the great buffalo range, eliminating the game and with it the foundation of the Plains Indians' way of life.[20]

With the completion of the transcontinental railroad in 1869, the advance of non-Indian settlers increased. Frontier movements had always upset Indian life, but this new movement destroyed forever the belief that Indians could escape inundation by the dominant culture through living beyond the borders of that civilization. Reservations soon represented sanctuaries in a hostile environment.

Few of the Plains tribes were ready by 1869 for a restrictive reservation life. Such tribes as the Sioux, Cheyenne, Kiowa, Comanche, and Arapaho were determined to continue their nomadic traditions just as the predominantly white settlers were intent upon the conquest of the plains. Cultural divergence only exacerbated attempts at mutual understanding and tolerance. Indians who agreed to adopt the invader's way of life became traitors to their people, no less subject to attack than the dominant Whites. For many people in the government and the military, it became increasingly apparent that subjugation of the Indians must precede any policy of their eventual assimilation. Subjugation could be accomplished either peacefully or forcefully depending upon the dispositions of the Indians. The reformers who adopted the cause of Indians following the Civil War rejected force out of hand.

In the decades after the Civil War, and especially during the last
two decades of the nineteenth century, federal Indian policy came to
be dominated by a group of earnest men and women who identified
themselves as "friends of the Indian." They recognized the crisis that
resulted from the increasing pressures put on the Indians and their
lands by frontier settlement. They brought with their efforts on behalf of the Indian a profound faith in the future and in Christianity,
but many reflected the ethnocentrism of their time and regarded
Indian cultures as vestiges of a barbarous state of civilization that
would quickly succumb to an enlightened and vigorous Christian
stewardship. Reformers would clash openly and recurrently with
people in and out of government who placed greater emphasis on
military force when dealing with Indians.[21] Reformers often intensified the struggle between the military and civilian agencies for control
of Indian affairs.

Friction between civilian and military authorities had increased by
the end of the 1860s. The northern and southern plains had erupted
into war in 1866. The army, disgusted over the failure of special committees of Congress to provide the requisite legislation demanded by
reformers so as to restore peace to the plains, grew increasingly critical
of the Indian bureau. Christian reformers, horrified by the bloodshed
in the Sioux War of 1866–68 and the campaigns against the Southern
Cheyennes, charged the army with usurpation of civilian control, and
with debauching and demoralizing Indians that came within the
range of their influence. Reformers further accused the military of
provoking unnecessary wars, and in failing to distinguish in their
wars between peaceful and hostile Indians. Army officers, in turn,
ascribed Indian troubles to the ignorance, incompetence, corruption,
mismanagement, and the rapid turnover of Indian bureau personnel.
The army also accused the reformers of preaching about Indian management, a subject with which they had little firsthand knowledge or
experience. Both charge and countercharge, as one historian has observed, contained enough substance to suggest credibility and enough
exaggeration and fabrication to kindle further controversies.[22]

The military proposed what they considered a simple solution to
the problems of Indian administration: return of the Indian service
to the War Department where it properly belonged. The transfer,
they reasoned, would eliminate the uncertainty and contention over

respective roles, responsibilities, and jurisdictions that plagued civilian control of Indian affairs. It was further argued that the military possessed the means by which force could be readily administered. To remove the anxieties of the reformers, who were fearful of the army's power of intimidation, military leaders explained that Indian appropriations and annuities could be managed more efficiently and more honestly through the army's commissary and quartermaster departments. Opponents to military transfer remained unconvinced of the army's good intentions despite such assurances. The reformers found abhorrent and rather ironic the notion that the army could provide sound moral and intellectual leadership in Indian affairs. "Our experience during the period when the Indians were under military care," wrote Indian Commissioner Nathaniel Taylor, "affords no ground for hope that any benefit to them or the treasury would be secured."[23]

Shortly after Ulysses S. Grant assumed the presidency in March, 1869, a series of measures that came to be labelled "Grant's Peace Policy" were put into effect. The measures adopted reflected some of the recommendations of the Doolittle Commission and clearly contemplated continued civilian control of the Indian bureau. Among its more prominent features were the nomination of agents and superintendents by church groups, a ten-person Board of Indian Commissioners appointed by the President and composed of philanthropists who would serve without pay in overseeing the disbursements of Indian annuities, and finally an end to the treaty system by which the government treated Indian tribes as domestic dependent nations. Reservations were, in a sense, to serve as manufacturing centers: their products would be literate, Christian, farmer-Indians. In time the "Indian" distinction would disappear.

The peace policy as originally conceived also contained much that would please the military. Only the newly created central and southern superintendencies that embraced the more hostile Plains tribes were to be staffed by church-nominated agents. Virtually all the remaining superintendents and agents were to be army officers detached for service to the Indian bureau. The army also had sole responsibility for all Indians off the reservations. Here seemed to be an objective basis for separating hostile from peaceful Indians and for delineating civilian and military responsibilities: the Indian bureau retained exclusive control and jurisdiction over all the Indians on the reservation, while the army received responsibility for all Indians off the reservations. Those Indians who refused to give up their tribal existence without a fight—and there were few as it turned out—and move onto the reservations were to be considered hostile. The army was, however, forbidden to interfere with the reservation Indians unless expressly requested to do so by the agent, or his superior in Washington. Under pressure from humanitarian groups, Congress in 1870 further modified the peace policy to prohibit army officers from serving as agents, thus returning the administration of all reservations to civilian control.[24]

The peace policy never achieved the success that its formulators envisioned. The Plains tribes vigorously resisted its implementation, especially the provisions for concentrating the tribes on ever smaller reservations. Only after Indians had been pacified by the army at considerable cost in lives and dollars did the question once again arise, what is to be done with the Indians?

Because the work of the Board of Indian Commissioners and the assignment of agents by church groups proved to be unsuccessful, reformers changed their emphasis. Rather than participate directly in the administration of Indian affairs, they would direct their efforts toward enlivening public concern and toward lobbying in Congress. Reform that would solve the Indian problem would naturally result from that agitation.

After a decade of the peace policy, and because of its failures, there arose a number of organizations that addressed themselves to the challenges of federal Indian policy reform. The Boston Indian Citizenship Committee was the first such organization. Founded in 1879, at the time Charles Eastman was enrolled at Knox College, when a group of distinguished Boston citizens organized to protest the forced removal of Ponca Indians from their homes in Dakota to Indian Territory, the committee later involved itself in all aspects of policy reform. In the same fashion a group of women in Philadelphia, alarmed by the loss of tribal lands in Indian Territory, founded a nationwide association, the Women's National Indian Association, to petition Congress for the benefit of Indians, eventually organizing over eighty state and local chapters. In 1882 a much more influential society was formed, again in Philadelphia, by men who called themselves the

Indian Rights Association. The association avoided the emotional-
ism of such reformers as Helen Hunt Jackson whose *A Century of
Dishonor* had recently appeared in print, concentrating instead on
specific efforts to correct injustices to particular tribes, and also lobbying in Washington for general legislation that would ultimately rectify, as they hoped, the problems in Indian affairs.[25]

These disparate groups were brought together in an annual October meeting where policy reform could be coordinated. Albert K.
Smiley, a Quaker and a member of the Board of Indian Commissioners, had been disturbed by the board's hurried meetings in Washington. He invited the board and other persons interested in Indian
policy to spend three days as his guest at the sprawling hotel he and
his brother owned at Lake Mohonk, near New Paltz, New York. The
Lake Mohonk Conference of Friends of the Indian, as these annual
meetings came to be called, influenced greatly the course of federal
Indian policy well into the twentieth century.

At the October meetings more than a hundred persons gathered to
hear reports and discuss the past year's Indian affairs. Out of these
discussions came a platform of recommendations. Representatives of
the reform organizations were joined by missionaries, high officials of
the Indian bureau, Protestant clergymen, writers, newspaper editors,
and, once in a while, even an Indian. Each year the conference published its proceedings, which contained edited versions of the papers,
the addresses of the president of the conference, minutes of the discussions, and the platform describing the projected program for reform during the coming year.

The reformers who gathered at Lake Mohonk Lodge concentrated
their efforts on a few broad programs. They believed that before civilization's allures could beguile the savage, his tribal relations had to
be destroyed and that the best means to accomplish this was through
the allotment of reservation lands. Once the Indian received his
homestead, communality would give way to individualism. And once
allotted land, the Indian would be granted citizenship with all the
rights and privileges of a citizen and without the special advantages
given to a ward of the government. Finally, the reformers believed
they should direct their energy toward establishing a universal government school system that would complete the transformation of
the Indian into good Americans.[26]

Frank Wood, who met Eastman's train in Boston, introduced the young man to the courteous world of the eastern reformers and counseled him on everything from proper dress to proper deportment. He was greatly impressed by what Eastman had already achieved, and was mightily concerned that nothing should impede the young man's progress or shorten his reach. Wood and his wife, trustees of Wellesley College, extended their concern for Eastman to financial matters as well and prevailed upon the other trustees of Wellesley to engage the Sioux for a lecture. Eastman received an honorarium for his speech before the women of Wellesley concerning the French and Indian War and Pontiac's Rebellion. The lecture was only the first for which he would receive money; in the future his lectures would account for a considerable portion of his income.

From his association with the Woods and his successful lecture at Wellesley, Eastman came to the attention of a larger community of persons interested in the advancement of Indians. He received an offer of a generous scholarship if he would forsake Dartmouth for Harvard. He conferred with Wood on the matter and decided to stick with Dartmouth, but instead of enrolling immediately, he attended Kimball Union Academy at Meriden, New Hampshire, for a year and a half, so that he might improve upon certain deficiencies in his preparation for the Ivy League. It was not until the fall of 1883, and at the age of twenty-five, that Eastman entered Dartmouth's freshman class.[27]

Eastman's course of study at Dartmouth would abash most of today's college students and many of their professors. He enrolled in the Latin scientific curriculum, which required extensive language courses in Latin, French, Greek, German, linguistics, and English. Other subjects included zoology, botany, chemistry, physics, natural history, philosophy, geometry, political science, and history. He distinguished himself in all his studies and graduated with honors,[28] but his successes went beyond the classroom.

The freshman class in the fall of 1883 elected him their football captain for the traditional rush against the sophomore class. When during the game, he mistakenly tackled a young philosophy professor who he thought was on the opposing side, newspapers played up the incident with obvious amusement, declaring that a new Sioux student at Dartmouth tried to "scalp" one of the professors. He also played baseball and tennis and boxed. He held the school record for long-distance running for three years, only to have it eclipsed in his senior year when he came in second in a two-mile race. He pledged Phi Delta Theta fraternity and acquired a partiality for a good game of whist.[29]

He remembered his four years at Dartmouth with nostalgia as rich and rewarding. He thought long thoughts and played hard. He was welcomed, if only for a few seasons, into the ranks of the privileged and well born, meeting such luminaries as Matthew Arnold and Francis Parkman. Even though he never felt at home in Hanover as did most of the other young men, Eastman was respected by his former college classmates, and at reunions of the class of '87, Eastman frequently led the procession, attired in Indian ceremonial dress. In later years, three beautiful portraits of him were presented to Dartmouth by his classmates. One life-size portrait shows a resplendent Eastman with his eyes fixed upward on some far-off horizon and his jaw set firmly but unmenacingly.[30]

He received his Bachelor of Science degree in June, 1887. He planned to return to his people as a medical missionary but was persuaded by the Woods and others within their circle of reform-minded Christians to enter Boston University School of Medicine. Again, he received financial aid from the university and from friends.[31] Information on his coursework there is extremely sparse. During his last two years of study he worked among the poor of Boston's South End, treating the common diseases of poverty as well as some rare medical cases. He also had surgical experience both at the dispensary and university hospital.[32] All the while, the Woods kept him abreast of pending legislation that would affect his people. Because of his increasing renown among the Sioux, he was consulted about the provisions of the General Allotment or Dawes Severalty Act of 1887.[33]

Eastman supported the Dawes Act and no doubt encouraged Indians to accept the allotment policy. After witnessing the devastating results of the act as well as related legislation which allowed Indians to sell their allotments, Eastman realized belatedly that the Dawes Act was not the panacea it was purported to be.[34] But in 1887 he believed that the only way for the Indians to survive was to adopt the white man's ways. All Indians could not be physicians, but most could be citizen-farmers.

The idea of land allotments for Indians goes back to America's colonial beginnings. Some tribes had undergone the process before the Civil War, and the movement gained momentum in the early 1860s with the urgent recommendations of Indian Commissioner William Dole. Neither treaties that guaranteed the Indians land in perpetuity nor individual certificates of occupancy were adequate for the protection of their land. The problem for reformers was, how to save the Indians' remaining patrimony and how to grant them the time needed for adjustment to the culture that was displacing their own. It was not until 1868, however, that the essence of the Dawes Act clearly emerged. In their first annual report, the newly created Board of Indian Commissioners recommended that Indians "should be taught . . . the advantage of individual ownership of property, and should be given land in severalty, . . . and the titles should be inalienable from the family of the holders for at least two or three generations."[35] In 1874, Commissioner of Indian Affairs Edward P. Smith drafted and sent to Congress a bill which would have made possible the granting of citizenship to individual Indians who could demonstrate before a federal judge sufficient intelligence and prudence in management of their lives.[36] Although Smith's bill failed in Congress, the following year Congress passed legislation allowing Indians to file claims to land under the Homestead Act of 1862 if they agreed to leave their tribe.[37]

Most reformers favored the extinction of the reservation system but they nevertheless understood that the immediate issuance of patents and the division of tribal lands would invite disaster. Without Congress providing safeguards in the form of inalienable rights of land, the Indians would not only lose that land but also never achieve adequate preparation for assimilation through the individual allotment. Furthermore, unless such legislation could be identified with the interests of white citizens, it would fail to pass Congress.

The General Allotment Act, which became law in February, 1887, was dependent as much upon western land-hunger to propel it through Congress as it was upon the efforts of Indian rights organizations. Many reformers, Senator Henry L. Dawes of Massachusetts among them, saw the new law as the solution to the "Indian problem." Reservations would be broken up, lands allotted, and the Indian cease to be an Indian. Everyone would benefit from the law.

Others of less noble persuasion saw new opportunities to acquire more Indian land. Both types were elated over its passage, and what resulted is a well-known story.

In its final form the Dawes Act gave the President discretionary power to make all reservation Indians, with the exception of the Five Civilized Tribes and a few others, landholders in severalty and citizens of the United States. Tribal lands were allotted in varying amounts, not to exceed 160 acres, to heads of families and to others. Since there was more land in relation to the number of Indians receiving allotments, the surplus reservation lands were sold to non-Indians. The proceeds from the sales would be held in trust for the benefit of the particular tribe. To prevent Indians from selling their holdings, title was retained in trust by the United States for twenty-five years. Indians accepting allotments and leaving their tribes were eligible for citizenship. A large number of Indians chose not to work their allotments, some being content just to lease most of their land to whites. Subsequent legislation, however, chipped away at the twenty-five year trust period. An act passed in 1902 permitted Indians to sell inherited land from deceased relatives, and the Burke Act of 1906 included a provision authorizing the Secretary of the Interior to judge Indians competent to own their allotments and manage their own affairs before the trust period ended. Tens of millions of acres of land were sold by "competent" Indians. For nearly fifty years, the principles of the Dawes Act and related pieces of legislation operated, until finally, in 1934, Indian land allotments ended, and most of the American Indians were still not assimilated into white society. The policy was a wretched failure.

The Dawes Act represented the culmination of the forced assimilation policies subscribed to by the humanitarian reformers of the 1880s. The rationale behind the act described the theory of assimilation then popular—an Indian who possessed land of his own, and who then no longer depended upon the government for his livelihood, would of necessity become a farmer or herder, but most Indians, contrary to the reformers' hopes, did not become independent farmers. They did, however, lose their tribal patrimony. Acreage owned by Indians decreased from 140 million acres in 1887, to 78 million acres in 1900, to 55 million acres by 1934, when allotment was finally abandoned as a federal policy.[38]

Eastman, no doubt influenced by his benefactors, and mindful of his own accomplishments, counseled his people to accept the act, reasoning that because he had lived in the white world for some years and had benefited from the association, so could his people.

Three years after the passage of the Dawes Act, Eastman completed the requirements for his medical degree, ranking high in his class of approximately sixty students. Elected unanimously as the class orator, he delivered an oration entitled, "The Comparative History of the Art of Healing," at Tremont Temple on June 4, 1890. The thirty-two year old graduate cast a striking figure, standing two inches under six feet tall with jet black hair combed in a high pompadour and speaking in a clear and forceful manner.[39]

The models who had influenced his life seemed to converge in that day to create the impressive figure of Dr. Charles Eastman. At times their contradictory instructions had caused great strains first in the boy and later in the man as he struggled for his own identity. His surrogate mother, Uncheedah, introduced her grandson to the spiritual core within the Indian world; his uncle, Mysterious Medicine, groomed his nephew to be a hunter and warrior and wary of whites; his Christianized father, Jacob Eastman, initiated his son into a new way of life fraught with great difficulty but holding out rewards for those who would conform; his teacher at Santee Normal Training School, Alfred L. Riggs, who saw the potentiality of an aspiring student encouraged him to obtain further education; and his benefactors, the Woods, who gave him financial and emotional support proudly introduced him to their influential eastern friends. Among those friends were many activists in the cause of Indian rights, from whom he learned about the great goal of assimilation, and from him they realized the principle's worthiness. He sat with them on Sunday mornings in their Congregational churches, and learned that ultimately there were no intercessors between God and man. Although salvation could not be achieved only through good works, it was nevertheless the duty of all Christians to help the less fortunate among them, like the Indians. And if Charles Eastman were to help his people, he would have to do so as an Indian. He was an acculturated Sioux rather than an assimilated one, but that discovery was yet to be made.

By 1890, Eastman was ready to put his newly acquired medical knowledge to work. He had spent nearly seventeen years obtaining an education, beginning at a small mission school that led circuitously to Boston University School of Medicine, mastering the English language and mastering himself. His blending of Indian and Christian teachings helped him to adjust to a world, not of his vision but of his father's.

It is unfortunate that he left no detailed records of this period other than his carefully edited memoirs. His autobiographies lack intimacy. What were his private thoughts and desires, say, during his four years at Dartmouth, or later during his dispensary practice in the slums of Boston's South End? The record that does exist represents only scattered impressions of a man in a reflective mood who is willing to forego even the remembered details in the interest of a larger purpose—to describe one man's, an Indian's, transition between cultures in conflict, and in the process to reveal truths common to humanity.

Whatever doubts and longing during those seventeen years of schooling Eastman may have had, he never faltered; or rather, if he did occasionally falter, his misfortunes and misgivings were never great enough to hinder his progress. It would not always be so. Having achieved some success in pursuit of an education and a worthy career, he would find it more difficult to sustain that success once free of the classroom. In the larger world outside higher education there would be fewer persons who would offer him encouragement; fewer still who would be willing to sponsor his life in the same way that Alfred Riggs or Frank Wood were willing to do.

NOTES

1. Eastman, *From the Deep Woods*, pp. 7–8.
2. Ibid., pp. 8–10; Mensel, "John, Charles, and Elaine Goodale Eastman," p. 19.
3. Eastman, *From the Deep Woods*, pp. 16–23.
4. Ibid., pp. 24–29.
5. Ibid., pp. 29–32, 40; *Holloway Herald* (Minnesota), June 1, 1916.
6. Richard L. Guenther, "The Santee Normal Training School," *Nebraska History* 51 (Fall, 1970): 359–62; Meyer, *History of the Santee Sioux*, pp. 176, 187; *Minneapolis Journal*, Oct. 28, 1917.

7. Guenther, "The Santee Normal Training School," pp. 365–68, 373; Meyer, *History of the Santee Sioux*, pp. 188–90.
8. Eastman, *From the Deep Woods*, pp. 32–40.
9. Ibid., pp. 40–50; Alfred L. Riggs to E. A. Hayt, Dec. 8, 1877, Records of the Bureau of Indian Affairs, Record Group 75, Letters Received, National Archives and Records Service; Stephen R. Riggs to Hayt, Mar. 19, 1878, ibid.
10. Mensel, "John, Charles, and Elaine Goodale Eastman," p. 20; Eastman, *From the Deep Woods*, p. 50.
11. Eastman, *From the Deep Woods*, pp. 51–53.
12. Ibid., pp. 54–57; Alfred L. Riggs to Hayt, Apr. 4, 1879, BIA, RG 75, LR, NA.
13. Mensel, "John, Charles, and Elaine Goodale Eastman," p. 21; Eastman, *From the Deep Woods*, pp. 57–58; Alfred L. Riggs to Hayt, Oct. 4, 1879, BIA, RG 75, LR, NA.
14. Eastman, *From the Deep Woods*, p. 59; Mensel, "John, Charles, and Elaine Goodale Eastman," pp. 21–22.
15. Mrs. Philip S. Haring, Curator at Knox College, to author, Sept. 9, 1975.
16. Eastman, *From the Deep Woods*, pp. 59–60.
17. Mensel, "John, Charles, and Elaine Goodale Eastman," pp. 22–23.
18. Ibid., p. 23.
19. Eastman, *From the Deep Woods*, pp. 62–63; Mensel, "John, Charles, and Elaine Goodale Eastman," p. 23.
20. Fritz, *Movement for Assimilation*, pp. 20–31.
21. Francis Paul Prucha, ed., *Americanizing the American Indians: Writings by the "Friends of the Indian," 1880–1900* (Cambridge: Harvard University Press, 1973), pp. 1–6.
22. Robert M. Utley, *Frontier Regulars: The United States Army and the Indian, 1866–1891* (New York: Macmillan, 1973), p. 195.
23. CIA, *Annual Report*, 1868, pp. iii–iv.
24. Utley, *Frontier Regulars*, p. 197; Robert Winston Mardock, *The Reformers and the American Indian* (Columbia: University of Missouri Press, 1971), pp. 53–54; Loring Benson Priest, *Uncle Sam's Stepchildren: The Reformation of United States Indian Policy* (Lincoln: University of Nebraska Press, 1975), pp. 1–5; CIA, *Annual Report*, 1869, pp. 5–6.
25. Prucha, *Americanizing the American Indians*, pp. 4–5.
26. Ibid., p. 6.
27. Mensel, "John, Charles, and Elaine Goodale Eastman," pp. 23–24; Eastman, *From the Deep Woods*, pp. 64–67, 71–72.

28. See Class of 1887 Merit Roll Book, Charles A. Eastman, Baker Library, Dartmouth College, Hanover, N.H.
29. Mensel, "John, Charles, and Elaine Goodale Eastman," pp. 25–26; Charles A. Eastman Folder, Baker Library, Dartmouth College, Hanover, N.H.; Charles A. Eastman Folder, Jones Public Library, Amherst, Mass.; Eastman, *From the Deep Woods*, pp. 67–68.
30. Charles A. Eastman Folder, Baker Library; Eastman, *From the Deep Woods*, p. 72.
31. Mrs. Frank Wood to M. S. Cook, Oct. 13, 1887, BIA, RG 75, LR, NA; Eastman, *From the Deep Woods*, p. 71.
32. Charles A. Eastman to T. J. Morgan, Aug. 20, 1890, BIA, RG 75, LR, NA.
33. Eastman to Secretary of the Indian Rights Association, Dec. 28, 1887, Indian Rights Association Papers, 1886–1901, Microfilm, Reel 12, Incoming Correspondence, Historical Society of Pennsylvania, Philadelphia, Penn., Scholarly Resources. Hereafter cited as IRA.
34. See Eastman, *The Indian Today*, p. 103; Eastman, *From the Deep Woods*, pp. 163–64.
35. As quoted in Fritz, *Movement for Assimilation*, p. 206.
36. CIA, *Annual Report*, 1874, pp. 324–27.
37. U.S., Congress, House, *Indian Citizenship Bill*, House Executive Document No. 228, Forty-Third Cong., First Session, vol. 16, Apr. 24, 1874.
38. Barbara Hetrick and Sar A. Levitan, *Big Brother's Indian Programs, with Reservations* (New York: McGraw-Hill, 1971), p. 30. See Wilcomb E. Washburn, *The Assault on Indian Tribalism: The General Allotment Law (Dawes Act) of 1887* (Philadelphia: J. B. Lippincott, 1975) for an excellent account of the Dawes Act.
39. Thomas Addison to Herbert Welsh, June 11, 1890, enclosure, IRA, Reel 18, Incoming Correspondence; Frank Wood to Morgan, May 19, 1890, BIA, RG 75, LR, NA.

CHAPTER 3

SERVICE AT PINE RIDGE
DURING THE GHOST DANCE

D R. CHARLES EASTMAN remained in the East for a few months after he received his medical degree in June, 1890. He stayed at the request of his friend and benefactor, Frank Wood, and kept the books for Wood's steam printing business while the regular book-keeper took his vacation. During this summer Wood introduced him to Commissioner of Indian Affairs Thomas Jefferson Morgan, appointed in 1889, in hope of securing for Eastman a position as a government physician on some Indian reservation. Formerly a practicing Baptist minister and a professional educator, Morgan, a Republican, retained his position until shortly before the inauguration of the second Cleveland administration.[1]

Wood stressed his protege's exemplary character and fastidious personal habits in arguing Eastman's cause to Morgan. He also pointed out that while Eastman was working in the dispensary during his last two years of medical school, he became so popular with his patients that they regularly requested to be treated only by the "Indian Doctor." But what most influenced the commissioner's decision to employ the Sioux physician was Wood's statement that he "is today the finest object-lesson of what Christianity and education will do for the Indian that can be found in this country." Commissioner Morgan, ever conscious of the value of object lessons, promised that he would use his power to obtain for Eastman an appointment somewhere as government physician.[2] In the meantime, Eastman would have to submit a standard application for government employment.

Eastman's ideas concerning the role he could play as government physician were explained in a letter accompanying his application.

As an Indian seeking employment among Indians, he could be of extraordinary service to the Indian bureau. "The government physician can be," he observed, "the most useful civilizer among the force of government officers placed in any Indian Reservation if he could understand the language and the habits of the people." Eastman believed that in order to gain the Indians' confidence, a physician "must feel at home with them, and must put forward no claim of superiority, but rather sympathy and kindliness in action and feelings."[3]

When Eastman was notified that he was to be sent to Fort Berthold Agency, North Dakota, he expressed his disappointment to Wood. At that agency he would be among the Gros Ventres, a tribe which was traditionally an enemy of the Sioux and whose language he did not speak. He questioned his usefulness among a people who might regard him with considerable resentment and suspicion. He had fondly hoped to be assigned to some Sioux agency, preferably Rosebud, Pine Ridge, or Standing Rock; and if this were not possible, he wished to be appointed to Sisseton, Santee, Yankton, or Devil's Lake, the homes of the central and eastern divisions of the Sioux.[4] Wood wrote on his behalf to the commissioner, supporting Eastman's objections to Fort Berthold. The Sioux doctor could, no doubt, learn the Gros Ventres' language "in a year's time," Wood told Morgan, but the doctor would be more useful to his own people. Wood firmly reiterated his belief that an appointment should be made where Eastman's "knowledge of the Sioux language and customs and character of that people could be utilized."[5]

Eastman was reassigned to Standing Rock Agency.[6] He was extremely pleased over this appointment and wrote the commissioner that as a child he had met James McLaughlin, the agent, and that McLaughlin's Indian wife was a distant relative.[7] But staunch opposition to the appointment soon developed. Apparently, Dr. James Brewster, the physician at Standing Rock, had little desire to be transferred to Fort Berthold and objected to the commissioner's solicitude. Agent McLaughlin himself supported Brewster's retention, arguing that Brewster was doing a fine job among the 4,000 Sioux at Standing Rock. Because of Eastman's inexperience as a doctor, McLaughlin thought it wiser to station him at a smaller agency, and, if this were impossible, to assign Eastman as Brewster's assistant.[8] Swayed by these arguments, Morgan notified Eastman that it would be better for all concerned if he accepted the original assignment at Fort Berthold.[9]

When news of Eastman's assignment to Fort Berthold reached Wood, he again protested, employing the same arguments as before. Besides, wrote Wood, Eastman's personal effects had already been sent to Standing Rock and train tickets had been purchased. Wood stressed that Eastman was "willing to go where he is sent, but naturally desires to work where he can do his work most efficiently," and this was, of course, only possible on a Sioux reservation. In his closing arguments, Wood praised Eastman's abilities and hoped something could be done to alter the decision and to get Eastman among his own people where he would be "of the greatest usefulness."[10]

The matter was finally resolved to everyone's satisfaction when Morgan appointed Eastman government physician at Pine Ridge Agency, South Dakota. He would assume his duties on November 1, 1890, at an annual salary of $1200. Apparently, there were no major objections to transferring the previous physician at Pine Ridge to the vacancy at Fort Berthold.[11]

Both Wood and Eastman, who were attending the Lake Mohonk Conference when they received the good news, were pleased with the appointment to Pine Ridge. Wood wrote that he believed Eastman "will prove a creditable representative both of the Government and his race," while Eastman declared, "I am happy to go among my own people to do what I can for them."[12] In addition, news of the appointment was greeted enthusiastically at the conference by such people as the Smiley brothers, Albert and Alfred, Senator Henry L. Dawes of Massachusetts, and Miss Sybil Carter, an Episcopal missionary at Pine Ridge. Eastman addressed a few pertinent remarks to those assembled wherein he affirmed his dedication to Christianity and the hope that he might in some small way help to rectify the wrongs committed against his people. In his closing remarks, he lapsed into sentimentality: "From Sky-Top [the name of one wing of Lake Mohonk Lodge] this morning I looked down upon the floating clouds all around us. But way up on the sides of the hills I could see specks of light here and there between the great clouds. The clouds were breaking up, and I had faith that they would move away. So I have faith that the clouds that shadow our people will move away."[13] Eastman's words enchanted the audience. When the conference ended, he returned to Boston where he prepared himself, with Wood's help, for the trip west.

When Eastman arrived at Pine Ridge during the first week of November, 1890, the starkness and desolation of the agency staggered him on first sight. He had grown accustomed to the verdure of the New England landscape and had acquired a taste for more gracious surroundings. Seeing the quarters he would inhabit hardly revived his flagging spirits. The agency dispensary had all the rustic charm of a large corn crib, and was about as effective in blocking the chilly winds.[14] It was furnished with two wood stoves improperly vented, four old chairs, and a desk. There were no tables, window curtains, carpets, or bed. The first thing Eastman did after dropping his suitcases inside the dispensary door was sign out an iron bed from agency supply. Once his books and other personal belongings arrived from the East, he felt less like an unwelcomed guest. He had received an offer his first day at the agency from a fellow employee to stay with him but he declined because he believed he should be nearer to his office, which adjoined his quarters in the dispensary, should he be needed by his Indian callers. Such Spartan idealism did, however, have its limit. He gladly accepted the money Frank Wood sent him for the purchase of furniture and household supplies.[15]

On the morning of his first full day as agency physician, he boarded up the small window from which his predecessor had doled out medicine. Eastman's practice, contrary to past procedures, would not be as a disbursing agent for nostrums. He was shocked that Indians had, for some time, been allowed to diagnose their own troubles. The previous physician, he complained, was little more than "a mere druggist who fills prescriptions" for them. He would see to it that Indians, before any drugs were prescribed, would first submit to an examination, and once their ailments were properly diagnosed, then he would treat them with properly prescribed medicine. He soon discovered why his predecessor had been so relaxed in his duties. Eastman was kept so busy his first week and a half, he wrote Wood, that he was only off his feet when asleep for a few hours every night. And if his patient load were not large enough already, Indians without ailments were appearing at his door at all hours, out of curiosity about the new Indian doctor.[16]

He also made several long trips to outlying districts during his first few weeks on the job. He resented having to make the trips on horse-back, when a team and wagon would have better suited his needs. With the large number of Indians around the agency and those in settlements scattered throughout the reservation, he wondered why the Indian bureau provided only one doctor for 6,000 Indians. But rather than despair, he plunged into his practice with renewed zeal. "My own inconveniences," he informed his Boston friends, "have not entered my mind since the first realization of the situation."[17]

By the end of December, Eastman reported with some satisfaction an improvement in sanitation at the reservation. He found, however, that scrofula, consumption, and indigestion were still the most preva-lent diseases among Indians, and he again noted the need for addi-tional medical staff to help care for the large Indian population. Many Sioux still patronized the old medicine men out of necessity because, as he knew, "they can not all have the government physician when they want him." A fully staffed and equipped hospital would also be a great blessing and would help solve the problem.[18]

Yet he persevered, and in a little over two years of service at Pine Ridge, Eastman performed his tasks most diligently. The number of patients he treated remained high, especially on issue days, usually bimonthly, when Indians gathered at the agency to receive their ra-tions. In time he even received a medical assistant to help with the work and also a team and buggy to use on his personal visits to his patients. He complained that two of the gravest problems which he faced in treating Indians were their reluctance to accept anesthesia and their great fear of amputation when circumstances proved neces-sary for such an operation.[19] He performed several other functions relating to health care: inaugurating a campaign, with the agent's assistance, to remove decaying livestock carcasses lying around the reservation; recommending a quarantine of Indians who had re-turned from European tours with Wild West shows until it could be established that they were free from cholera;[20] verifying the sick claims of Indian students, and conducting health inspections of gov-ernment and mission schools. Wherever possible, he initiated im-proved ventilation of dormitories but was unsuccessful in eliminating overcrowding. He could do little more than protest the way in which Indian children were stuffed into every available space at the board-ing schools.[21]

Despite his demanding schedule, Eastman did find time occasionally for socializing with colleagues of the agency community. On just such an occasion early in his tenure at Pine Ridge he met his future wife. Shortly after his arrival at the agency, at a reception given by the Reverend Charles Smith Cook, an Episcopal missionary and, like Eastman, a mixed-blood Sioux, he was introduced to Elaine Goodale, government supervisor of education for the Sioux. Their meeting coincided with the increase in tensions at Pine Ridge over the Ghost Dance Religion, or "Messiah Craze" as it was referred to at the time. Many Sioux had adopted the religion, which held out the lush promise that very soon all Indians would be free from disease, despair, and death, white civilization would disappear miraculously, and Indians living and dead would be reunited upon a regenerated earth. Coupled with recent crop failures, illness in epidemic proportions, and a lingering resentment over the breakup the previous year of the Great Sioux Reservation into six smaller reservations, was a recent reduction in rations. Hundreds of Sioux were ready that season for such miracles as the Ghost Dance promised. Within several weeks of Eastman's arrival at the agency, half the U.S. Army would be detailed to the Sioux country by the President to put down what was perceived as a rebellion. The collapse of authority at the agency, the arrival of troops, and the bloodletting that resulted, accelerated the courtship of Charles and Elaine, who were engaged within a month of their first meeting.[22]

Elaine Goodale was born on October 9, 1863, at Sky Farm, the home named by her father, Henry Sterling Goodale. It was an old house built by Dutch farmers halfway up a mountainside in the small township of Mount Washington nestled in the Berkshires of western Massachusetts. Her mother, Dora Hill Read Goodale, named their first-born daughter Elaine for Tennyson's lovelorn character. Both Elaine's parents were Yankee to the marrow, each one able to trace an American forebear to the early seventeenth century.

Dora Goodale perhaps most influenced the young girl's mind. "My mother was the pretty, youngest daughter of an old colonial family," Elaine remembered. "Though straitened in means, they were people of some pretensions and she was a city-bred girl of fastidious tastes, unused to hard work and hardly born to fit so primitive a setting" as Sky Farm. Dora Goodale would not send her daughter to the district

school a mile or so away from their home, but instead taught Elaine
herself. Dora was a good teacher: Elaine could read fluently at the
age of three.

Elaine's was a sheltered childhood. Lacking schoolmates and companions and with few excursions away from home, Elaine and her
two younger sisters—a brother, the youngest child of the Goodales,
was born when Elaine was fourteen—created a world of their
own where their imaginations were free to wander beyond their
mountainside.[23]

Elaine and her sister Dora, the second eldest, developed an un-
rivaled intimacy. Since their education had been primarily literary,
they achieved some facility with poetry. They composed their poems,
mostly about the discoveries of the natural world around them, and
read them to an admiring audience gathered around the dinner table.
Their parents encouraged them and were instrumental in publishing
many of the poems, first in magazines and later in a collected volume.
In the years after the Civil War, a period rich in sentimentality, the
young women of Sky Farm acquired fame. Six of their compositions
under the title "Poems by Two Little American Girls," were introduced to a juvenile audience in the pages of *St. Nicholas* in 1877,
when Elaine was fourteen. The two sisters published their first book,
Apple-Blossoms: Verses of Two Children, in 1878.

In the next few years, when it became clearer to their mother that
Elaine and Dora would need a more disciplined education to sharpen
their wits and hone their style, they were enrolled in a small, select
boarding school in New York City. They stayed there only one year,
long enough for homesickness to trigger their youthful reverie, and
long enough to meet the entrance requirements for Radcliffe College. But the year in New York had considerably diminished their
parents' finances so there would be neither college nor an entree into
middle-class society by way of an exclusive women's college. Instead
Elaine and Dora returned home where their mother, described as a
"nervous invalid" by then, prepared her elder daughters for adulthood with admonitions and aphorisms: "the beauty of service,"
"plain living and high thinking," and "our own duties and others'
rights."[24] Such wisdom, whether embroidered in a sampler or falling
from the lips, simple and direct, may not have satisfied her mother in

the end, but they provided Elaine with vivid memories of her mother's sacrifices that both satisfied and sanctified.

When it came time for Elaine to choose a career, she accepted her mother's wish that she teach at Hampton Institute in Virginia. "The altruistic motive appealed to us both," Elaine recalled, "and a post in a missionary school was no doubt less wounding to [mother's] pride than the alternative suggestion of tutoring small children in a private family." Elaine was then twenty. Sky Farm had been sold, her father moved to New York and a salaried post, and her mother, with the younger children, returned to her childhood home in rural Connecticut.[25]

Hampton Normal and Agricultural Institute had been founded in 1868 by General Samuel C. Armstrong, who had been a commander of Negro troops during the Civil War and afterward served as an agent of the Freedmen's Bureau. Armstrong had recognized a need for mental and manual training of the freedmen. Hampton Institute, as it was more commonly called, was founded for that purpose with generous support from the American Missionary Association and private philanthropy. Armstrong became an acquaintance of the Goodales when he visited Sky Farm in the summer of 1878, though in her memoirs, Elaine never explained what prompted the visit. He, it may be presumed, was taken with the young girl's precocity and remembered her five years later when a position was added in the Indian department at Hampton. Perhaps it was her mother who approached the general, though Elaine implies it was the reverse. However it happened, the young Miss Goodale joined Armstrong's staff in the fall of 1883, assigned to the sewing room as an instructor but quickly taking on additional classroom duties.

During the final military conquest of the Plains tribes in the 1870s, many reformers, wishing for an end to the violence and hoping for a solution to the "Indian problem," came to see similarities between the needs of Negroes and those of Indians in preparing them for eventual assimilation into American society. Accordingly, space was provided for Indians at Hampton. When the Red River War of the southern plains ended in 1875, Captain Richard Henry Pratt took a group of seventy-two Indian prisoners to Fort Marion in Florida. Pratt, after seeing considerable frontier service as an officer of the

Tenth Cavalry, a Negro regiment, and later as a commander of Indian scouts at Fort Sill, Indian Territory, while at Fort Marion decided that it was useless to imprison the more troublesome Indians unless they learned more from their experience than the power of intimidation possessed by the Whites. He persuaded his superiors to assign him the task of educating the prisoners, and achieved some dramatic successes. When the imprisonment ended in 1878, Pratt was reassigned to Hampton Institute and took with him seventeen of his former charges who were supported at Hampton by private benefactors.

Pratt, however, had a grander vision. He did not enjoy subordination to Armstrong. Although both agreed on principles of education, Pratt believed that Indians should have their own school. He also feared that prejudice against the assimilation of Blacks might proscribe the assimilation of Indians were they to be too closely associated with each other. Both men possessed strong personalities and were fiercely proud, but Armstrong was the more conciliatory and diplomatic of the two. Pratt, temperamental and unforgiving, found a sympathetic ear with Carl Schurz, Secretary of the Interior, and received permission to establish an Indian industrial school at the abandoned army barracks at Carlisle, Pennsylvania. Pratt left Hampton late in 1879, but Hampton retained its expanded mission for the education of both Negro and Indian. In between Pratt's stay at Hampton, and Elaine Goodale's appointment in the fall of 1883, the Indian division at the Virginia school enlarged the number of Indian students, and it became virtually a school within a school.[26]

Elaine's first "academic" class was "adult primary," where she taught rudimentary English to Indian men, many of whom were her seniors. She thankfully recognized her inexperience in the classroom, let alone a classroom filled with Indians, and learned to soften her demands for discipline.

> The appearance of a slip of a girl in the role of taskmaster, issuing mysterious orders and requiring instant obedience, must have been to these potential warriors a bewildering anomaly. Much hung on our sympathy, ingenuity, and quick appreciation of the struggle to relearn, in maturity, such fundamental tools as a new language, new

conventions, new social attitudes. It was a struggle of the will and the emotions, no less than of the intellect, in which both teacher and pupils engaged as pioneers.[27]

She was also soon engaged as a pioneer in public relations for Hampton. Shortly after Elaine arrived at Hampton, General Armstrong asked her to put her literary talents to work at promoting the school. Public support for Hampton was slow in developing, so Elaine wrote articles that trumpeted the success of educating Indians and enjoined the readers to support the enterprise with more than their prayers. "It was," she wrote, "a short step from verse suffused with serious purpose to prose animated by the zeal of a recent convert."[28]

Armstrong approved of all she wrote, and he introduced her to a widening circle of reformers interested in the uplift of Indians. On one such occasion, Anniversary Day at Carlisle, she met Captain Pratt. His encouragement, coupled with that of the general's, hardened her resolve to spend her life as an Indian educator.

After a year at Hampton, deciding it was time she visited Indian country, she informed General Armstrong of her desire and he obliged her by arranging for her safe escort on a tour of the Great Sioux Reservation agencies. Florence Bascom, a volunteer at Hampton, agreed to accompany Elaine. Florence was then at her father's home in Madison, Wisconsin, where her father was president of the University of Wisconsin. In Madison the two young women were joined by Herbert Welsh, of the recently formed Indian Rights Association, and his brother-in-law. Elaine found the tour "golden and memorable." "While little English was spoken among [the Sioux]," she wrote, "their friendly ways, and dark, smiling faces made a pleasant impression." She also met Bishop William H. Hare, Episcopal Bishop of Minnesota and Dakota Territory, and saw, firsthand, his model schools among the Sioux. At a settlement of "blanket Sioux," as she called them, on the White River a few miles above Lower Brule Agency, Elaine discovered an opportunity. In the midst of the forlorn community stood an abandoned government schoolhouse. A new tent, its canvass elaborately decorated by the Indians, was pitched close by the unpainted, broken-windowed school. Inside the tent, or "Ghost Lodge," were kept a sacred bundle of holy objects and plates filled daily with food for a recently deceased member of the community. Elaine grasped the dilemma of her calling, for there on White River "stood dramatically side by side the symbols of two opposed and irreconcilable cultures." On her return trip to civilization, she awakened to her mission: it was her duty to see that the tent was struck and the school opened. She arrived at Hampton, or so she remembered lapsing into third-person, "deeply committed to her task as she saw it."[29]

She told her story at the Lake Mohonk Conference that same October, and she repeated it shortly afterward to the Commissioner of Indian Affairs at Armstrong's suggestion. If the bureau would provide the funds, she would open an industrial training school and community center at White River. The commissioner, John D. C. Atkins, agreed, though he harbored certain misgivings about the ability of a young woman, just twenty-two, to make a success of the project. He overruled, however, the appointment of Laura Tileston, a teacher at Hampton and a close friend of Elaine, who had also volunteered. Undaunted, Tileston secured a commission as "lady missionary" from Bishop Hare with the understanding that she would assist Miss Goodale.[30]

A year after her first tour of Indian country, Elaine opened the school on the west bank of the Missouri at the mouth of White River. She and Laura soon had fifty children between the ages of six and sixteen in attendance. The two women attempted to teach their students the values of the dominant society. In the summer months when Laura would visit relatives in the East, Elaine would roam around the reservation and visit the agencies. By the close of the second term Laura had lost her missionary zeal and resigned her post in the summer of 1888. Elaine tried to replace Laura with Dora Goodale, her younger sister, but Dora demurred. Instead, Elaine's maiden aunt on her mother's side agreed to carry on the work at White River. For Elaine, however, the enterprise lost its charm during the third year: "The community center was moving smoothly, quite according to plan," but with success came disappointment, for Elaine knew that she "was no longer pioneering."[31]

Bishop Hare, sensing her restlessness, offered her a remote mission outpost among "the wilder Teton Sioux" and also hinted broadly that she might soon receive the superintendency of one of the smaller government boarding schools. Elaine, however, had pinned her hopes on the development of a system of community day schools. "I told myself that I would resign and go East . . . go to Mohonk . . . to Washington! I would put the whole case before people with influence and see what could be done." In the meantime, she spent the summer of 1889 traveling among the "wilder" Sioux. She accompanied a hunting party to the sand hills of Nebraska, south of the newly established Rosebud Reservation. Two days out from White River settlement, the party was met by a lone traveler, Chasing Crane, just returned from Rosebud, who joined the group gathered around the newly raked campfire and a boiling pot of coffee and told a wonderful story. "God," Chasing Crane explained, "has appeared to the Crows across the Stony Mountains." Because God could abide no longer the parents' crying for their children who were dying from the whites' diseases, Whites would disappear and the buffalo would return. The Indian messiah who promised these things was beautiful to look upon.[32]

All in the hunting party except Elaine listened transfixed by Chasing Crane's good news. The men in the party began to sing, and the monotonous, muffled beat of a ceremonial drum soothed the saddle-weary Elaine to sleep. She did not dream that night, but if she did, she could never have dreamed the "strange and cruel events destined to grow out of Chasing Crane's fantastic story."[33]

Elaine resigned her commission in the autumn of 1889 and returned to the East, jobless and without money. Her mother had moved to Northampton, Massachusetts, to be nearer to her two younger daughters, who were attending Smith College. She allowed Elaine to share her modest home and to use it as a headquarters for a campaign in support of day schools for Indians. Elaine supported herself on the honoraria she received for speaking to Indian rights groups and to college audiences, frequently sharing the same rostrum with Thomas Jefferson Morgan, President Benjamin Harrison's newly appointed Commissioner of Indian Affairs. Morgan heard much truth in the young woman's plea. An advocate of a comprehensive school system for Indians which would eventually lead to their complete integration into the public schools of the nation, Morgan believed that the public school was the bright star around which all Indian reform revolved. It was truly the polestar that had risen in this night of the Indians' cultural despair to guide, with a cool, clear light, their journey out of darkness towards a future illumination. The boarding schools, the Carlisles and Hamptons, had their place in the constellation, but they were only a few intensely bright spots in a much grander assemblage. Morgan warmed to Elaine's suggestions and promised to include her in his administration of the Indian bureau.[34]

True to his promise, in March, 1890, he named her as the first Supervisor of Education in the two Dakotas. As supervisor, she was directed to "systematically visit all the schools among the Sioux, ascertain what they need, report the deficiences, advise inexperienced teachers, devise ways of reaching the children, introduce industrial training into the day schools, and, in general, systematize, extend, and improve the schools as far as possible."[35] And it was in this capacity that she visited Pine Ridge Agency in the fall of 1890 and met Charles Eastman.

Although Charles and Elaine had never met before, both had heard about each other's work from their mutual friends and associates.[36] At the reception they were instantly drawn to each other, and shortly after their first meeting Elaine promised to marry Eastman. They decided to announce their engagement on Christmas Day, just a few weeks away.[37]

But the middle of November, 1890, at Pine Ridge was a "time of grim suspense," Elaine wrote. "We seemed to be waiting—helplessly waiting—as if in some horrid nightmare, for the inevitable catastrophe."[38] Chasing Crane's wonderful story, told a year before around a campfire in South Dakota, had since become the nightmare of which Elaine wrote. Newspapers throughout the country carried lurid stories of imminent Indian uprisings. The Sioux appeared the most rebellious and, in consequence, troops arrived at the Dakota reservations so as better to preserve order. The cause of all the disorder was a religion known as the Ghost Dance, but referred to in the popular press as the "Messiah Craze." Although its origins were vague, its presumed consequences were not. The government feared that people, probably white people, were in danger of their lives.

Wovoka, or Jack Wilson, as he was known among the Whites of Mason Valley, Nevada, was the person responsible for the Ghost

Dance of 1890. The religion of this Paiute holyman centered on the belief of the annihilation of the white race and the survival and glorification of all Indians in communion with all their past generations. The date for the millennium was originally set by Wovoka for the spring of 1891. To insure that the revitalization of the world would take place, Wovoka told his followers that they must be industrious, honest, and above all peaceful. At certain intervals they must also perform a dance, a slow, side-step to the left around a circle, that became the most prominent feature of the religion.

The historical roots of the Ghost Dance Religion lay deep in the protracted cultural destruction of America's native race. Wovoka's religion, first proclaimed in January, 1889, spread rapidly from his own Paiutes to the Washos, Bannocks, Mohaves, Walapais, Chemehuevis, Havasupais, Shoshonis, Utes, Gosiutes, Arapahoes, Cheyennes, Kiowas, Pawnees, and Sioux. The doctrine and rituals were flexible enough that those tribes which adopted the religion often incorporated their own beliefs into a larger and sometimes confused theology. Yet as taught by the prophet, the pristine religion professed nonviolence. God would deliver a righteous punishment to non-Indians. In only one tribe, the Sioux, did the doctrine assume violent proportions. Before the slaughter of the Sioux at Wounded Knee on a bleak December morning in 1890, the religion had swept across the western United States. In just under two years—from January, 1889, to December, 1890, the Ghost Dance Religion had covered the interior West, from a rather small reservation, Walker River, in western Nevada, to the banks of the Missouri. From estimates made by James Mooney, the chronicler of the religion, out of a total reservation-Indian population of 146,000, approximately 60,000 of them adopted the religion.[39]

For American civilization the year 1890 has been given a measure of significance by many historians. In that year the superintendent of the census announced the official closure of the frontier. In that year Native Americans reached the nadir of degradation in their centuries-old struggle for the survival of their cultures. Not only did the bloodletting at Wounded Knee signal the end of the Ghost Dance as a major religious movement among Indians, but it also represented the ultimate defeat of the once-feared Plains tribes, preeminently represented by the Sioux, to a circumscribed status and subordinate status within the dominant society. Indians were now confined to an existence which demanded an uncritical acceptance of the ways of American culture.

One implication of the Ghost Dance largely overlooked at the time was its dimensions. Before its suppression, the religion had unified a very great number of American Indians in a common belief extraordinary in its hopefulness—what two hundred years of Christianization and civilization had failed to accomplish. Of particular significance also was the development of a Pan-Indian response to assaults on their cultures. American Indians had for millennia identified themselves exclusively in tribal terms. American Indians began, as a result of the Ghost Dance, to look upon themselves as "Indians," ironically as the Whites had been doing for centuries. Wovoka told his followers that they were members, not of individual tribes, but of one Chosen People.

For the Sioux the Ghost Dance had tragic consequences. The rumors of the previous summer, 1889, were confirmed when a delegation of Sioux returned to their reservations late in March, 1890. The Sioux apostles of Wovoka added their own message to that of the prophet's. The religion soon became a militant confrontation between many of the Sioux and their white keepers. Wovoka had continually stressed the avoidance of violence, even in thought, and though other tribes seemed to absorb the message, "it was only where chronic dissatisfaction was aggravated by recent grievances," James Mooney explained, "that the movement assumed a hostile expression."[40]

The plight of the Sioux by the close of the 1880s was grim. Their herds of cattle were diminished by disease in 1888; their crops failed in 1889; and epidemics of influenza, measles, and whooping cough devastated the Indian camps. During this same period a government commission negotiated a surrender of 11,000,000 acres of land.[41]

With the passage of the Dawes Act, Congress moved quickly in the passage of a special Sioux Bill in April, 1888. The Dawes Act had stipulated that the President, either before or after allotment of a tribe, could negotiate with that same tribe for surplus lands. For the Sioux it meant that such a transaction would have to follow the provisions under Article XII of the Treaty of 1868. It required three-quarters of all adult males to approve any cession of land. According to the Sioux Bill, the Great Sioux Reservation was to be divided into six smaller reservations and the surplus lands were to revert to the public domain.

The Secretary of the Interior appointed a special commission headed by now Colonel Richard Henry Pratt of Carlisle, to take the document to the Sioux. Difficulties plagued the Pratt Commission almost from the moment it arrived in the Dakotas.[42] Many of the promised benefits incorporated in the new bill were simply repetitions of older, unfulfilled treaty provisions. Failing to receive the required number of signatures, the Pratt Commission left the reservation and returned to Washington, where its leader penned a scathing report in which he denounced the Sioux for their obstinate refusal to recognize something so clearly in their interest.[43] On March 2, 1889, the lame duck session of the Fiftieth Congress passed a revamped Sioux Bill, signed by President Grover Cleveland just two days before he left office, which held to many of the same principles of the earlier one, but with added compensations which the Indians had demanded from the Pratt Commission and later during a visit of Sioux chiefs to Washington.[44] On May 19, 1889, President Benjamin Harrison sent a new commission under the leadership of General George Crook.

The Crook Commission left Chicago in May, stopping first at the Rosebud Agency, where they opened the council with a barbecue of fifteen beeves. Despite strenuous opposition from a few leaders regarded as "nonprogressives," the Crook Commission obtained a good number of signatures. Although the commissioners listed the signers of the bill by agency, the Indian bureau calculated the signatures on the basis of the entire reservation. The signers supposedly numbered 4,482 out of a possible 5,678 eligible males, or more than the three-fourths required by the 1868 treaty, and on this basis the agreement, though fradulent, was passed by Congress.[45]

The land cession of 1889 left the Sioux dazed and insolent. To make matters worse, their government rations were cut by more than half due to a recent census.[46] Because of the bruised sensibilities of the Sioux, the Ghost Dance Religion appreared as balm.

The stories of the Sioux delegates upon their return from Nevada sped to the remotest corner of each of the newly created reservations. The "progressive" Sioux, many of whom were younger and remembered little of the previous way of life, found dubious the more remarkable tenets of the religion. The "nonprogressives," those of middle and advanced age who had suffered most from the conflict between the old and the new values, embraced the religion. The glowing promises gave them renewed hope, and they looked eagerly to Wovoka's Sioux apostles for instruction in the Ghost Dance.

As the summer of 1890 dragged on, any hope that the Sioux would be able to subsist on their own crops evaporated like a drop of water in a desert. Hunger continued to plague the reservations. The growing season, which had begun so auspiciously in the spring, was ruined by the July drought. The loss of crops that summer exceeded that of the previous year.[47] Ghost Dances began at Pine Ridge early in August and spread to the other reservations. The cult seized the Rosebud Sioux in September. In the second week of October one of the Sioux apostles took his message to Sitting Bull's people along the Grand River at Standing Rock Reservation. Agent McLaughlin had the Sioux missionary ejected from the reserve and warned Sitting Bull that he would not tolerate any ghost dancing on his reservation.[48]

From October until late December and Wounded Knee, conditions at four of the Sioux reservations—Pine Ridge, Rosebud, Cheyenne River, and Standing Rock—became tenser. On October 31, for example, Short Bull, one of the Sioux delegates to Wovoka, addressed a large gathering of ghost dancers at Pine Ridge, proclaiming that, because the Whites were interfering so much in the Indians' religion, he was personally advancing the date of the great change to the new moon in December.[49] The Sioux were then holding dances in direct violation of their agents' orders.

The newly appointed Republican agent at Pine Ridge, Dr. Daniel F. Royer, began calling for the army almost from the moment he arrived at the agency in early October. He earned from the Oglala Sioux at Pine Ridge the sobriquet "Young Man Afraid of His Indians." His most frantic telegram to the Indian bureau was sent on November 15. "We need protection and we need it now," he pleaded. "The leaders should be arrested and confined in some military post until the matter is quieted and this should be done at once."[50] The President, however, had already issued orders to the War Department and the army to take such steps as necessary for the maintenance of order.[51] Accordingly, on the morning of November 20, soldiers arrived at the Sioux agencies. At Pine Ridge alone, five companies of infantry and three companies of cavalry marched into the agency.[52]

At seeing so many soldiers, the frightened Pine Ridge Sioux, progressives as well as nonprogressives, fled to the Badlands northwest of the reservation, where they joined with Short Bull's band of ghost dancers. As the Indians fled north and west, foraging as they went, the settlers in the recently opened lands fled east. Indian agents could not distinguish between those Indians who believed in the religion and those who were simply running from the army.[53]

Dr. Eastman had been against the summoning of troops. Agent Royer, on the evening of the same day he frantically wired for troops, called together agency employees to ask their opinions on what should be done to restore order. Eastman believed that there was no "widespread plot, or deliberate intention to make war upon the whites." If troops were sent for it would only serve as a challenge to the ghost dancers. His view, however, was clearly in the minority.[54] But should the use of troops prove necessary, Eastman had already pledged to support the government. It was his duty and, furthermore, no one could then brand him disloyal.[55] The anticipated use of force troubled him. He hoped to avoid a confrontation and believed that resorting to intimidation might bring on the clash of arms which all people at Pine Ridge hoped to avoid.

Eastman suspected that if the Sioux ghost dancers were left alone, their enthusiasm for messiahism might wane naturally in a few months.[56] And though he was not fully aware, at first, of the many grievances that the Sioux had, he soon became aware of the hunger and famine, and also of the government's unresponsiveness. Humane and conciliatory measures would, he came to believe, have accomplished much more with less violence than all the soldiers called from all the military posts throughout the country.[57] Eastman's voice of moderation unfortunately, as well as those of a few others, were overwhelmed by the more pugnacious.

Efforts to implement the newly adopted policy of isolating the "troublemakers" resulted in the death of Sitting Bull. On December 15, officers of the Indian police at Standing Rock Reservation arrested the Hunkpapa leader at his home on Grand River. A fight broke out between his followers, some of whom were ghost dancers, and the Indian police. In a gunfight at close quarters, Sitting Bull, though unarmed, was shot by the Indian police.[58] News of his death alarmed both friendly and hostile bands of Sioux.

Another Sioux leader, Big Foot of Cheyenne River Reservation, was also feared by government authorities because they believed, wrongly, that he too supported the Ghost Dance. Although he had encouraged adoption of the religion in October and November, by December he had become disillusioned with the movement. The military and agency officials, however, were unaware of Big Foot's apostasy. When it was discovered that Big Foot and his Miniconjou band, which included refugees from Sitting Bull's Standing Rock Sioux, planned to march to Cheyenne River Agency for rations and annuities and then move on to Pine Ridge where the chief was promised 100 ponies by the headmen of that reservation if he could restore order, the commander of the soldiers at Pine Ridge dispatched a unit to intercept the Indians. Big Foot's band was found, and at a council with the officer-in-charge, Big Foot agreed to return to his camp. The soldiers then withdrew. Pressured by a number of the men in his band, Big Foot violated his pledge and resumed the trek to Pine Ridge on December 23. Once again, the army intercepted him and the chief and his people were ordered on December 28 to head for a camp on Wounded Knee Creek. Colonel James W. Forsyth and soldiers from the Seventh Cavalry, Lieutenant Colonel George A. Custer's former regiment, were sent to guard the camp.[59]

Back at Pine Ridge Agency, government employees and their families were gathered together; they had been fearful of an uprising of the Oglala Sioux. To help ease tensions, Eastman and Elaine planned activities for the agency in celebration of the Christmas season. The doctor recalled that the morning of December 29, 1890, was sunny and mild. Suddenly, echoes of gunfire were heard from the direction of Wounded Knee, and it became apparent that the dreaded confrontation between the military and Indians had happened. Messengers, both military and Indian, brought news of the fight to the agency. Chaos ensued, and gunfire was exchanged between Indian police and Indians. Brigadier General John S. Brooke, commander of the troops sent to the Sioux agencies, and Eastman ran out from the agency headquarters, and the general screamed, "Stop, stop! Doctor, tell them they must not fire until ordered!"

Eastman, in the Sioux language, relayed the order to the Indian police "as bullets whistled by us, and the General's coolness perhaps saved all our lives, for we were in no position to repel a large attacking force." Moreover, because of Brooke's later refusal to employ an armed attack against these Indians, another major confrontation was avoided.[60]

Yet many people at the agency, including Eastman, were certain that their lives were in danger and the agency would be attacked at any moment. "Every married employee," Eastman wrote, "was seeking a place of safety for his family." Indeed, he had tried to persuade his fiancee to leave the agency for her own safety. Elaine refused and, with Eastman and others, helped care for panic-stricken men, women, and children.[61]

As night approached, the Seventh Cavalry arrived at the agency with the results of the day's violence. Although the exact numbers of the dead and wounded Indian men, women, and children cannot be accurately ascertained, final reported figures indicated a total of 153 dead and 44 wounded. Twenty-five soldiers had been killed, in some instances by the shots from the troops who ringed the Indian camp. Thirty-nine soldiers had been wounded in the encounter.[62] Military casualties were taken to an army field hospital, while most of the wounded Sioux were placed in the Reverend Charles Cook's Episcopay mission chapel, which had been converted into a hospital. Eastman, who was placed in charge of the wounded Indians by General Brooke, sadly wrote:

> We tore out the pews and covered the floor with hay and quilts. There we laid the poor creatures side by side in rows, and the night was devoted to caring for them as best we could. Many were frightfully torn by pieces of shells, and the suffering was terrible.... Although the army surgeons were more than ready to help as soon as their own men had been cared for, the tortured Indians would scarcely allow a man in uniform to touch them. Mrs. Cook, Miss Goodale, and several of Mr. Cook's Indian helpers acted as volunteer nurses. In spite of all our efforts, we lost the greater part of them, but a few recovered, including several children who had lost all their relatives and who were adopted into kind Christian families.[63]

The day after the Wounded Knee disaster, a raging two-day blizzard blanketed Pine Ridge with snow. In the midst of the blizzard, on December 30, Eastman and several Indian police unsuccessfully attempted to locate an injured policeman, who was reported wounded and lying about two miles from the agency.[64]

On the morning of January 1, 1891, a far more important search took place. The blizzard had finally ended and an expedition of over one hundred men, mostly Oglala Sioux, began their journey to Wounded Knee Creek, eighteen miles away. They were eager to know if there were any wounded Indians who might have survived the fight on December 29 and the devastating blizzard which followed. In charge of the expedition was Dr. Eastman.[65]

As the party approached the site of the battle, the startling realization of what had happened became apparent. Before them lay the remains of Big Foot's campsite. The Indians on the expedition began their mourning chants. Eastman was also deeply moved. The Whites, fearing repercussions, were deployed to search the foreboding mounds for any possible survivors. To the surprise of most of the searchers, seven Indians—five adults and two children—were found still alive and were transported back to the mission chapel hospital.[66]

Eastman personally found an old blind woman and an infant girl, both of whom had lived through the grueling ordeal. The woman had been discovered under a wagon which protected her from the elements, while the girl was found lying near her dead mother. She had survived the three days of extremely low temperatures because she had been warmly wrapped. Ironically, on her head she wore a fur cap embellished with a beaded embroidery of an American flag.[67]

Observing the activities of the search party from nearby hills were Indian warriors, who were, according to Eastman, friends of the victims. Fear of an armed attack from the hostile band resulted in Eastman's riding back to the agency for a military escort. He later wrote, "I covered the eighteen miles in quick time and was not interfered with in any way, although if the Indians had meant mischief they could easily have picked me off from any of the ravines and gulches."[68] Extra soldiers arrived, and the expedition, after burying all the dead Indians in a large, rectangular pit, returned to the agency.[69]

Eastman and others continued looking after the ailing Indians, and he received much needed aid from individuals and organizations throughout the country, including the powerful Indian Rights Association.[70] The pace must have been rigorous because the Reverend Cook suffered a nervous breakdown while caring for Indian survivors. Praise of the role Eastman and Elaine Goodale played in their untiring service to the sick and wounded echoed from the halls of the Lake Mohonk Conference of Friends of the Indian.[71]

In explaining the tragedy at Wounded Knee, Eastman once again expressed his views candidly. He was profoundly disturbed by what had happened, and perhaps for the first time in his life really felt the torment of an Indian operating in white society. "All this was a severe ordeal," he lamented, "for one who had so lately put all his faith in the Christian love and lofty ideals of the white man." Corrupt politicians and their improperly trained political appointees, declared Eastman, were responsible for the troubles and subsequent battle because they "first robbed the Indians, then bullied them, and finally in a panic called for troops to suppress them."[72] Moreover, he believed Big Foot and his people were not hostile; they were simply frightened of not only having to surrender their weapons to the soldiers but also of the large Hotchkiss guns directed at them. He agreed that an Indian fired the first shot which sparked the disaster at Wounded Knee, but he could not in any way condone the indiscriminate killing of women and children.[73]

Elaine Goodale also reported on what had happened. Her views concerning the facts that Big Foot's band "did not deliberately plan a resistance" and that an Indian bore the responsibility for firing the initial shot corresponded with Eastman's statements. On the matter of the random killing of women and children, she declared that although there might have been a few attempts not to fire on them, "it was in many cases deliberate and intentional," and "the Seventh Cavalry, Custer's old command, had an old grudge to repay." This letter, which was an answer to Commissioner Morgan's request for her observations on the battle, later appeared in a number of newspapers.[74]

By the middle of January, 1891, the entire affair had ended, costing the government approximately $1,200,000, money which could have been used to relieve the hunger and distress of the Indians, and to save over 350 lives. On January 21, Major General Nelson A. Miles, commander of the Division of the Missouri, assembled the 3,500 troops at Pine Ridge and ordered a grand review. It was an effective display of military might.[75] By March, Eastman could write to Commissioner Morgan that dangers of another Indian outbreak were slim. By that time also, more pleasant thoughts began to occupy the doctor's mind. His wedding day was fast approaching and preparations were underway. Elaine resigned her position in March and went East to help with the details.[76]

Eastman followed later, receiving leave time from his duties as government physician.[77] The wedding took place on June 18, 1891, at the Church of the Ascension, an Episcopal church, in New York City. Frank Wood and his wife gave the newlyweds a lavish reception. After visiting with friends and relatives in New York, Massachusetts, and Connecticut, the Eastmans returned to the West. At Flandreau, they were received by John Eastman. They all raised glasses to the future and unbridled happiness.[78]

NOTES

1. Wood to Morgan, May 19, 1890, BIA, RG 75, LR, NA; Wood to David Dorchester, July 18, 1890, ibid.
2. Wood to Dorchester, July 18, 1890, ibid.
3. Eastman to Morgan, Aug. 20, 1890, ibid.
4. Ibid.; Wood to Morgan, Aug. 18, 1890, ibid.
5. Wood to Morgan, Aug. 18, 1890, ibid.
6. Morgan to James McLaughlin, Aug. 22, 1890, Records of the Bureau of Indian Affairs, Record Group 75, Standing Rock Agency, Box 517170, Misc. Letters, Federal Archives and Records Center, Kansas City, Mo. Hereafter cited as KC.
7. Eastman to Morgan, Aug. 29, 1890, BIA, RG 75, LR, NA.
8. McLaughlin to Morgan, Sept. 3, 1890, James McLaughlin Papers, Microfilm, Reel 21, Assumption Abbey Archives, Richardton, N.D.; James Heisney to Secretary of the Interior, Sept. 6, 1890, ibid., Reel 34.
9. Morgan to R. H. Best, Oct. 1, 1890, telegram, BIA, RG 75, LR, NA.
10. Wood to R. V. Belt, Oct. 4, 1890, ibid.
11. Belt to D. F. Royer, Nov. 6, 1890, BIA, RG 75, Pine Ridge Agency, Box 11, LR and gen. file, KC.
12. Wood to Belt, Oct. 9, 1890, BIA, RG 75, LR, NA; Eastman to Belt, Oct. 9, 1890, ibid.
13. Henry L. Dawes to Belt, Oct. 10, 1890, ibid.; *Proceedings of the*

Eighth Annual Meeting of the Lake Mohonk Conference of Friends of the Indian, 1890, p. 46. Hereafter cited as LMC.

14. Eastman, *From the Deep Woods*, pp. 76–77.
15. Ibid., p. 77; Wood to Belt, Nov. 15, 1890, BIA, RG 75, LR, NA; Wood to Belt, Nov. 17, 1890, enclosure, Records of the Bureau of Indian Affairs, Record Group 75, Special Case Number 188, The Ghost Dance, 1890–98, Microfilm, Reel 1, National Archives and Records Service.
16. Wood to Belt, Nov. 17, 1890, enclosure, Special Case No. 188, Reel 1.
17. Ibid.
18. "Monthly Sanitary Report of Sick and Wounded at Pine Ridge Agency, South Dakota," Dec., 1890, BIA, RG 75, LR, NA. A hospital was eventually built through the aid of contributions primarily collected by the Indian Rights Association.
19. Eastman, *From the Deep Woods*, pp. 87, 120–21.
20. Eastman to Captain Charles G. Penney, Apr. 26, 1891, BIA, RG 75, Pine Ridge Agency, Box 3, vol. 10, 1891, Letters Sent, KC; Captain George Le Roy Brown to Eastman, Sept. 17, 1892, BIA, RG 75, Pine Ridge Agency, Box 4, vol. 15, 1892, Misc. LS, KC.
21. Brown to Eastman, Sept. 27, 1892, BIA, RG 75, Pine Ridge Agency, Box 4, vol. 15, 1892, Misc. LS, KC; Eastman to Penney, Nov. 10, 1891, BIA, RG 75, Pine Ridge Agency, Box 12, 1891, LR and gen. file, KC; Penney to CIA, Nov. 11, 1891, BIA, RG 75, Pine Ridge Agency, Box 3, vol. 11, 1891, LS, KC.
22. Eastman, *From the Deep Woods*, pp. 85–86.
23. Kay Graber, ed., *Sister to the Sioux: The Memoirs of Elaine Goodale Eastman, 1885–1891* (Lincoln: University of Nebraska Press, 1978), pp. 1–4. See also Elaine Goodale Eastman, "All the Days of My Life," *South Dakota Historical Review* 2 (July, 1937): 171–84.
24. Graber, *Sister to the Sioux*, pp. 8–10, 13–14.
25. Ibid., pp. 16–17.
26. Ibid., pp. 16–22; Priest, *Uncle Sam's Stepchildren*, pp. 141–44; Francis Paul Prucha, *American Indian Policy in Crisis: Christian Reformers and the Indian, 1865–1900* (Norman: University of Oklahoma Press, 1976), pp. 271–74.
27. Graber, *Sister to the Sioux*, p. 19.
28. Ibid., pp. 20–21.
29. Ibid., pp. 23–26, 29.
30. Ibid., pp. 29–31.
31. Ibid., pp. 32, 40, 63–64, 86, 94.
32. Ibid., pp. 94–97.

33. Ibid., p. 97.
34. Ibid., pp. 114–17.
35. Ibid., p. 117; quoted from her first report following Eastman, "All the Days of My Life," p. 188.
36. Mensel, "John, Charles, and Elaine Goodale Eastman," pp. 28, 33; Eastman, *From the Deep Woods*, p. 86.
37. Eastman, "All the Days of My Life," p. 181; Eastman, *From the Deep Woods*, pp. 105–6; *The Red Man*, Dec. 1890–Jan. 1891.
38. Graber, *Sister to the Sioux*, pp. 151–52.
39. James Mooney, "The Ghost Dance Religion and the Sioux Outbreak of 1890," *Fourteenth Annual Report of the Bureau of American Ethnology* (Washington: Government Printing Office, 1896), p. 926.
40. Ibid., p. 777. See also L. G. Moses, "James Mooney and Wovoka: An Ethnologist's Visit With the Ghost Dance Prophet," *Nevada Historical Society Quarterly* 23 (Summer, 1980): 71–86.
41. Fritz, *Movement for Assimilation*, p. 218.
42. "Treaty With the Sioux, Fort Laramie, April 29, 1868," in Washburn, *The American Indian and the United States*, vol. 4, p. 2524; George Hyde, *A Sioux Chronicle* (Norman: University of Oklahoma Press, 1956), pp. 184–228.
43. For activities on the Pratt Commission, see CIA, *Annual Report*, 1888.
44. Utley, *The Last Days of the Sioux Nation*, p. 47; James C. Olson, *Red Cloud and the Sioux Problem* (Lincoln: University of Nebraska Press, 1965), pp. 310–19.
45. Olson, *Red Cloud*, p. 319.
46. Fletcher W. Johnson, *The Red Record of the Sioux: Sitting Bull and the History of the Indian War of 1890* (Philadelphia: Edgewood Publishing, 1891), pp. 513–20.
47. Olson, *Red Cloud*, pp. 320–21.
48. Stanley Vestal, *Sitting Bull, Champion of the Sioux* (Norman: University of Oklahoma Press, 1957), pp. 268–71.
49. Hyde, *A Sioux Chronicle*, p. 266.
50. Royer to CIA, Nov. 15, 1890, telegram, Special Case No. 188, Reel 1.
51. Benjamin Harrison to Secretary of War, Nov. 13, 1890, ibid.
52. Olson, *Red Cloud*, pp. 326–27.
53. Vestal, *Sitting Bull*, p. 287.
54. Eastman, *From the Deep Woods*, pp. 97–98.
55. Ibid., pp. 96–97.
56. Ibid., p. 99. See Utley, *The Last Days of the Sioux Nation*, p. 76 for similar views.

57. Utley, *The Last Days of the Sioux Nation*, p. 76.
58. Ibid., pp. 146–66.
59. See ibid., Chapters 9–11 for a complete and detailed account of these events.
60. Eastman, *From the Deep Woods*, pp. 107–9; Utley, *The Last Days of the Sioux Nation*, pp. 232–33.
61. Utley, *The Last Days of the Sioux Nation*, pp. 232–33.
62. Ibid., pp. 227–28.
63. Eastman, *From the Deep Woods*, pp. 109–0; Utley, *The Last Days of the Sioux Nation*, pp. 234–35.
64. Eastman, *From the Deep Woods*, pp. 110–11.
65. Ibid., p. 111; Utley, *The Last Days of the Sioux Nation*, pp. 1–2.
66. Utley, *The Last Days of the Sioux Nation*, *pp.* 2–4; Eastman, *From the Deep Woods*, pp. 111–13.
67. Utley, *The Last Days of the Sioux Nation*, p. 3; Eastman, *From the Deep Woods*, p. 113.
68. Eastman, *From the Deep Woods*, pp. 113–14.
69. Utley, *The Last Days of the Sioux Nation*, p. 4.
70. Eastman, *From the Deep Woods*, p. 114; Welsh to Goodale, Apr. 8, 1891, IRA, Reel 5, Outgoing Correspondence.
71. Welsh to Goodale, May 29, 1891, IRA, Reel 5, Outgoing Correspondence; LMC, 9th sess., 1891, pp. 8–9.
72. Eastman, *From the Deep Woods*, pp. 114, 117.
73. Eastman to General Eliphalet Whittlesey, Jan. 30, 1891, Selected Documents from the Records of the Board of Indian Commissioners, Microfilm, Reel 201, Doris Duke Oral History Project, History Department, University of New Mexico, Albuquerque, N.M. See also Eastman to Wood, Jan. 31, 1891, pp. 33–34, in Elaine Goodale Eastman's manuscript copy of "The Ghost Dance War and Wounded Knee Massacre of 1890–91," Sophia Smith Collection (Women's History Archive), Eastman Collection, Y Eastman, file 2, Smith College Library, Northampton, Mass. This material, carefully edited by Elaine Goodale Eastman, contains very little on Charles A. Eastman.
74. Goodale to CIA, Jan. 12, 1891, McLaughlin Papers, Reel 35. See also Eastman Scrapbook Number 1, Eastman Collection, Smith College Library and Elaine Goodale Eastman, "The Ghost Dance and Wounded Knee Massacre of 1890–91," *Nebraska History* 26 (Jan., 1945): 26–42.
75. Utley, *The Last Days of the Sioux Nation*, pp. 260, 267–70.
76. Eastman to Morgan, Mar. 27, 1891, BIA, RG 75, LR, NA; Eastman, *From the Deep Woods*, p. 115.

77. Wood to Morgan, May 9, 1891, BIA, RG 75, LR, NA; Eastman to Morgan, May 11, 1891, ibid.
78. Eastman Scrapbook No. 1, Eastman Collection, Smith College Library; Charles A. Eastman Folder, Baker Library; Eastman, *From the Deep Woods*, pp. 125–26.

CHAPTER 4

PHYSICIAN VERSUS AGENT

AT THE HEIGHT of the Ghost Dance at Pine Ridge Reservation Elaine Goodale had pledged herself to marry Dr. Charles Eastman. She gave her promise, she later reminisced, "with a thrilling sense of two-fold consecration." She gave herself to the traditional duties of wife and mother, and at the same time she "embraced with a new and deeper zeal the conception of life-long service to my husband's people." And in that moment of consecration, how simple it all seemed, compared to "how far from simple has been the event."[1]

When the Eastmans returned to Pine Ridge Agency, Charles resumed his duties as physician, and Elaine began her journey down "the old and well-worn road, trodden by women's feet throughout the ages."[2] But of the prolonged happiness of a new life which both had anticipated, and which both had toasted, there proved to be precious little. Controversy soon swirled about the newlyweds, involving a long, drawn-out, and complicated series of charges between them and the acting Indian agent, Captain George Le Roy Brown, a Civil War veteran.

The controversy had its origin in the payment of a $100,000 congressional appropriation to those Sioux at Pine Ridge, identified as "nonhostiles," for losses to their property and livestock during the Ghost Dance troubles. Commissioner Morgan placed Special Agent James A. Cooper in charge of the disbursement. At first Cooper received the cordial support of the Eastmans.[3] In fact, Dr. Eastman suggested to Commissioner Morgan that Cooper should make the payments because of his previous extensive work among the Sioux and his personal knowledge of many of the claimants.[4] Cooper later approached Eastman and asked him to serve as one of three witnesses during the actual payments, an assignment the doctor was reluctant to accept at first because of his busy schedule, but when assured by the special agent that his duties would be few, Eastman relented.[5]

No sooner had Cooper begun making payments than Indians began complaining to Eastman that they were not receiving their rightful share. They intimated that Cooper was involved in questionable activities with other Whites at the agency, notably James A. Finlay, the Indian trader, and George P. Comer, the chief clerk. Eastman accepted existence of a "ring," though he was not sure of its designs.[6]

Eastman erred in his response. Instead of reporting the Indians' complaints to Agent Brown, which was the proper thing to do, he wrote to others concerning the discontent among a few Pine Ridge Sioux. Cooper was himself aware that some Indians were dissatisfied and asked Brown to investigate their complaints. The agent called Eastman into his office and proceeded to inquire about the accusations of fraud. Brown's account of this meeting and subsequent meetings with Eastman are contradictory to Eastman's recollections of them.

Brown, according to the report submitted to Commissioner Morgan, asked the doctor "if he knew, of his own personal knowledge, anything in any way derogatory to the character of" Cooper, Finlay, and Comer. Eastman answered in the negative, but said he had received complaints against them from others whose names he gave to Brown. Brown reported that he "duly investigated in the Doctor's presence" all of the charges made, and found that some Indians denied ever making such statements, that one Indian was in error about the amount he should have received, and that Eastman misunderstood others. Brown declared that Cooper "performed his duties faithfully and conscientiously." He wrote that his investigation also cleared the other men involved. He concluded that everyone, including Eastman, was satisfied with the investigation, which proved that the charges were groundless and based on "unfounded and absurd rumors." Moreover, Brown expressed his belief that Eastman was only trying to help his people, but his enthusiasm had gotten the better of him, and though his intentions were honorable, he had been indiscreet. Brown hoped that, in the future, the doctor would come directly to him with such complaints.[7]

Cooper, who was present during Brown's investigation of the charges, also filed a report which explained that making depredation payments to Indians was fraught with difficulty. Yet despite the inherent problems, most of the Indians with whom he had spoken, including Sioux leaders Red Cloud and Young Man Afraid of His Horses, had heard no complaints whatsoever and were indeed pleased with the special agent's work. Cooper, with mock surprise, wrote also that the doctor had never offered one word of complaint throughout the time he served as witness to the payments. He concluded his report with feigned candor, suggesting that Eastman, as an educated Indian, should "set an example" for other less fortunate brethren to follow, and not be in the vanguard promoting "groundless charges."[8]

Eastman's version of Brown's investigation, sent to the commissioner two months after the agent's, challenged not only Brown's right to hold such an investigation but also several statements made by Brown in his report. The doctor thought that Cooper had no legal right to ask the agent to direct such an investigation. Such authority, Eastman believed, should have come only from Washington. With Brown in charge, Eastman viewed the entire matter as a "snap investigation," one in which "the poor Indians will receive no fair deal." He declared that Brown had improperly allowed Cooper and Finlay to question some of the Indians that Eastman named, and worse still, that the agent made it appear in his letter to the commissioner that the plaintiffs were all questioned by the agent in the doctor's presence. There seems to be a valid complaint here because Brown's report strongly suggests that he questioned all the Indians himself, and he does not mention Cooper's and Finlay's interrogations of them. Eastman further stated that he was not satisfied, as Brown reported, with the investigations, and he still believed that the Indians' charges should be properly investigated. He concluded by criticizing Brown of bias in favor of Cooper, for only helping those who could help him in return.[9]

Eastman's letter to Morgan was written after the doctor confronted Brown. In reporting their tense meeting, Eastman had written that Brown denied ever suggesting that the witnesses were questioned in front of the doctor. Brown had explained that he hoped to save the doctor much embarrassment by excluding him from the meetings. There was no malice in the decision. Eastman accepted with equanimity the agent's protestations that he "did not intend to do me injustice," but by writing a bogus report, Brown had indeed done him an injustice.[10] Since both Brown and Eastman had challenged the veracity of each other in letters to the commissioner, both men quickly attempted to reinforce their positions by calling to mind, for the commissioner's benefit, all the past indiscretions of the other. The original controversy involving depredation payments was quickly submerged in a sea of charges and countercharges. Eastman struck first. He wrote Morgan that Brown had attempted to lure him into a scheme in which he would buy cattle from the Sioux at a low price, pasture them on reservation lands, and then sell them to the government for almost double the original price. Actually, Eastman was anxious, at first, to get involved and wrote to Wood for a loan. Wood not only discouraged the venture but also was suspicious of Brown's motives. He persuaded Eastman not to get involved. Both later believed that Brown tried to compromise Eastman by making him indebted to Brown for his financial gains, and thereby prevent the doctor from ever criticizing him.[11]

Eastman protested that he had been harassed by Brown "very wickedly." Such anguish was caused him that he found it increasingly difficult to perform his duties properly. Brown's tormenting, asserted Eastman, ranged from the agent belittling him as a non-Christian to accusing him of doing an inefficient job as the government physician. Eastman explained that on several occasions he was sent miles from the agency to care for an allegedly sick Indian and before getting there would be overtaken by an Indian policeman with orders to return to the agency at once. Upon returning, he would be reprimanded by Brown for racing his horses.[12]

Brown countered that Eastman's team was in wretched condition because of excessive if not inhuman driving." He concluded for the benefit of the commissioner that this was either due to Eastman's deficient knowledge of how to take care of horses, or to his disregard for government property, or perhaps both. Brown explained that he had directed Eastman to be, in the future, more "careful and humane" toward his team.[13]

Brown decided that the source of the doctor's resentment against him stemmed from his not supporting Eastman in a real estate deal involving land in Denver which Eastman and others would buy from heirs at Pine Ridge. Brown said that because he did not know that much about the value of the property, he refused to use his influence, as the doctor desired, in persuading such Indians to sell their land. Since his refusal, he found that Eastman began circulating rumors about him in an effort to undermine his authority.[14] It reached the point, Brown complained, where he had been forced to refuse to speak with Eastman without a witness present because of the doctor's repeated statements that he either misunderstood what the agent said to him or what others had said. "I am thoroughly convinced," wrote Brown, "either that his knowledge of the English language is utterly at fault, or that he wilfully mis-states facts."[15]

By the end of September, 1892, and continuing into the new year, Brown sent formal requests to Commissioner Morgan that Eastman be transferred to another agency. In most of these requests, Brown repeated that he hoped such a transfer might "be effected without detriment to the Doctor's future well-being."[16] As reasons for the transfer, Brown declared that Eastman had "done all in his power to weaken my management or to throw obstacles in the way of successful conduct of affairs." Therefore, for the "best interests of the service," Brown asked that Eastman be sent to another reservation.[17]

Eastman did indeed receive offers of transfers to other agencies from Morgan. On November 23, 1892, the commissioner asked Eastman if he would either accept the position of school physician at Fort Lewis, Colorado or a position at some other agency where, Morgan hinted broadly, "your work would be lighter and your relations more agreeable." Eastman, on November 28, answered that he would like to be sent to the Indian school at Flandreau.[18] Within four days, however, he had changed his mind. "I have now fully decided," he wrote, "to stand my ground—not for a personal advantage or any desire of my own benefit by staying here for there is no advantage for me to stay, but for sake of principle and self respect."[19] Meanwhile Morgan notified Eastman, apparently before he had received Eastman's second letter, that he would be sent to Flandreau. Eastman declined the transfer.[20]

Brown must have been overjoyed when he first learned of Eastman's transfer to another agency. He did not learn about Eastman's refusal until several days later.[21] On Christmas day, 1892, a disappointed Brown asked Morgan if Eastman could be "transferred else-

where without delay." Morgan replied that "Eastman will not be
transferred from Pine Ridge at present."[22] Brown answered that
he inferred by the words "at present" that the doctor would be
transferred "in the near future." In this letter and others which followed, Brown cited Eastman's disrespect and insubordination to his
management at Pine Ridge and hoped that the transfer would be
forthcoming.[23]

In time both Eastman and Brown received support from some
powerful individuals—men who were in the vanguard of Indian reform and normally united. In Eastman's corner were such prominent
figures as Commissioner Morgan and Senator Dawes. He was also
supported by his wife and by Wood. Brown had on his side the influential Herbert Welsh, secretary of the Indian Rights Association,
and Theodore Roosevelt, who was then a Civil Service commissioner
studying the effects of the spoils system in the Indian service. Both
he and Welsh favored the extension of civil service rules to include
Indian service employees.

Morgan and Dawes pleaded Eastman's case in Washington. The
commissioner wrote to John W. Noble, Secretary of the Interior, that
Eastman "is one of the finest specimens of Indians I have ever met,
and is a sample of what can be done for these people by education."
He expressed high praise of Eastman's efficiency as a physician labor-
ing to the needs of 6,000 Indians, which was an extremely difficult
assignment that would keep any three to five doctors very busy. Morgan believed that the strain between the two men was doubtless due
to Eastman's inexperience, youth, and heavy work load. "He may
have been indiscreet perhaps in some respects," explained the commissioner, "and may not have been as careful in his words relating to
Capt. Brown as he might have been." Yet Morgan could not help
feeling that Brown was "possibly playing the role of a petty tyrant"
and was attempting "to revenge himself upon Dr. Eastman for his
attitude by crushing him with work." Morgan concluded, however,
that if Eastman were "guilty of offences" against the agent, he would
not "sustain him in any improper conduct."[24] Dawes, on the other
hand, told Wood that he had met with President Benjamin Harrison
and presented testimony on Eastman's behalf. Dawes agreed with
Wood in "admiring the pluck of Dr. Eastman more than his wisdom

in determining to stay at Pine Ridge and fight the hosts of darkness there" instead of going to Flandreau, where he would be with his brother and where conditions would be more pleasant.[25]

Wood, as was typical, expressed his untiring loyalty to Eastman. He wondered why the commissioner allowed Brown "to continue his outrageous persecutions of a man who is his superior in every respect." Calling Brown a "hypocritical military upstart" bent on destroying Eastman because he would not remain silent about injustices done to his people, Wood boasted that he had "the reputation of being a pretty good and persistant [sic] fighter" himself and would defend Eastman to the end.[26]

Eastman's wife, remembering her public relations campaign for Hampton Institute, turned to the press to vindicate her husband. In a number of articles published throughout the country, she attacked conditions at Pine Ridge under Brown's administration and supported her husband's allegations against Brown. Wood also adopted similar methods, using his considerable prestige on behalf of Eastman.[27] Brown became outraged when he saw these accounts and sought allies that could counter the printed charges. Herbert Welsh was one of those who came to Brown's defense.[28]

Welsh had initially assured Elaine Eastman, at the time she began her campaign, that he would examine the whole matter impartially. When he sided with Brown rather than her husband, Elaine felt betrayed.[29] Welsh based his support for the agent on letters he had received from people who resided at or had been to Pine Ridge recently, from Brown himself, who kept a steady stream of correspondence flowing to Welsh, and from a trip to Pine Ridge which Welsh made in late September, 1892. Welsh later published a pamphlet that contained information on this trip, and it is interesting to note that he does not mention in it the strained relations nor that he spent some time with the Eastmans. He does, however, praise Brown's service as agent.[30]

Throughout the controversy Welsh declared that Eastman and his wife failed to prove any definite charges against Brown. According to Welsh, when he asked them for proof, they declined to give it, protesting that it would not be worthwhile since he already supported Brown. "I can only infer," wrote Welsh, "that their attack is animated principally by personal feeling, and rests upon no solid basis of fact." As a parting shot, he also added that he had an unpleasant time with the Eastmans while at Pine Ridge.[31]

Another interesting reason for Eastman's alleged conduct was suggested by the Reverend William J. Cleveland, an Episcopal minister among the Sioux and an Indian Rights Association investigator who conducted an investigation of the Wounded Knee tragedy. Cleveland wrote that Eastman was urged on by his wife in an effort to remove Brown and get Eastman appointed agent. Brown agreed that certain people, unnamed, encouraged Eastman to keep up the fight with this goal in mind, although such a charge was not found in his official letters to Morgan and only appears in his personal correspondence to Welsh.[32]

Upset with Morgan's support for Eastman, Welsh enlisted the help of Theodore Roosevelt, who had also been to Pine Ridge in August, 1892. Roosevelt believed the Eastmans were entirely at fault, and he wrote in Brown's defense, "There certainly has not been a scintilla of proof advanced by them to show him guilty of any misconduct worth taking into account."[33] Roosevelt got nowhere with Morgan but was successful with Secretary Noble. After a meeting with him, Roosevelt wrote Welsh that the secretary thought Brown was doing a fine job and was a "first-class man."[34]

In an effort to resolve the matter, Noble, at the request of Morgan, ordered another investigation. In asking for it, Morgan sent a letter from Senator Richard F. Pettigrew of South Dakota, a close friend of Eastman, who wrote that not only were there irregularities in the Cooper payment but also that some government employees were associated with improper activities. Noble assigned Indian Inspector Benjamin H. Miller to investigate. Miller's report indicated that "the payment was not squarely and properly made." However, Noble, after reviewing Miller's findings, decided that they did not fully warrant such conclusions. Accordingly, he ordered Inspector James H. Cisney, on November 11, 1892, to conduct a thorough reinvestigation. Cisney's report completely exonerated Cooper, and Noble wrote that he was satisfied "that each and every Indian beneficiary received from Special Agent Cooper the amount allowed and receipted for and that Mr. Cooper did not retain or cause to be retained, any portion of the moneys entrusted to him to disburse."[35]

Noble explained that Miller based his report on Indians who were operating under the misapprehension that they should have received the sums they claimed instead of what was paid them by Cooper's scaling down of individual claims to within the amount appropriated by Congress. An important additional reason for Miller's confusion was the man he employed as his interpreter. Noble said that his name was Weston, and he was Eastman's uncle. Weston was totally incompetent, wrote Noble, because he misinterpreted Indian testimony. From the ninety Indian depositions taken by Miller and translated by Weston, Cisney, in his reexamination of the evidence, found that sixty-six Indians claimed they were inaccurately translated during their testimonies.

Regarding Eastman's testimony, Noble stated that Eastman disclaimed "knowing of any irregularities, of his own knowledge, on the part of Special Agent Cooper," and that "all he knew emanated from Indians complaining that they had not received the amount which appeared on the rolls, or the amounts which they thought they ought to have received." Of the fourteen Indians he identified as complainants, all except two, who failed to testify, told Cisney that they made no such charges. However, it was possible, concluded Noble, that Eastman as well as Senator Pettigrew truly believed that the Indians had been cheated, even though this was not the case.[36]

Inspector Miller's report only verified the Eastmans' suspicions of irregularities in the Cooper payment. Dr. Eastman, however, was annoyed with Miller because he failed to condemn Brown. This was due, the doctor believed, to Miller's opposition to Senator Pettigrew's campaign to rid the Indian service of military officers serving as agents. When Eastman discovered that Noble had not accepted Miller's findings and ordered another inspection, he was outraged. He called Cisney's investigation a sham because it not only cleared Cooper of all charges but similarly found no foundation to his allegations against Brown.[37]

Eastman complained bitterly that Cisney treated him and his wife improperly during the investigation. He said that the inspector compelled them to answer every question put to them no matter if it were relevant or not to the case but afforded Brown the privilege of objecting to questions addressed to him he felt were improper. As a result, Eastman asked Morgan for a leave of absence so that he could come to Washington to present his case. Morgan granted him thirty days' leave.[38] As it turned out, Eastman's request was needless because on January 5, 1893, Morgan received an order from Noble to notify Eastman that President Harrison "directs him to report to the Secretary of the Interior upon business that will be made known to him on his arrival."[39]

When word reached Brown that Eastman was going to Washington, he wrote to Morgan and demanded the same consideration. Endorsement for such a request came from Welsh, who told Brown that Senator Dawes was trying to get Eastman an audience with the President and that he would keep Brown informed on Eastman's activities.[40] In additional letters to Morgan and Welsh, Brown brought to their attention that Eastman left the agency without notifying him; he obtained a substitute doctor who was unqualified in Brown's estimation; he continued to be disrespectful; and he was responsible for the publication of articles containing false and malicious statements against him. For these unbecoming actions, Brown once again requested Morgan to remove Eastman from his duties as physician at Pine Ridge.[41]

Brown's uneasiness about the possible success of the doctor's trip to Washington to plead his case soon diminished. Eastman's efforts proved futile, and he returned to Pine Ridge on January 23, 1893. Brown, at first, denied Eastman entrance to his physician's office because he had received no formal orders to place him back on duty. The next day, Brown reported that Eastman continued to display disrespect toward him.[42] Something had to be done to terminate the strained relations between agent and physician.

On January 25, 1893, Secretary Noble finally took action. He wrote to Morgan that he had thoroughly examined the controversy between Eastman and Brown and concluded that for "the good of the service" Eastman "shall be suspended" and "unless he can be assigned or appointed to another place that he is willing to accept within fifteen days, he must resign or he will be removed." Noble further asserted that he found no improprieties in Brown's conduct in the matter. He praised Eastman's many excellent qualities and stated, "I do not take this action in condemnation of him." Yet Noble believed that Brown's supremacy as agent had to be maintained, and this was the basis for his decision. Eastman's reply was, "I prefer to resign."[43]

Reaction from Wood over Eastman's resignation perhaps best illustrates the sentiment of those who backed the doctor. He wrote to Welsh, who was Brown's most persistent supporter, a curt note. "Are you not proud," he exclaimed, "of having secured the removal from the Indian service of the best educated Indian this country has yet produced, who is also a Christian gentleman of the highest-type, whose highest purpose in life was to Christianize, civilize, and help his people?" In two other letters, Wood told Welsh that Brown had deceived him and that Welsh would eventually realize this. Welsh replied, "My only object has been to protect the agent at Pine Ridge from attacks made upon him with the evident design to drive him from his position and discredit his character." He stated that he had no personal animosity against the Eastmans and thought that Dr. Eastman should have accepted a transfer in the first place.[44]

Elaine Eastman also singled out Welsh and condemned him for the role he played against her and her husband. She tendered her resignation from the Indian Rights Association and released to the press her reasons for doing so. Her statement created quite a stir among the supporters of Indian policy reform. She considered Welsh's behavior "unjust and partisan," noting specifically the articles he had written as highly personal attacks on her character. Commenting on this, Welsh, once again, wrote that he was only repelling assaults against Brown in these articles, and he presumed Mrs. Eastman's news release about her resignation to be a vengeful attack on him.[45]

Eastman's first venture as an educated Indian in the government Indian service ended in a personal disaster. There was little doubt that in the beginning he performed his duties as physician well. He received high praise for the part he played during the Wounded Knee tragedy, and his firsthand observations, as well as his wife's, are important sources for historians. But after Brown's arrival in December, 1891, his troubles truly began. Eastman and Brown carried on a bitter, and sometimes farcical, feud between May, 1892, and January, 1893. The confusion and contradictions involved in the controversy are most trying and make it difficult to ascertain the validity of their

respective accusations. Both adversaries had the support from powerful and influential people in the Indian service and in the Indian
rights organizations. Eastman's most ardent supporters were close
friends, such as Frank Wood.

The conflict between Eastman and Brown first flared over the
Cooper payment and blazed with them accusing each other of hor-
rendous conduct until the original controversy was consumed in a
larger conflagration of pride. In fairness to Brown, Eastman should
have gone directly to him instead of writing to others, which perhaps caused Brown to become suspicious of Eastman's motives.
Eastman, influenced by his strong-willed wife, may indeed have
hoped to oust Brown and get himself appointed as agent. This charge,
however, never appeared in official government correspondence on
the matter. Noble's decision ordering the doctor's transfer did not
severely indict Eastman; rather, he praised Eastman's qualities and
gave him an opportunity to go elsewhere. Perhaps the uniqueness of
Eastman's achievements and political overtones involved in remov-
ing him compelled Noble's action. Eastman, whose fierce pride had
been wounded, chose instead to withdraw. To accept the proffered
transfer was, in his mind, an acceptance of guilt. Life, it seemed,
would no longer be as simple as it once was during his college years
where success awaited his every effort and his associations with people helped to confirm his uniqueness. To Brown he was only the upstart physician.

Although his first experience with the Indian service ended in
failure, Eastman would, nevertheless, hold other government positions throughout his long life. He decided to move his family, which
now contained the first of their six children, a girl named Dora
Winona, born on May 31, 1892, to St. Paul, Minnesota, where he
planned to start a private medical practice.[46] If he could not serve his
people unencumbered of tyranny and political jobbery, he would
serve himself and his family in more polite surroundings. Others
could question his motives, but few could question his credentials.

NOTES

1. Graber, *Sister to the Sioux*, p. 172.
2. Ibid.

3. Eastman Scrapbook No. 1, Eastman Collection, Smith College Library; Eastman to Morgan, Feb. 25. 1892, BIA, RG 75, LR, NA.
4. Eastman to Morgan, Feb. 25, 1892, BIA, RG 75, LR, NA.
5. Eastman, *From the Deep Woods*, p. 128.
6. Eastman to Philip Garrett, June 14, 1892, BIA, RG 75, LR, NA.
7. Brown to Morgan, June 25, 1892, ibid.
8. James A. Cooper to CIA, July 22, 1892, ibid.
9. Eastman to Morgan, Aug. 28, 1892, ibid.
10. Ibid.
11. Wood to Morgan, Aug. 31, 1892, BIA, RG 75, LR, NA.
12. Eastman to Morgan, Nov. 28, 1892, ibid.; Eastman to Morgan, Dec. 2, 1892, ibid.; Eastman, *From the Deep Woods*, p. 133.
13. Brown to Morgan, Oct. 18, 1892, BIA, RG 75, Pine Ridge Agency, Box 5, vol. 16, 1892, LS, KC; Brown to Eastman, *ca.* Nov. 29, 1892, BIA, RG 75, Pine Ridge Agency, Box 4, vol. 14, 1892, Misc. LS, KC.
14. Brown to Benjamin H. Miller, Sept. 26, 1892, BIA, RG 75, LR, NA.
15. Brown to Morgan, Nov. 27, 1892, BIA, RG 75, Pine Ridge Agency, Box 5, vol. 17, 1892–93, LS, KC.
16. Brown to Morgan, Sept. 26, 1892, BIA, RG 75, LR, NA.
17. Brown to Morgan, Sept. 30, 1892, BIA, RG 75, Pine Ridge Agency, Box 5, vol. 16, 1892, LS, KC; Brown to Morgan, Sept. 26, 1892, BIA, RG 75, LR, NA.
18. Morgan to Eastman, Nov. 23, 1892, BIA, RG 75, LS, NA; Eastman to Morgan, Nov. 28, 1892, BIA, RG 75, LR, NA.
19. Eastman to Morgan, Dec. 2, 1892, BIA, RG 75, LR, NA.
20. Morgan to Eastman, Dec. 10, 1892, BIA, RG 75, LS, NA; Eastman to Morgan, Dec. 18, 1892, BIA, RG 75, LR, NA.
21. Morgan to Brown, Dec. 10, 1892, BIA, RG 75, Pine Ridge Agency, Box 5, vol. 16, 1892–93, Misc. LS, KC; Brown to Eastman, Dec. 10, 1892, ibid.; Eastman to Brown, Dec. 18, 1892, BIA, RG 75, LR, NA.
22. Brown to Morgan, Dec. 25, 1892, telegram, BIA, RG 75, LR, NA; Morgan to Brown, Dec. 27, 1892, telegram, BIA, RG 75, Pine Ridge Agency, Box 13, 1892, LR and gen. file, KC.
23. Brown to Morgan, Dec. 28, 1892, BIA, RG 75, Pine Ridge Agency, Box 5, vol. 17, 1892–93, LS, KC; Brown to Morgan, Dec. 31, 1892, BIA, RG 75, LR, NA.
24. Morgan to Secretary of the Interior, Nov. 23, 1892, BIA, RG 75, LS, NA.
25. Dawes to Wood, Dec. 31, 1892, BIA, RG 75, LR, NA.
26. Wood to Morgan, Dec. 3, 1892, ibid.
27. See for example, *New York Evening Post*, Nov. 16, 1892; *Omaha*

Daily Bee, Nov. 20 and 21, 1892; Samuel Chapman Armstrong Collection, Folder E-G, Williams College Library, Williamstown, Mass.

28. Brown to Morgan, Nov. 23, 1892, BIA, RG 75, LR, NA; *New York Evening Post*, Dec. 8, 1892.
29. Welsh to Mrs. Eastman, Aug. 26, 1892, IRA, Reel 6, Outgoing Correspondence; Welsh to Garrett, Aug. 31, 1892, ibid.
30. Herbert Welsh, *Civilization among the Sioux Indians* (Philadelphia: Indian Rights Association, 1893).
31. Welsh to E. L. Godkin, Nov. 28, 1892, IRA, Reel 6, Outgoing Correspondence; Welsh to J. George Wright, Oct. 28, 1892, ibid.
32. Welsh to Charles C. Painter, Jan. 30, 1893, IRA, Reel 6, Outgoing Correspondence; Brown to Welsh, Feb. 8, 1893, IRA, Reel 20, Incoming Correspondence.
33. Theodore Roosevelt to Welsh, Feb. 14, 1893, IRA, Reel 20, Incoming Correspondence.
34. Welsh to Roosevelt, Jan. 11, 1893, IRA, Reel 6, Outgoing Correspondence; Roosevelt to Welsh, Jan. 12, 1893, IRA, Reel 20, Incoming Correspondence.
35. John W. Noble to CIA, Jan. 9, 1893, BIA, RG 75, LR, NA.
36. Ibid.
37. Wood to Morgan, Aug. 31, 1892, enclosure, BIA, RG 75, LR, NA; Mrs. Eastman to Welsh, Aug. 4, 1892, IRA, Reel 19, Incoming Correspondence; Welsh to Brown, Jan. 11, 1893, IRA, Reel 6, Outgoing Correspondence; Eastman, *From the Deep Woods*, p. 131. In *From the Deep Woods*, Eastman presented his side of the story. However, he is guilty, at times, of not adequately answering or developing poignant points that would cast doubt on the validity of some of his arguments.
38. Eastman to Morgan, Dec. 18, 1892, BIA, RG 75, LR, NA; Morgan to Eastman, Dec. 19, 1892, telegram, BIA, RG 75, Pine Ridge Agency, Box 5, vol. 16, 1892–93, Misc. LS, KC.
39. Noble to CIA, Jan. 5, 1893, BIA, RG 75, LR, NA.
40. Brown to CIA, Jan. 16, 1893, BIA, RG 75, Pine Ridge Agency, Box 5, vol. 17, 1892–93, LS, KC; Welsh to Brown, Jan. 11, 1893, IRA, Reel 6, Outgoing Correspondence.
41. See Brown to CIA, Jan. 3, 1893, telegram, BIA, R675, LR, NA; Brown to CIA, Jan. 5, 1893, telegram, ibid.; Brown to CIA, Jan. 9, 1893, ibid.; Brown to CIA, Jan. 10, 1893, BIA, RG 75, Pine Ridge Agency, Box 5, vol. 17, 1892–93, LS, KC; Brown to Welsh, Jan. 6, 1893, IRA, Reel 20, Incoming Correspondence; Brown to Welsh, Jan. 10, 1893, ibid.

42. Brown to CIA, Jan. 23, 1893, telegram, BIA, RG 75, LR, NA; Brown
    to CIA, Jan. 24, 1893, BIA, RG 75, Pine Ridge Agency, Box 5, vol.
    17, 1892–93, LS, KC; Brown to Welsh, Feb. 8, 1893, IRA, Reel 20,
    Incoming Correspondence.
43. Noble to CIA, Jan. 25, 1893, BIA, RG 75, Pine Ridge Agency, Box 5,
    vol. 17, 1893, LS, KC; Eastman to Morgan, Jan. 26, 1893, telegram,
    BIA, RG 75, LR, NA.
44. Wood to Welsh, Jan. 25, 1893, IRA, Reel 20, Incoming Correspon-
    dence; Wood to Welsh, *ca.* Jan. 26, 1893, IRA, Reel 20, Incoming
    Correspondence; Wood to Welsh, Feb. 1, 1893, ibid.; Welsh to
    Wood, Jan. 27, 1893, IRA, Reel 6, Outgoing Correspondence.
45. Welsh to Mrs. W. W. Crannell, Feb. 15, 1893, IRA, Reel 6, Out-
    going Correspondence; Welsh to Mrs. William Welsh, Feb. 16, 1893,
    ibid.
46. Eastman, *From the Deep Woods*, pp. 127, 135. Charles A. and Elaine
    G. Eastman had five girls—Dora Winona, Irene Taluta, Virginia,
    Eleanor, and Florence—and one son, Ohiyesa II. All attended
    schools of higher learning, and, at the time of this writing, Eleanor
    and Virginia are the only surviving children. They were all on the
    tribal rolls.

CHAPTER 5

INDIAN SECRETARY FOR THE YMCA

THE EASTMANS ARRIVED in St. Paul, Minnesota, with renewed hopes of starting a new life, resolving to put the unpleasant-
ness of life at Pine Ridge far behind them. Their finances, however,
were in disarray, since they had very little money and had been forced
to sell their furniture to obtain enough cash to finance their move./
The government still owed Charles money for his last month's salary
and for expenses incurred on his trip to Washington, but it was late
in coming because of Brown's apparent confusion over when Eastman's pay ceased and when his resignation took effect. Eastman resigned on January 26, 1893, but his resignation did not become
effective until February 8. Brown, however, wanted to pay him only
for the first nine days in January, even though he was notified to continue Eastman's salary until February 8. After considerable correspondence, including several letters from influential people on Eastman's behalf, he finally received the full amount that was due him.[1]

In the meantime Eastman took his three-day state medical board
examination. After he passed it and began his practice, he wrote that
he was approached by several people who attempted to get him involved in illegal schemes which would exploit his Indian heritage at
the expense of patients seeking special Indian cures and medicine. He
refused to have anything to do with such escapades.[2]

Eastman claimed his practice was steadily improving, but toward
the end of 1893, he began writing letters in hopes of again obtaining
a position as government physician among Indians. He worried that
his resignation, less than twelve months ago, might hurt his chances
for reemployment but believed that his reasons for resigning were just
and were appreciated by the Indian service. Eastman said that his

decision to return to the Indian service was governed by appeals from
friends to do so as well as by his overwhelming desire to help his people. If possible, he wanted to go to the Santee Agency in Nebraska or
the Lower Brule Agency in South Dakota, but there were no positions
available for Eastman. He soon received, however, an offer from the
Young Men's Christian Association to head a program which extended their movement to Indians.[3]

Eastman learned that because of initial successes of organizing
associations at Carlisle Indian School in Pennsylvania and later at
Indian schools and reservations throughout the country, someone
was now needed to supervise and instruct these groups as well as
organize additional associations. When Charles K. Ober, secretary of
the International Committee of the YMCA, asked if he would accept
such a position, Eastman hesitated at first because he questioned his
qualifications for such work. Ober assured him that his credentials
were in order, so Eastman accepted Ober's offer with the condition
that he be allowed to name his successor. Ober agreed to Eastman's
choice of Arthur Tibbetts, a Sioux, who then enrolled in a three-year
program at the International Secretarial Training School in Springfield, Massachusetts.[4]

Eastman began his duties as Indian secretary of the International
Committee of the YMCA on June 1, 1894, at a salary of $2,000. He
spent his first ten months in almost constant travel, by early September making a rapid tour of all the associations on the Sioux reservations in South Dakota, North Dakota, and Nebraska in an effort to
obtain a comprehensive view of the work being done there before the
annual meeting of these associations at the Indian Missionary Conference held at Cherry Creek, South Dakota, on September 13–16.
Almost two thousand Indians attended this meeting, which included
both day and night sessions devoted to the promotion of Christianity
among their race. The body firmly endorsed Eastman's employment
and pledged their cooperation.

An interesting and significant sidelight to the meeting was a statement by Ober condemning rumors that Eastman and his wife had
separated. Branding the rumors as malicious and false, Ober declared
that the couple were happily married. In later years, however, the
Eastmans did indeed separate—a fact that has been almost completely concealed in the documentation on their lives and a subject

which most members of the family contacted steadfastly refuse to discuss.[5]

After this conference Eastman traveled to such places as Manitoba, Canada, Indian schools in Pennsylvania, Kansas, and Indian Territory, and special conventions in Minnesota, Texas, and New York. After ten months of extensive field work, he wrote a report that contained his recommendations on how to improve association work among Indians. Eastman discovered that although the associations contained many willing and enthusiastic members, they were limited in scope and needed competent professionals to direct them. He suggested that annual Indian summer workshops be used to train leaders and that perhaps several men could be sent to the YMCA training schools in Chicago and Springfield. He also recommended a stronger bond be developed between associations on reservations and ones at Indian schools. This would not only strengthen the movement but would also provide returning Indian students with meaningful employment.[6]

All of these suggestions were put into effect and proved successful. For example, the first YMCA Indian summer school workshop, held at Big Stone Lake, South Dakota, was a ten-day affair, from June 26 to July 5, 1896. A brochure, written in both English and Sioux, advertised the event, which included lectures and special sessions conducted by such persons as Eastman, Ober, and the Reverend Alfred L. Riggs. To help meet expenses, those attending the program were asked to contribute one dollar as well as to supply their own Bible, hymn book, provisions, tent, and cooking and camping equipment.[7]

Commenting on this unique affair was none other than Herbert Welsh, who happened to be on a western tour of Indian reservations. He reported that the Indians engaged in daily hymns and prayers and attended both morning and evening religious meetings, which sometimes involved informal question-and-answer sessions. Eastman, Riggs, and other competent people were employed as translators because many of those in attendance could not understand the English language. Meetings were held in a large round tent. Welsh observed, "It was hard to believe that this class of young men, clad in citizens' dress and preparing themselves for missionary work among their contemporaries in their tribe, were only one remove from aboriginal barbarism." All, however, was not work, and the Indians participated in outdoor sports and recreational activities. Welsh viewed the entire conference as "a very interesting spectacle, and a noteworthy sign of the times in the field of Indian civilization."[8]

Eastman's wife encouraged and supported her husband's work for the YMCA. She wrote that the extension of the movement to Indians could only result in improving conditions among them, by uniting them, producing self-confidence and strength, and providing education and instruction. She believed that Indians, once possessed of such virtues, could cope better with white society and defend themselves against graft and corruption. She also went with her husband to the Lake Mohonk Conference in 1895, where she hoped to secure financial support for the continued development of associations among Indians. Addressing the conference, she again stressed the importance of the YMCA movement among Indians.[9]

Dr. Eastman noted in his speech to the conference that while there were many good Christian Indians, denominationalism proved a hindrance by obstructing progress. Eastman wanted to foster cooperation among Indians simply as Christian brothers and avoid the frequent sectarian squabbles among those people who insisted on identifying themselves as Baptists, Methodists, Episcopalians, and the like. Let each man cleave to his denomination; but let each man first remember that he was a Christian. He also warned that many of the Indians he encountered on his trips suffered from lack of exercise, excessive use of tobacco and liquor, and the effects of widespread gambling. To combat these vices, Eastman stated, "My method is to meet the young men, and call their attention to Bible study, and try to arouse their sympathy for one another. I also talk simply of their bodies,—how to keep them clean, pure, and to take care of them so as to make the most of them, warning them of all the evils that they blindly go into, which destroy their bodies as well as mind and soul." By combining Biblical studies with exercise or wholesome sports as lacrosse and pony polo, Eastman hoped to check degeneration and help the Indian develop both in mind and in body.[10]

Eastman's efforts, for the most part, proved fruitful among the Sioux. At Pine Ridge Agency in 1895, Eastman reported to Ober the existence of three Indian associations and another in the making. He said that he was cordially received and his suggestions on new activities were warmly accepted. Eastman believed that the Indians' participation in "wild dances" and other "degrading things" was on the decline at Pine Ridge because of the associations' work: they had just procured football and baseball equipment and eagerly played the games almost every evening. Pleased with these encouraging developments, Eastman was perhaps further gratified when several Indians "begged" him to return as their agency physician. Ober expressed his confidence and pleasure in Eastman's performance.[11]

At the end of his second year of service, Eastman reported, "From every point of view this department of the International Committee's work is growing and at the same time performing a kind of Christian service that is thoroughly missionary in practice." To demonstrate additional achievements and dedication, Eastman cited the Minniska association on the Lower Brule Agency for their "faith and fidelity." They continued to hold regular weekly meetings while subjected to harassment from government officials attempting to remove them to another location. Another good sign was the increasing participation of returning Indian students in reservation associations.[12]

There were, however, Indians with whom Eastman had little or no success, like the Crows in Montana. After visiting their reservation, Eastman abandoned the plan of organizing associations similar to the ones among the Sioux. "I found," he lamented, "that the religious work there was still in its infancy, and that it would require much of the time of an experienced man to get them into proper form." He urged returning Crow students, who were familiar with the movement, to attempt to organize weekly sessions "for the purpose of bringing the subject before the young men of the tribe."[13]

Eastman wrote that one of the severest rebukes he ever encountered in his work came from the Sac and Fox in Iowa. At the time he was also serving as secretary on a committee which was to select officers for a newly created Indian Rights Association of Iowa, which in conjunction with the YMCA movement tried to promote Christianity among these Indians. He was warmly welcomed by the tribe and detailed his work in a speech emphasizing the advantages to be gained by adopting Christianity. An old chief, said Eastman, responded to his address, criticizing the white man for his disrespect toward nature and God. "We shall," the chief concluded, "still follow the old trail." Eastman respected their wishes, although disappointed by their rejection. Later he wrote that while among these people he had unknowingly lost his wallet containing a considerable amount of valuables. When the wallet was returned to him with its contents intact, he was extremely impressed and stated that if the same had happened in the streets of a Christian city, he would most likely never have seen the wallet again.[14]

This significant episode reflects the inherent pressures he faced in this work. He was a Christian, yet how could he promote a religion and teach about the doctrines of Jesus Christ to a subjugated people who envisioned almost everything associated with white men as another step toward their annihilation? Eastman recognized this, and more importantly that the original doctrines of Christianity were professed in theory, but not in practice. He believed that Christianity was too closely linked with white civilization's emphasis on competition and materialism. In his travels, Eastman was shocked when he saw the poor living conditions and slums in the white Christian world. He was further dismayed when he heard profanity and God's name being used in vain. Yet, as a product of both Indian and white religious teachings, Eastman reconciled his position and conversion to Christianity by declaring, "It is my personal belief, after thirty-five years' experience of it, that there is no such thing as 'Christian civilization.' I believe that Christianity and modern civilization are opposed and irreconcilable, and that the spirit of Christianity and of our ancient religion is essentially the same."[15]

Indeed, this was the cord which bound him to Christianity. To Eastman there was no real difference between theoretical Christianity and the Indian concepts on religion. He cited both believed in miracles, revered nature, recognized a supernatural force behind every action, and believed in an afterlife. Although his comparisons and opinions were far from original, he, nevertheless, was personally satisfied with them and could draw parallels between both cultures' religious beliefs in his own mind and in his work. He tried to impress upon the Indians that Christianity was not "at fault for the white man's sins, but rather the lack of it" was to blame, beliefs shared by other Indians he met.[16]

These years were pleasant to Eastman, who wrote that he was "unhampered by official red tape in the effort to improve conditions among my people." He believed, as did others in the YMCA movement, that the future of the country lay with the young men who had to be Christianized, taught a profession, and educated. This was especially true for Indians, who could never again return to their former way of life. Only through accepting the good aspects of white civilization could Indian people achieve success, and one of the best ways to instruct and encourage them in this direction was YMCA Indian associations. Expressing these views in a speech before an International Convention of YMCAs of North America, Eastman stated, "I sometimes forget my color when I stand before audiences. And then I sometimes wish we were color blind; how much easier it would be for us to do Christian work. But never mind; we will do the best we can. It is only through the young men that we can save the Indian race, and the Young Men's Christian Association can be made a great power in their behalf if it is rightly fostered."[17]

Because of Arthur Tibbetts's graduation and the need to devote more attention to another project, that of representing his tribe's claims in Washington, D.C., Eastman resigned on April 1, 1898. Tibbetts continued Eastman's work, although the program was now mainly concentrated on the Sioux. He still employed summer workshops, Bible study sessions, and returning Indian students in developing needed local leadership and participation.[18]

In evaluating Eastman's years with the YMCA, several observations should be made. He believed that by adopting Christianity Indians could operate better in the technologically advanced white world. To Eastman, who believed that the Christian God was the same supreme deity Indians held sacred, this would not dramatically alter their basic religious beliefs. This blending of religions on Eastman's part was, however, perhaps an oversimplification, since there existed many differences between Indian religious customs and Christianity, differences which Eastman never really addressed himself to, especially in his writings. Yet, this reconciliation satisfied Eastman; it seemed to be a convenient way for him to join the religious training he had received from both cultures.

The extension of the YMCA ideals to Indians, although experimented with during the mid-1880s, reached its maturity when Eastman assumed the office of Indian secretary. Although he never mentioned having any previous contact with the YMCA before going to St. Paul and before accepting the position in 1894, Eastman most probably knew of the organization while attending schools in the East and from meeting white reformers. It was not an easy job traveling extensively and facing, at times, unreceptive groups. Eastman's efforts proved most fruitful among his own people, which can be explained, in part, by his familiarity with their customs.

It is worth noting that Eastman's uncle, Mysterious Medicine, had become a Christian farmer in Canada. Although vague regarding his uncle's conversion, Eastman had learned about it from a white missionary he had met. On one of his YMCA Canadian trips, Eastman was able to visit his uncle, and though over twenty years had passed since nephew and uncle had seen each other, their reunion was a pleasant one. Before departing, Eastman visited the grave of his beloved grandmother, Uncheedah.[19]

By the time of Eastman's resignation as Indian secretary, he had helped in organizing over forty Indian associations. When asked to pioneer a project which would help his people, Eastman responded to the call, perhaps partly because he needed money, but more because he truly believed in the merits of the work. Conditions on reservations were deplorable, and Eastman thought that the extension of the YMCA movement to Indians would improve matters. "I do not know," he wrote after his resignation, "how much good I accomplished, but I did my best." Commenting on Eastman's performance, Richard C. Morse, consulting general secretary of the International Committee of the YMCA, wrote, "The personal contribution Dr. Eastman brought as an Indian of conspicuous ability was invaluable."[20] Indeed, Eastman deserved such recognition for a job well done.

NOTES

1. Morgan to Brown, Feb. 7, 1893, BIA, RG 75, Pine Ridge Agency, Box 14, 1892–93, LR and gen. file, KC; Brown to Eastman, Mar. 30, 1893, BIA, RG 75, Pine Ridge Agency, Box 7, vol. 22, 1893, Misc. LS, KC; Morgan to Belt, Apr. 11, 1893, BIA, RG 75, LR, NA; Garrett to CIA, June 6, 1893, ibid.; Eastman to J. H. Kyle, Dec. 8, 1893, ibid.
2. Eastman, *From the Deep Woods*, pp. 136–38.
3. Eastman to Kyle, Dec. 8, 1893, BIA, RG 75, LR, NA; Eastman to Kyle, Jan. 5, 1894, ibid.; Richard F. Pettigrew to D. M. Browning,

Jan. 19, 1894, ibid.; C. H. Howard to Browning, Jan. 26, 1894, ibid.; Eastman, *From the Deep Woods*, p. 139.

4. See "The Indian Work. Its Latest Development," *Young Men's Era* 43 (Oct. 25, 1894): 5 in Charles A. Eastman Materials, YMCA Historical Library, New York, New York; Robert C. Morse, *My Life with Young Men: Fifty Years in the Young Men's Christian Association* (New York: Association Press, 1918), pp. 404–7; Eastman, *From the Deep Woods*, pp. 139–40.

5. "The Indian Work. Its Latest Development," Eastman Materials, YMCA Hist. Lib.; "Charles A. Eastman's Work among American Indians; Excerpts from Year Books of the YMCAs of North America," 1895, Eastman Materials, YMCA Hist. Lib.; *Omaha World Herald*, Sept. 22, 1894.

6. "Charles A. Eastman's Work among American Indians," 1895, Eastman Materials, YMCA Hist. Lib.; "The Indian Work. Its Latest Development," ibid.

7. "Indian Young Men's Christian Association Summer School," 1897, ibid.

8. *The Fourteenth Annual Report of the Executive Committee of the Indian Rights Association* (Philadelphia: Office of the Indian Rights Association, 1897), pp. 42–45.

9. Eastman Scrapbook No. 1, Eastman Collection, Smith College Library; LMC, 13th sess., 1895, pp. 92–94.

10. See LMC, 13th sess., 1895, pp. 15–16, 66–68.

11. Eastman to Charles K. Ober, June 26, 1895, Carlos Montezuma Papers, Microfilm, Correspondence, 1892–1907, Reel 1, State Historical Society of Wisconsin, Madison, Wis.; Ober to Richard H. Pratt, July 5, 1895, ibid.

12. "Among the Indians. The Tour of Indian Secretary Eastman among the Associations of South Dakota. Some History," *Young Men's Era* 2 (Jan. 10, 1895): 21, Eastman Materials, YMCA Hist. Lib.; "Charles A. Eastman's Work among American Indians," 1897, ibid.

13. "Charles A. Eastman's Work among American Indians," 1899, ibid.

14. Eastman, *From the Deep Woods*, pp. 148–49; "The Sac and Fox Indians of Iowa," undated, IRA, Reel 23, Incoming Correspondence.

15. Charles A. Eastman, *The Soul of the Indian: An Interpretation* (1911; reprint ed., New York: Johnson Reprint Corp., 1971), p. 24; Eastman, *From the Deep Woods*, pp. 147, 193–95.

16. Charles A. Eastman, "The Sioux Mythology," *Popular Science Monthly* 46 (Nov., 1894): 88; Eastman, *The Soul of the Indian*, pp.

16–17; Eastman, *From the Deep Woods*, pp. 142–43, 149; Charles A. Eastman, "Great Spirit," *American Indian Teepee* 1 (1920): 3–4.

17. "For Indian Young Men," *Young Men's Era* 20 (May 16, 1895): 323, Eastman Materials, YMCA Hist. Lib.; *Proceedings of the Thirty-first International Convention of YMCAs of North America*, held at Springfield, Mass., May 8–12, 1895, p. 9, Eastman Materials, YMCA Hist. Lib.; Eastman, *From the Deep Woods*, pp. 145, 194–95.

18. "Charles A. Eastman's Work among American Indians," 1899, Eastman Materials, YMCA Hist. Lib.; "Arthur T. Tibbetts' Work," 1900–1905, ibid.; LMC, 18th sess., 1900, pp. 100–101.

19. Eastman, *From the Deep Woods*, pp. 143–45.

20. Ibid., pp. 141, 150; Morse, *My Life with Young Men*, p. 407.

CHAPTER 6

EASTMAN AND THE SANTEE CLAIMS

W HILE STILL EMPLOYED by the YMCA, Eastman became involved with the Santee Sioux claims case, concerning the restoration of annuities for the lower Santee Sioux (Mdewakantons and Wahpekutes), the Indians held primarily responsible for the 1862 Santee Sioux Uprising in Minnesota. Causes of their discontent were many—broken promises, widespread hunger, and white encroachment on their lands. The foolish actions of several young Indians sparked the short-lived, unsuccessful uprising.[1] On February 16, 1863, Congress passed an act which abrogated all previous treaties made with them and ended payments of government annuities to the Santees, forcing most of the Santees to leave Minnesota. The proscriptions against the Santees compounded their already considerable losses. The tribe, meeting in council at Santee, Nebraska, in December, 1884, and hoping to recover their annuity payments from Congress according to the Treaties of 1837 and 1851, decided to petition Congress for a restoration of payments. According to an 1863 statute, special congressional legislation was needed before an Indian tribe could enter suit in the U.S. Court of Claims. Nothing came of the council's resolution of 1884 until Charles Eastman and others went to Washington to lobby for the restoration of these annuities in the 1890s.[2] Eastman's designation as advocate for the tribe's claims was not without difficulty.

Problems soon arose within the tribe as to who could best represent the Santees in Washington. Two factions developed, one headed by Charles and John Eastman, the other led by a mixed-blood clergyman and former teacher at Santee Normal Training School named James Garvie. Both groups attempted to persuade the tribe to sign an agreement making their faction the tribe's recognized legal agents responsible for the prosecution of these claims against the United States. Such factionalism within tribes involved in claim suits was common, frequently pitting "progressive" Indians—those embracing civilization programs—against "non-progressive" Indians—those preferring to retain their traditional ways. At other times it typically involved who would represent the tribe in the suit, entitling those representatives to a certain percentage of the cash settlement for their services. The factionalism created among the Santees over their claims against the United States was largely due to the bitter rivalry between Charles Eastman and James Garvie, which contributed to significant and recurring delays. The original Santee claim was argued in Congress intermittently for over two decades before the suit reached the U.S. Court of Claims, where the controversy continued.

The matter of which faction was to represent the tribe was temporarily settled on November 27, 1896, when the Santees signed a contract with Charles Hill, a former Indian agent to the Santees from 1885 to 1890 and later a banker in Springfield, South Dakota, and Charles Eastman. Neither man was a trained attorney. The Hill-Eastman contract was to last for ten years, during which the Santees agreed to pay them 10 percent of all monies received up to $250,000, and an additional 5 percent of any payments over that sum. These percentages were not extravagant and were, in fact, quite similar to contracts negotiated by legal representatives of other tribes. The Hill-Eastman contract was sent to Washington and received approval from the Commissioner of Indian Affairs on June 29, 1897, and from the Secretary of the Interior on July 1, 1897.[3]

During this period Eastman attempted to obtain additional contracts with other Sioux tribes, visiting Standing Rock, Cheyenne River, and Pine Ridge agencies, where he met with Indians and asked them to appoint him as their legal representative in Washington to handle tribal affairs. Contracts were negotiated, but none became effective because of opposition from Indian agents and certain Indians. For example, some agents expressed contempt for the manner in which Eastman tended to excite Indians at their agencies, while other believed that the contracts would not benefit their wards. Paul White Swan, a Cheyenne River Sioux, declared in a letter to the commissioner that the majority of Indians at his agency did not favor the proposed contract with Eastman and hoped it would not be accepted.[4]

Eastman recognized an opportunity to put his talents to work in behalf of Indians and, in the process, secure adequate remuneration for himself and his growing family. Income from such contracts would justify the sacrifices he would be asked to make, especially in his abandonment of medicine. He was unsuccessful in securing contracts with these tribes. Despite his disappointment, he pressed ahead on the Santee claims. Eastman moved his family to Washington, where he could concentrate his efforts to persuade Congress to pass legislation allowing the U.S. Court of Claims to adjudicate the Santee case. Elaine frequently joined her husband in lobbying. Factionalism, discontent, and unresponsiveness of congressmen, however, hampered their effectiveness. Complaints against Eastman came from Santees associated with the Garvie faction. Writing in broken English to Commissioner William A. Jones, Andrew Goodthunder cautioned the commissioner not to listen to Charles Eastman because he would "try to fool you about those Medawakanton Money."[5]

Garvie, on the other hand, tried to challenge Eastman's credibility as tribal representative. He brought to Jones's attention Eastman's acceptance of government benefits both as a Santee and Flandreau Sioux. This was patently illegal, Garvie maintained. Jones apparently agreed because he directed Eastman either to relinquish the eighty acres of land given him as a Santee by the act of March 3, 1863, or to refund the $160 paid him as a Flandreau under the act of March 2, 1889. Over a year and a half elapsed before Eastman responded to this directive, the delay due in part to Eastman's belief that he was entitled to both benefits. The commissioner remained unconvinced.[6]

Because of Eastman's reluctance to reply to additional correspondence, the matter dragged on. It was finally decided at the bureau to withhold all interest payments from Sioux trust funds owed to Eastman and his children as well as any monies due him as a government employee until the sum was recovered. An outraged Eastman finally paid the $160.[7] Eastman remained dissatisfied and wrote to President Theodore Roosevelt, explaining that the allotment of eighty acres to him was done without his knowledge or consent. Moreover, because the Flandreaus had decided to accept $160 in cash payments instead of allotments of 160 acres, he felt cheated, especially in having to pay back the $160. Eastman asked that he be allowed to relinquish his eighty acres at Santee for an allotment of 160 acres in either Gregory County, South Dakota, or on another western Sioux reservation. He also wanted his children to receive allotments.[8]

Although Roosevelt hoped that such arrangements would be granted to Eastman, both the commissioner and Secretary of the Interior disapproved. The only way in which Eastman and his children could legally be entitled to further allotments, wrote Jones, was by special legislation. Eastman temporarily accepted this ruling; however, after Jones was replaced as Indian commissioner by Francis E. Leupp, he wrote to Leupp in hopes of reversing the decision. Leupp, however, concurred with his predecessor and denied Eastman's requests, going so far as to summarize the laws, statute by statute, in denying additional allotments.[9]

Controversy still raged over the Hill-Eastman contract. To end for all time the complaints from the Garvie faction, the Secretary of the Interior ordered Indian Inspector James McLaughlin, formerly agent at Standing Rock, to go to the Santee Agency and conduct a thorough investigation.[10] The chief protestor during the investigation was none other than James Garvie. He claimed that because of irregularities in the manner in which the contract was made, it should be declared null and void. Both sides had legal counsel present, which attests to the gravity of the allegations.[11]

The Garvie faction accused Hill and Eastman of not giving proper notice for the meeting at which the contract was discussed; of misrepresenting themselves as legal attorneys; of having obtained illegal signatures of minors or people who had not been on the reservation; and of purposely confusing many Indians in regards to the length of the contract and their fees.[12] McLaughlin painstakingly investigated these allegations and obtained a considerable number of affidavits, submitting his findings and recommendations to the secretary on July 18, 1903.[13]

McLaughlin wrote that Garvie was responsible for all the protests against the contract, by either preparing them himself or instigating others to do so. The reason for Garvie's actions, explained McLaughlin, was because Eastman and Hill did not make him their partner in the contract. He further stated that Garvie's testimony, "together with all other evidence elicited, fails to show any influence was exerted or any misrepresentations made by the Contractors in obtaining the consent of the Indians nor in the execution of the contract." McLaughlin discovered that according to several affidavits proper notice had been given; Eastman and Hill had not attempted to pass themselves off as lawyers; no minors had signed the petition ratifying the contract; and only two of the several signatures in question were erroneous—one name had appeared twice, while the other was discounted because she was not a family head. The people who had been absent from the reservation explained that they had authorized others to sign their names. According to all evidence gathered, McLaughlin stated that the charges regarding confusion over the terms of the contract and the percentage granted to Eastman and Hill of monies recovered were "in no instances proven."[14]

McLaughlin concluded that besides Garvie's personal motives, some Indians had become unhappy because Eastman and Hill had said that they would receive their payments possibly in a year, or at the very latest within three years. Six years had passed without results. Nevertheless, McLaughlin wrote that a clear majority had approved the contract, and furthermore three-fourths of the Santees "are now in favor of the contract." He believed that Eastman and Hill had "done everything that was possible under the circumstances for the restoration" of the annuities, and in the best interests of the Santees, McLaughlin recommended that the contract be continued for the remaining four years.[15]

Although the contract remained effective, Eastman and others failed to get Congress to act until several years after its expiration. The major reason for this indifference on the part of Congress involved disagreement over attorney fees. The House wanted the U.S. Court of Claims to fix the amount at no more than 5 percent of the final judgment and in no event to exceed $25,000. The Senate, however, favored a higher percentage for the attorneys, similar to the terms in the Hill-Eastman contract. There were other points of contention: some congressmen harbored suspicions that a certain congressman would benefit from the payment and questioned whether or not the Santees should be allowed to recover their annuities, since they had participated in an insurrection against the United States.[16]

In discussing the reasons for congressional inactivity, Eastman at first neglected to mention the conflicting views regarding attorney fees. He wrote that he went to Washington expecting to meet men of high integrity who would give him a fair hearing, but he soon became dismayed because of dishonest politicians and lawyers demanding kickbacks in return for their help. Eastman's pleas before several committees and subcommittees fell on deaf ears. Frustrated and in need of finding regular employment to support his family, he turned to his brother for assistance. They made an arrangement whereby John would continue bringing the matter before Congress while Charles would serve in an advisory capacity. Eastman left Washington in 1899 for a job at Carlisle Indian School in Pennsylvania. For the next ten years he held two other positions in the Indian service (see following chapters). Eastman claimed that although he was involved in other pursuits during those ten years, he devoted considerable time to the case and kept informed as to how it was progressing.[17]

Eastman's finances at the time of his departure from Washington were considerably strained. He owed a debt of $500 for room and board, the amount Mrs. C. B. Cutler, his landlady, claimed Eastman and his family owed for staying at her place. She was unable to get Eastman to pay for well over a year after he left Washington and finally wrote to both the Indian commissioner and the Secretary of the Interior in hopes that they would intervene on her behalf. Eastman had since resigned from Carlisle and had taken a position as physician at Crow Creek Reservation in South Dakota. The commissioner wrote to the agent at Crow Creek, asking him to tell Eastman to pay the bill. Eastman agreed to pay Mrs. Cutler monthly installments, but when he defaulted on the payments, she hired attorneys, and the matter was again brought to the attention of the commissioner, who was greatly disturbed over the entire incident and harshly reprimanded Eastman. He told the doctor that he was sick and tired of receiving correspondence on the subject and objected to his office serving as a collection agency against one of its employees. Again, Eastman replied that he would try to pay Mrs. Cutler as soon as he could. The bill was finally settled in the spring of 1906, much to the relief of Mrs. Cutler and officials in Washington.[18]

Several months later, in October, 1906, John Eastman met with

the Santees to discuss the Hill-Eastman contract. He told them that
they would not seek a renewal of it but would continue their efforts
to obtain the confiscated annuities. Once the restoration was secured, they expected to receive their percentage just as if a new contract had been signed. This aroused criticism from Indians and
Whites alike, and later resulted in further financial losses for Charles
Eastman after a decision was rendered by the U.S. Court of Claims.[19]

W. E. Meagley, superintendent at the agency, and Special Agent
Ralph Connell commented on John Eastman's meeting with the
Santees. They criticized his statements and expressed low opinions
of him and Charles Hill. Connell declared that expecting to collect
a percentage on an expired contract was a cheap tactic devised by
them because they realized it was impossible to have the contract
renewed. He advised the Santees to have nothing to do with John
Eastman and Hill. Meagley agreed and also condemned Hill's pecu-
liar banking methods, stating that Hill was not only guilty of cheating
a poor Indian woman on a debt incurred by her deceased husband
but also an old Indian man who had purchased, on account, two
coffins. Curiously, nothing was said about Charles Eastman.[20]

Notwithstanding these criticisms, the Eastmans, without a contract, continued lobbying for congressional action on the Santee
claims. Charles Eastman, in an appearance before a House Subcommittee on Indian Affairs on August 15, 1916, gave a history of the
case and declared that the Santees had suffered enough, comparing
their treatment and losses to the depredations against the people of
Europe by German soldiers in The Great War. Eastman reminded
the subcommittee that he had made the original contract with the
Santees, and for the last twenty years he and his brother had been
involved in the case. He claimed that the Indians stood by the contract even though it had ended. Eastman concluded that attorney
fees had been the major stumbling block responsible for congressional delay and hoped that Congress would come to an agreement
on a proper percentage and would recognize the role he and his
brother played in the entire affair.[21]

At long last Congress resolved its disagreement over attorney fees.
Meeting in a joint conference committee, they reached a compromise: it was agreed that attorneys could not receive more than 10

percent of the final award, nor an amount exceeding $50,000. On March 4, 1917, Congress passed an act granting jurisdiction to the U.S. Court of Claims "to hear, determine, and render final judgment" on the Santee claims.[22]

Because nothing specifically was said about the part Eastman had performed in the case, he went to Santee Agency in order to have the Indians confirm him as their legal representative. Eastman encountered opposition not only from C. E. Burton, the superintendent, but also from Indians who were either confused about the proper course to follow or most likely belonged to the Garvie faction. Burton complained to the commissioner "that this reservation is in a turmoil" because of Eastman's visit.[23] According to Burton, Eastman tried to obtain a written declaration from the Santees attesting to their recognition of his assistance in getting the act passed. He also suggested that a six-man delegation accompany him to Washington, at his expense, to promote the case. When Indians asked Burton for his advice on these matters, he told them that he did not think it was wise to do either one. A written statement, he advised, might be used for unauthorized purposes, and such a delegation would most likely be too much under Eastman's influence.[24]

Burton reported that when Eastman learned that he had disapproved of his requests, he began "talking very rough about me and my administration." Confronting Eastman, he asked him if he had authority to hold councils with the Santees. Eastman replied that as a Santee he did not need permission to speak to his own people.[25] At a loss as to what to do next, Burton sent a telegram to Indian Commissioner Cato Sells. He wrote, "Dr. Eastman here holding councils without my permission, accusing all Government officials as being against the Santee receiving money from the Big Santee Bill. Has he Office permission and approval to do this? He is working to get the lion's share of attorney fees. Wire quick instructions."[26]

The commissioner wrote to Eastman and requested him to explain his actions in writing to Burton. Instead, Eastman wrote directly to Sells, denying all the statements made by Burton in the telegram, and respectfully chastising the commissioner for wanting him to answer such charges to the subordinate making them. He claimed that Burton was fully aware of the councils and originally made no objections.

Although not going into any details, Eastman believed that Burton's change of attitude was apparently caused by his favoring others who were trying to negotiate new contracts with the Santees.[27]

Sells wrote to both Eastman and Burton, telling them he would study the matter thoroughly. In addition, he ordered Burton to submit any evidence or other materials supporting his position. Although Burton sent affidavits from "5 reputable Santees" supportive of his statements, the commissioner apparently took no further action on the subject.[28]

Confusion about and outright resistance to Eastman's efforts to garner recognition from the tribe came from Indians as well. Isaac Redowl said that Eastman wanted a new contract by which he would receive $25,000. Redowl quickly added, however, that there were hardly any Santees who supported such an agreement. He was extremely misinformed on the details regarding the act passed by Congress but believed that officials in the Indian service would help and protect his people.[29] Napoleon Wabashaw, another Santee, declared that the tribe did not like Eastman or any one else associated with the Hill-Eastman contract and hoped that the Santees were not bound to pay these men. If another contract were required, wrote Wabashaw, the Santees were willing to grant one to individuals who had no connections with Hill and Eastman.[30]

The struggle over who represented the Santees persisted. When the U.S. Court of Claims finally rendered a decision on June 5, 1922, the attorneys representing the Santees were Marion Butler and J. M. Vale, men associated with the Garvie faction.[31] The U.S. Court of Claims determined that the amount the Santees had a right to recover from the United States under the Treaties of 1837 and 1851, without interest, was $386,597.89. The Santees were unhappy with this judgment and wanted a settlement more in line with one given to the Sissetons and Wahpetons in 1907, who received $788,971.53. Butler and Vale advised that they accept the payment and present other claims at a future date. Eastman, however, suggested that if the Santees appointed him as their attorney, he would attempt to convince Congress to pass legislation increasing the sum paid to them.[32]

Confused as to what would be the best path to follow. Thomas H. Kitto, tribal chairman, asked the Indian commissioner for advice. He acknowledged that Butler and Vale were their attorneys yet believed

their position on pressing for additional claims at a later date would
prove futile. Kitto said that the majority of Santees favored Eastman's proposals but wondered if there would arise a conflict of interest between their present attorneys and Eastman.[33] He was perhaps too naive to realize that such a predicament already existed.

When Eastman learned of this letter, he wrote to Kitto and said
that the chairman's statements could be misconstrued. "It is true,"
stated Eastman, "that Butler and Vale have been attorneys in the
Santee case, but it is also true that I have myself acted personally
and through appointment of counsel in the same case." He condemned the advice given the Santees by Butler and Vale. Eastman
stated that if the Santees furnished some written evidence which
authorized him to introduce a proposal for amendatory legislation,
his "friends in Congress" gave their assurance that it would pass.[34]

Acting Commissioner Edgar B. Meritt replied to Kitto's inquiry.
He wrote that their acceptance of the payment "would not prevent
them from obtaining additional legislation later, should they be able
to make a showing that they have additional meritorious claims
against the Government." Since they already had attorneys, the
commissioner concluded that he saw no reason for nor advantage in
making Eastman their attorney.[35]

Unable to secure recognition from the Santees, Eastman turned
to people in Washington for assistance, explaining in a letter to the
commissioner his long association with the case and his fears of not
receiving a fair deal from Hill, Butler, and Vale. Apparently Eastman and Hill had a falling out because he complained that Hill had
not lived up to his agreement with him to help defray expenses while
in Washington. Eastman further noted that his brother John had
alienated the Santees by accepting payments for himself and his family from the Sisseton and Wahpeton settlement in 1907.[36]

Eastman believed he had a right to one-half of the attorney fees,
which were $38,659.78, but he said he would accept $15,000. He
wanted the Secretary of the Interior to hold a hearing on the distribution of fees with all the parties claiming to represent the Santees.
Failing at this, Eastman called upon friends in the Senate and House
for help.[37] On February 14, 1923, Massachusetts Senator Henry
Cabot Lodge, Sr., proposed an amendment to an appropriation bill
which would authorize the Secretary of the Interior to deduct

$15,000 from the restored Santee annuities and pay that sum to Eastman. Two days later, Representative Frederick H. Gillett, also from Massachusetts, introduced a bill for the relief of Eastman which contained the same provisions. The House bill was referred to the committee on Indian Affairs while the Senate appropriations committee considered Lodge's amendment. Neither measure was reported out of committee.[38]

The Santees protested Eastman's attempt to get legislation passed, which would take an additional $15,000 from their settlement. Chairman Kitto and Garvie declared that attorney fees were fixed at 10 percent, and adding another $15,000 to the amount already given in fees was illegal. Besides, they stated that Butler and Vale had informed the Santees that they had paid Eastman $5,000 for his services. If this were true, Kitto and Garvie further observed, it was more than an adequate payment for the work Eastman may have rendered.[39] Unfortunately, nowhere in the materials searched does Eastman state he received this amount.

Eastman's involvement with the entire affair, which lasted for more than twenty years, cost him a great deal in time, money, and trouble. Although deeply concerned over the Santees' right to recover their confiscated annuities, it is certainly clear that Eastman had more than just their interest at heart. He expected a large sum of money for his services. Congressional delay and factionalism hampered his efforts and resulted in the Santees not renewing the Hill-Eastman contract. He continued, nevertheless, to represent the tribe unofficially, hoping that they would reward him in the end. When other attorneys were hired, he tried unsuccessfully to combat their influence. It must be remembered, however, that Eastman believed he was entitled to at least one-half of the attorney fees. Butler and Vale apparently had paid Eastman $5,000, but he was obviously dissatisfied with his share and sought congressional legislation when it became apparent that he would not receive a larger settlement. Had Congress approved one of the relief measures, coupled with the $5,000 he apparently received from Butler and Vale, Eastman would have been paid $20,000.

It was indeed unfortunate that the case was riddled with factionalism and several unpleasant occurrences. Eastman and others must share the blame for practicing divisive maneuvers which not only undermined their effectiveness as tribal representatives, but also prolonged congressional action. There remains little doubt that Eastman played a major role in the case. Notwithstanding his ulterior motive of receiving a considerable profit from the undertaking, Eastman's participation in the Santee claims case is demonstrative of his efforts to help his people.

NOTES

1. See Folwell, A *History of Minnesota*, II, 212–41; Meyer, *History of the Santee Sioux*, pp. 109–32; Eastman, *Pratt*, p. 128.
2. Folwell, A *History of Minnesota*, II, 258, 437–39; Meyer, *History of the Santee Sioux*, pp. 301–2.
3. William A. Jones to Charles Hill and Charles Eastman, Sept. 28, 1897, BIA, RG 75, LS, NA; A. C. Tonner to Robert J. Gamble, Oct. 4, 1898, ibid.
4. See George H. Bingenheimer to CIA, Jan. 4, 1899, BIA, RG 75, LR, NA; James G. Reid to CIA, Jan. 6, 1899, ibid; Tonner to Secretary of the Interior, Jan. 18, 1899, BIA, RG 75, LS, NA; Paul White Swan to CIA, Feb. 1899, BIA, RG 75, LR, NA; Reid to CIA, Mar. 30, 1899, ibid.; Reid to CIA, May 2, 1899, ibid.
5. Andrew Goodthunder to Jones, Jan. 10, 1898, BIA, RG 75, LR, NA; Red Cloud et al. to CIA, Jan. 13, 1898, ibid.
6. See Jones to Secretary of the Interior, June 15, 1904, BIA, RG 75, LS, NA and Francis E. Leupp to Eastman, Feb. 8, 1906, ibid. for information regarding this entire matter.
7. Ibid.; Eastman to CIA, June 3, 1904, BIA, RG 75, LR, NA.
8. Jones to Secretary of the Interior, June 15, 1904, BIA, RG 75, LS, NA.
9. Ibid.; Leupp to Eastman, Feb. 8, 1906, BIA, RG 75, LS, NA.
10. Ethan A. Hitchcock to McLaughlin, June 20, 1903, BIA, RG 75, LR, NA.
11. See McLaughlin Papers, Reel 26, Letterbooks 1903–4 for the entire proceedings. For Garvie's bias account of his role in the case see *Niobrara Tribune*, July 22 to Sept. 9, 1920.
12. See for example, James Garvie's testimony, July 2, 1903, McLaughlin Papers, Reel 26, Letterbooks 1903–4.
13. McLaughlin to Secretary of the Interior, July 18, 1903, ibid.
14. Ibid.
15. Ibid.
16. See footnote 9 in Folwell, A *History of Minnesota*, II, 437–38 for references to congressional hearings regarding this bill.

17. Eastman, *From the Deep Woods*, pp. 155–58; Eastman to CIA, Feb. 15, 1923, BIA, RG 75, Central Files, NA.
18. See Tonner to J. H. Stephens, Feb. 25, 1901, BIA, RG 75, LS, NA; Stephens to CIA, Apr. 25, 1901, BIA, RG 75, Crow Creek Agency, Box 5, vol. 16, 1900–1901, LS, KC; C. F. Larrabee to Eastman, Nov. 27, 1905, BIA, RG 75, LS, NA; Eastman to CIA, Dec. 1, 1905, BIA, RG 75, LR, NA; William H. White to CIA, Feb. 14, 1906, ibid.; Eastman to Leupp, Sept. 7, 1906, ibid.
19. W. E. Meagley to CIA, Oct. 24, 1906, BIA, RG 75, LR, NA.
20. Ibid.
21. U.S., Congress, House, Subcommittee on Indian Affairs, *Restoration of Annuities to Medawakanton and Wahpakoota (Santee) Sioux Indians, Hearings*, 64th Cong., 1st sess., Aug. 15, 1916, pp. 3–10.
22. Folwell, *A History of Minnesota*, II, 437–38.
23. C. E. Burton to CIA, Aug. 2, 1917, BIA, RG 75, CF, NA.
24. Burton to CIA, Aug. 20, 1917, ibid.
25. Ibid.
26. Burton to Eastman, July 13, 1917, BIA, RG 75, CF, NA.
27. Eastman to CIA, July 21, 1917, ibid.
28. Cato Sells to Eastman, Aug. 11, 1917, ibid.; Sells to Burton, Aug. 11, 1917, ibid.; Burton to CIA, Aug. 20, 1917, ibid.
29. Isaac Redowl to Edgar B. Meritt, July 30, 1917, ibid.
30. Napoleon Wabashaw to Franklin K. Lane, Nov. 5, 1917, ibid.
31. Medawakanton Indians et al. v. U.S., 57 C. Cls. 357 (June 5, 1922); Stephen Blacksmith to Eastman, Sept. 25, 1922, BIA, RG 75, CF, NA.
32. Medawakanton Indians et al. v. U.S., 57 C. Cls. 379 (June 5, 1922); Sisseton and Wahpeton Indians v. U.S., 47 C. Cls. 416 (May 13, 1907); Thomas H. Kitto to CIA, Sept. 26, 1922, BIA, RG 75, CF, NA.
33. Kitto to CIA, Sept. 26, 1922, BIA, RG 75, CF, NA.
34. Eastman to Kitto, Oct. 6, 1922, ibid.
35. Meritt to Kitto, Oct. 14, 1922, ibid.
36. Eastman to CIA, Feb. 15, 1923, ibid.
37. Ibid.; Eastman to Charles H. Burke, Jan. 16, 1923, BIA, RG 75, CF, NA; Burke to Eastman, Jan. 18, 1923, ibid.
38. U.S., *Congressional Record*, 67th Cong., 4th sess., p. 3605 (Feb. 14, 1923); U.S., *Congressional Record*, 67th Cong., 4th sess., p. 3817 (Feb. 16, 1923); Meritt to Eastman, Mar. 19, 1923, BIA, RG 75, CF, NA.
39. Kitto and Garvie to CIA, Feb. 24, 1923, BIA, RG 75, CF, NA.

Class photo of Eastman at Dartmouth College.

Eastman during college days at Dartmouth College.

All-around Athletic Team, Dartmouth College. Eastman, upper left.

Eastman in 1890 at Boston University School of Medicine.

Elaine Goodale shortly before her marriage to Eastman in 1891.

Camp Oahe.

Eastman teaching archery at Camp Oahe.

Irene Taluta Eastman, soprano.

Dr. Charles A. Eastman and daughter Dora, 1892.

Five of the six Eastman children: left to right, Ohiyesa II (Charles Alexander), 4 years old; Dora, 10 years; Irene, 8 years; Virginia, 5 years; and baby Eleanor. The youngest, Florence, was not yet born.

Mark Twain's seventieth birthday party, 1905. Eastman in lower photo, bottom right.

Eastman with Stanley Johnson, a classmate, at their fortieth reunion in Hanover, N.H., 1927.

Eastman in Sioux regalia on waterfront of Camp Oahe, ca. 1918.

Eastman in woods around Camp Oahe, ca. 1918.

Eastman, c. 1916.

CHAPTER 7

GOVERNMENT PHYSICIAN AT CROW CREEK, 1900-03

IN THE LAST TWO YEARS of the nineteenth century, after his resignation as Indian secretary of the YMCA, Charles Eastman began again to seek employment with the Indian service. He had suffered financial setbacks while representing the Santees in Washington and needed to recover these losses. Through the influence of Colonel Richard Henry Pratt, superintendent of Carlisle Indian School in Pennsylvania, Eastman became outing agent for that institution on November 9, 1899, with a salary of $800 a year.[1]

Carlisle Indian School, established in 1879, was not a college, though many writers have referred to it as such. It was actually an elementary school which stressed industrial training, which Pratt believed would enable the Indian students to adjust better to the white world. Pratt, an ardent assimilationist, was not, however, a racist. He wanted Indians and Whites to live together harmoniously and even supported intermarriage as a means to eradicate problems between the two races. The famous outing system, invented by Pratt, further demonstrated his goals. Pratt would send his Indian pupils to live with good Christian families, and the students would be treated as members of the household. "The boys," wrote Pratt, "live in the families, eat at the same tables, share in the work of the farm, and in all respects are treated like young Anglo-Saxons under the same circumstances." As outing agent, Eastman checked on the progress of the students and also any problems they encountered while living with white families and going to school with white children. Besides helping to select the white families with which the Indians were to live, Eastman made sure that both parties were free of difficulties in their adjustment to one another. Other duties involved Eastman's traveling to different reservations to select and then to escort new pupils to Carlisle. During the time the Eastmans resided at Carlisle, Elaine served as editor of the school newspaper, *The Red Man*.[2]

Returning from one of his trips to the West with new students in late December, 1899, Eastman became seriously ill with a severe case of pneumonia and for the entire month of January was bedridden. Seriously concerned about Eastman's welfare, Pratt wrote that he thought Eastman would die. Eastman made a miraculous recovery, however, and soon after he was able to return to his duties.[3]

Desiring a better position as well as a higher salary, Eastman submitted an application to Commissioner Jones in June, 1900, for a combined position of superintendent and physician at a nonreservation school. Eastman stressed his educational achievements. "I may call myself," he wrote, "a living contradiction of the arguments against Indian education. I went from the camp into college life without a common-school education, and succeeded; and that in the same year that Sitting Bull annihilated Custer." He included recommendations from several friends and hoped Jones could find him a position.[4] Jones wrote in reply that there were no vacancies, but that he would place Eastman's application on file.[5]

Eastman remained at Carlisle for three more months. On September 5, 1900, he was offered the position of government physician at Crow Creek Agency, South Dakota, at a salary of $1,200 a year. Eastman sent his letter of acceptance two days later, pleased with the prospect of working once again on a Sioux reservation.[6] Although Eastman was more than qualified to handle such work, Jones wrote that Senators William B. Allison and John H. Gear, both from Iowa, were instrumental in helping him secure the appointment, because they regarded Eastman as a "stalwart republican," and a man who could help the party.[7] This situation typifies the manner in which many people gained employment with the Indian service. Partisan influence often dictated who received appointments, and the Indian service remained a bastion of patronage years after civil service was enacted. Frequently, these appointees had never seen an Indian or had never been on a reservation, which helps explain why agencies were often mismanaged and fraught with corruption. Although Eastman apparently secured the appointment because of his

party affiliation, he should not be classified among the group of incompetent and ill-prepared individuals working on reservations.

According to an article in *The Red Man*, the Eastmans' trip to
Crow Creek was hampered by cold and rainy weather. They arrived
on September 19, and Eastman began his duties on October 1.[8] His
years at Crow Creek resembled, in many ways, the ones he had spent
at Pine Ridge. Once again, Eastman faced a rigorous work schedule,
caring for the general medical needs of both Indians and Whites and
serving as school physician for Indian students attending the three
reservation schools.[9]

One of his responsibilities involved conducting an extensive program to protect the inhabitants at Crow Creek against smallpox.
Eastman received orders to disinfect all agency buildings and to
initiate a vaccination program in an effort to combat an expected outbreak of this dreaded disease to which countless Indians fell prey.
Confronted with such a difficult task, Eastman requested more for-
maldehyde generators and supplies in order to carry out effectively
these directives. He wrote that by having additional generators "we
can easily cope with the disease, and will save the home of many from
burning."[10] Eastman reported that Indians feared the side effects
which accompanied the shots, and he had to travel extensively about
Crow Creek in a campaign to convince them of the need of vaccination. These precautions against a smallpox epidemic proved successful not only at Crow Creek but also at other Sioux agencies.[11]

The Eastman family, now including three daughters and a son,
passed their first winter at Crow Creek without much trouble. Their
living quarters, which adjoined Eastman's office, were cramped, but
the bureau promised to build a new physician's office.[12] When the
new office was finally completed in December, 1901, Eastman expressed his deep appreciation to Commissioner Jones. "I wish you
could see," boasted Eastman, "how neat and businesslike the office
is. Even the worst tasting drugs looked tempting." Elaine must have
been gratified as well since it gave her an extra room for her growing
family.[13]

Eastman served as physician at Crow Creek for nearly two and
one-half years, during which medical services and health conditions
improved. For example, because of complaints against the perfor-

mance of his old, sickly, and rotund hospital nurse, Eastman brought the matter to the attention of the commissioner, who, in turn, promised Eastman a new nurse who would be more qualified to hold the position.[14]

Following his previous policy at Pine Ridge, Eastman made himself accessible at any time for ailing patients.[15] Eastman observed in his last annual medical report in 1903 that the general health of the Crow Creek Sioux had been "fairly good this year." He indicated that no Indian deaths resulted from the vaccination program administered in the fall or from a measles outbreak in June. Eastman concluded his report by proudly announcing that for the first time in several years there was an increase in births over deaths among these people.[16]

Eastman's rapport and close personal contact with his patients helped bring about improvements in their general health. Unfortunately, his relationship with Harry D. Chamberlain, the Indian agent, began to deteriorate, and Eastman again found himself involved in a controversy reminiscent of his Pine Ridge days, this new confrontation not on the same scale as the embroilment between him and Brown, but nevertheless a ghastly affair, replete with charges and countercharges.

Before Eastman accepted his position at Crow Creek, there existed an atmosphere of discontent and distrust toward Agent James H. Stephens, Chamberlain's predecessor. Investigated in December, 1899, for such charges as trading illegally with Indians and neglecting his duties, Stephens managed to hold on to his position until April, 1901.[17] Among those expressing their contempt for Stephens's mismanagement and corrupt activities were White Ghost, a local leader at Crow Creek, the Reverend Hachaliah Burt, an Episcopal priest at Crow Creek, and Bishop William H. Hare, the nationally known Episcopal bishop and Indian rights figure. They called for his removal and convinced Secretary Herbert Welsh of the IRA to demand the same.[18]

Stephens was agent at Crow Creek when Eastman arrived. Eastman served under him for six months. The doctor surely knew about the troubles and discontent at the agency, yet nowhere in his letters to Commissioner Jones did he mention these matters. Moreover, his name never appeared in the IRA correspondence regarding the

Stephens case. Perhaps Eastman, remembering his past associations with agents, did not want to become involved and so instead decided to keep a low profile.

When Chamberlain took over as agent in June, 1901, Eastman observed that he "seems to be a good and well meaning man. I believe he will handle these people very well."[19] Eastman's expectations proved too optimistic; strained relations continued. The doctor wished to remain at Crow Creek and assured Jones, who was concerned over his well-being, that he would keep out of all affairs unrelated to his official duties. If, however, Chamberlain sought his advice on agency matters, wrote Eastman, he would, of course, gladly cooperate in any way possible.[20]

Here for the first time in his government correspondence, Eastman, without going into details, hinted at the discord and uneasiness at the agency, where the mounting tensions finally erupted in July, 1902. Although Eastman had made a pledge for noninvolvement unless officially asked, Chamberlain accused him of being responsible for "stirring up contention among the Indians of this agency."[21]

Chamberlain was particularly disturbed over a letter written to Jones by White Ghost, displeased with conditions and government policies at the agency, especially attempts by the agent to make Indians self-supporting. White Ghost also blamed Chamberlain for several misdeeds and asked Commissioner Jones if he could bring a delegation with "a good interpreter" to Washington to discuss these matters. This could only mean Eastman, Chamberlain inferred. The agent believed Eastman had encouraged White Ghost to write this letter because Eastman wanted to visit Washington at government expense on other matters. Furthermore, Chamberlain claimed that Eastman was guilty of other serious offenses which he could substantiate. Chamberlain would not press the matter, however, if Eastman would "let the Indians alone, or use his influence to help carry into effect the new policy of making Indians self supporting." He requested that Jones direct Eastman "to attend to the duties pertaining to his office" and to refrain from agitating Indians.[22]

Exactly one week later, Chamberlain requested that Eastman be transferred to some other agency. Another defamatory letter, signed by White Ghost and sent to Senator Alfred B. Kittredge of South Dakota, caused his sudden change of mind. The letter criticized the way Chamberlain disposed of lands belonging to heirs of deceased Indians. Summoning White Ghost to his office for questioning, Chamberlain reported that White Ghost denied, under oath, writing or signing the letter. This led Chamberlain to conclude that Eastman wrote the letter and forged White Ghost's signature, actions that he said made it impossible for him to work with Eastman. He reminded Jones of Eastman's involvement in a "similar experience" at Pine Ridge. If it were necessary to prefer specific charges in order to remove Eastman, Chamberlain stated that he would submit them.[23]

Meanwhile, Senator Kittredge and South Dakota's other senator, Robert J. Gamble, also requested Eastman's transfer, supporting Chamberlain's charges in a letter marked personal. Kittredge and Gamble complained that Eastman opposed certain Republican party candidates in different campaigns throughout the state. It should be recalled that one of the reasons given for appointing Eastman as physician was his usefulness to the party, but apparently Eastman had not been actively supporting Republicans as strongly as they thought he should. The senators hoped that Eastman would be sent to an agency outside their state.[24]

On August 2, 1902, Indian Inspector J. E. Edwards was sent to Crow Creek to investigate not only the troubles between Eastman and Chamberlain, but also other contentious matters involving Chamberlain, White Ghost, and J. Thomas Hall, superintendent of Crow Creek Boarding School.[25] Edwards received from Chamberlain ten reasons why Eastman should be removed: Chamberlain accused Eastman of creating turmoil at the agency, neglecting his duties, taking undue liberties with a female patient and attempting the same with others; he claimed Eastman told Indians they could perform dances, regardless of Chamberlain's order to the contrary; Eastman participated in writing certain letters, containing misrepresentations to the commissioner and Kittredge; and Eastman and Hall met late at night on several occasions to plot against him.[26]

As for the charges of negligence, Chamberlain declared that Eastman frequently left the agency for extended periods of time without notifying him of where he went or when he would return. He further asserted that Eastman had not only improperly cared for an Indian woman who died with her breasts infested with maggots, but had also refused treatment to a blind Indian boy. The allegations of immorality, on the other hand, concerned Eastman's sexual involvement with a patient, the wife of James Fire Cloud, an agency employee, and vague indications that Eastman had made sexual advances toward employees of Crow Creek Boarding School.[27]

Eastman emphatically denied every charge. "I have never incited nor created," declared Eastman, "any disturbance among the Indians of this Agency." Eastman stated that he had always discouraged Indian dances, particularly on Sundays and for exhibitions; had neither written nor dictated any of the letters in question; and had not engaged in any conspiratorial meetings with Hall.[28] In his denial of the allegations regarding negligence of duty, Eastman explained that even though he was never required to report his whereabouts to the agent, he always left word at his home where he could be reached in case of emergency. He further explained that he had been treating the woman, who was inflicted with an advanced stage of cancer, ever since his arrival at Crow Creek, but she had resisted his care and had not followed directions. "I could scarcely cleanse her wounds," he wrote, "unless by force," and all she wanted were opiates to arrest the pain. He never refused treatment of the blind youth, but there was little he could do for the boy. He said that he told the boy's father that perhaps an operation by a specialist might prove successful.[29]

Addressing the immorality charges, Eastman stated that he had never conducted himself unprofessionally with Mrs. Fire Cloud or any other patient. In his defense, he presented as proof Mrs. Fire Cloud's statement, corroborated by her husband and mother, and witnessed by the Reverend Burt, the Reverend John P. Williamson, and Hall.[30] Eastman awaited Edwards's report confident in his denial of Chamberlain's ten charges.

Before Edwards concluded his investigation of these allegations, however, Chamberlain made an additional charge against Eastman. He accused the doctor of immoral conduct with another agency employee, Miss Augusta S. Hultman, superintendent of Grace Boarding School. Edwards enlarged the scope of his investigation to include this new charge, which tended to overshadow all of the others. Based on affidavits collected from employees at the school and other agency personnel, Edwards's preliminary findings indicated "that there is no reasonable doubt of the existence of relations between" Eastman and Hultman. He reported that Hultman, who was approaching her fortieth year, had "not conducted herself as becomes a lady" and recommended her immediate removal. He also advised that the school should be abandoned because of low enrollments and the proximity of other schools in the vicinity to handle the pupils. As for Eastman, Edwards praised his achievements as an educated Indian, his abilities as a physician, and his efforts to encourage Indians to accept proper medical treatment. Because of these attributes, Edwards recommended that he should be reprimanded for his involvement with Hultman, warned that no other dishonorable actions would be tolerated, and transferred to another agency.[31]

Jones's response was that if Eastman and Hultman were guilty of such conduct, they should be removed. He advised Edwards to conduct a thorough investigation and to obtain written statements from Eastman and Hultman. Meanwhile, Chamberlain continued to complain to Washington about the demoralizing effects of the scandal and hoped that Eastman and others—principally Hall—would be removed.[32]

It is important to note that Edwards had a low opinion of Chamberlain's performance. On September 29, 1902, Edwards criticized Chamberlain's lack of executive ability. He reported that the agent had violated government regulations and had lost the respect and confidence of Indians under his control. He singled out Chamberlain's ineptness as directly responsible for all the troubles. In addition, Edwards exonerated Superintendent Hall of any misdeeds but recommended his transfer. Hall continued to harbor ill feelings toward Chamberlain.[33]

Edwards proceeded under Jones's directive and compiled more evidence on the immorality charges. Eastman, whose confidence began to wane, positively denied the charges.[34] Moreover, Eastman sent his explanation directly to Jones, claiming that Chamberlain had induced three female employees at Grace Boarding School, women who were personal enemies of Hultman and who possessed "very loose characters," to file these derogatory allegations. He pointed to the contradictions in their statements regarding where he slept when forced to spend the night at the school. Eastman went on to explain that his wife and baby often accompanied him on these visits. Eastman reported that when at the school Hultman allowed him to use her quarters as an office and as a bedroom when he stayed the night. She, of course, found other accommodations. Concluding his letter, Eastman believed that Chamberlain and the three ladies had "joined forces" in an effort to discredit the reputations of him and Hultman. He counted on Jones's support to rectify matters.[35]

Eastman also solicited statements from friends who praised his character and work, among them the Reverend John P. Williamson, a friend of Eastman since he began his formal education in the white man's school, who cited Eastman's abilities and declared "that his moral character is above reproach." Williamson believed that the charges against the doctor "were started with base and slanderous intent, and are propagated by those who are seeking his downfall."[36]

On October 13, Edwards submitted the first of three reports regarding the affair. Edwards wrote that he had suspended Hultman but allowed Eastman to remain on active duty because he was treating patients in the agency hospital. He also questioned the validity of statements made by several witnesses who spoke on Eastman's behalf. Once again, he recommended Hultman's dismissal, the closing of the school, and Eastman's transfer.[37]

Nine days later, Edwards sent his final two reports to Washington, criticizing Eastman's and Hultman's attempts to discredit the character of school employees who made statements sustaining the immoral conduct allegations and disclosing why at least one of the employees held these views. According to the affidavit of Henrietta Freemont, a mixed-blood teacher at the school, she found Eastman and Hultman together in the superintendent's quarters late one evening. When Edwards asked Hultman about this incident, she explained that Eastman had been measuring her for a truss and that he had examined her hernia on three separate occasions without the presence of a third party. Because of the absence of another person in the room during such examinations, Edwards told Hultman "that she was most indiscreet to say the least."[38]

Edwards's other report contained his conclusions on the ten original charges Chamberlain had made against Eastman on August 7. Edwards found Eastman guilty of frequent consultations with Indians, of several conspiratorial meetings with Hall, and of leaving the agency without notifying Chamberlain. All of the other charges were unsubstantiated. Edwards wrote that Eastman had neither neglected his patients nor taken certain liberties with Mrs. Fire Cloud or employees at Crow Creek Boarding School. He also exonerated Eastman on the charge of writing derogatory letters to influential people. White Ghost confessed to Edwards that Homer Clark, a mixed-blood member of the tribe, had written the letters in question.[39]

While awaiting the final decision from Washington, Hultman, who had been suspended, complained to her superiors that she had been discriminated against, while Eastman remained on active duty. Commissioner Jones agreed that she had not received equal treatment and recommended to the Secretary of the Interior that she be allowed to return to her duties.[40]

Hultman's return to Grace Boarding School resulted in further complications for her and Eastman. On Friday, December 19, Eastman went to the school, at Hultman's request, to examine a sick pupil. On the following morning, while Eastman was preparing to leave, an altercation took place between Eastman, Hultman, and Henrietta Freemont. Freemont, extremely disturbed because she believed Eastman and Hultman had assaulted her personal honor and good name, exchanged harsh words with them. A quarrel ensued, and Freemont struck Hultman twice. The enraged Freemont was finally restrained, and Chamberlain suspended her for striking a superior. The entire incident was reported to Inspector Frank C. Churchill, who had been conducting an examination of the conditions at Grace Boarding School.[41]

Churchill, who had also been ordered to reinvestigate all of the other troubles at Crow Creek, recommended that the school be closed and all of its teachers, including Freemont, transferred to other agencies. He believed, as did Chamberlain, that Freemont's attack was wrong, yet they expressed sympathy towards her. Churchill agreed with Edwards's view of Hultman's immodesty and indiscretion in allowing Eastman to examine her hernia and fit her for a truss without another party present and also found her to be "a high-strung, quick tempered person, with an erratic and uneven disposition." He recommended that she take a reduction in salary and be given a teacher's position at another agency.[42]

Of far greater significance was Churchill's disagreement with Edwards's substantiation of the immoral conduct charges against Eastman and Hultman. Churchill believed all of the evidence presented was circumstantial and declared that they had not been guilty of such actions.[43] Although Eastman and Hultman must have been elated when they learned of this, Eastman's enthusiasm soon diminished when Churchill filed his other report and recommendations on the overall dissension at the agency.

Unlike Edwards, Churchill had a low opinion of Eastman. He found Eastman to be "adroit and crafty" and "a dangerous man to have on a reservation where the Dakota or Sioux language is spoken." He believed Eastman, Hall, White Ghost, and others had conspired against Chamberlain in an effort to obtain his removal. Churchill recommended that Hall be sent to a smaller agency and that Eastman be transferred to another agency where the Sioux language was not spoken. All of the complaints against Chamberlain were dismissed.[44] White Ghost, however, remained displeased and continued to attack Chamberlain's administration after Eastman and Hall had left the agency.[45]

Churchill's recommendations were accepted. Grace Boarding School was abandoned, and several agency employees eventually received transfers. Eastman did not appeal Churchill's findings but instead requested thirty days' leave, to begin on January 5, 1903, which Jones granted despite Chamberlain's protest. Eastman went to New York and gave several lectures and talked with friends about his future. After Eastman's return to Crow Creek, Chamberlain complained to Jones that Eastman was again actively engaged in creating discord at the agency.[46]

On March 5, 1903, Jones conveniently offered Eastman a permanent position to revise the Sioux allotment rolls. Eastman, who had been asked by Jones and others late in 1902 to experiment with the possibilities of such work, which would help correct Indian surnames, accepted the appointment. Eastman hoped that he could remain at Crow Creek until April 1, which would allow him to work on the rolls there and at the Lower Brule Agency; to help treat patients who he claimed were afflicted with an epidemic of grippe, a type of influenza; and to delay his departure to Minnesota until the weather improved. Chamberlain expected his immediate resignation and informed Jones that there were only a few cases of the disease. The commissioner, undoubtedly weary and tired of the constant bickering between the two men, denied Eastman's request. Eastman resigned on March 12, 1903.[47] On the following day, Chamberlain, gloating over his victory, wrote to Freemont, who had been transferred to Fort Shaw, Montana. "I have the pleasure of informing you," boasted Chamberlain, "that Dr. Eastman has been removed from this Agency, and that Supt. Hall will go next."[48]

Eastman's second and final venture as a government physician had again been an unpleasant experience. Although he had been found innocent of immoral conduct with Hultman and others, he nevertheless participated in an attempt to undermine Chamberlain's authority. Eastman had pledged that he would not become involved in the turmoil at Crow Creek, but trouble seemed to attract him like filings to a magnet. His ability to communicate with the Sioux, at first considered by him and others an asset, became a liability. Indians undoubtedly voiced their complaints to him. Having a man like Eastman in the field seemed to be a good idea, yet his recurrent conflicts with white agents cast doubts on his effectiveness. Perhaps they were affronted or threatened by an educated Indian physician, or on the other hand, perhaps Eastman believed he was their intellectual superior. The answers remain obscure.

It should be emphasized that Indian agents on reservations throughout the United States possessed almost absolute power and often became embroiled in controversies with other employees at their agencies as well as their Indian wards. A plethora of material exists regarding these complaints and subsequent investigations of them. Eastman's confrontations are unique because they involved an educated Indian protesting what he believed were injustices inflicted upon his people and upon himself by Indian agents and other government employees. Although he was unable to serve his people as government physician at Crow Creek, Eastman's new job of revising the Sioux allotment rolls proved far more pleasant and rewarding.

NOTES

1. Pratt to CIA, Nov. 9, 1899, BIA, RG 75, LR, NA; Jones to Pratt, Nov. 21, 1899, BIA, RG 75, LS, NA.
2. Pratt to CIA, Nov. 9, 1899, BIA, RG 75, LR, NA; Hazel W. Hertz-

berg, *The Search for an American Indian Identity: Modern Pan-Indian Movements* (Syracuse: Syracuse University Press, 1971), pp. 16–17. For detailed information on Pratt and Carlisle see Eastman, *Pratt*; Everett Arthur Gilcreast, "Richard Henry Pratt and American Indian Policy, 1877–1906: A Study of the Assimilation Movement," (Ph.D. dissertation, Yale University, 1967); Carmelita S. Ryan, "The Carlisle Indian Industrial School," (Ph.D. dissertation, Georgetown University, 1962).

3. Pratt to CIA, Jan. 31, 1900, BIA, RG 75, LR, NA.
4. Eastman to Jones, June 15, 1900, ibid.
5. Jones to Eastman, June 21, 1900, BIA, RG 75, LS, NA.
6. Tonner to Eastman, Sept. 5, 1900, ibid; Eastman to Tonner, Sept. 7, 1900, BIA, RG 75, LR, NA. Eastman continued occasionally to escort students to Carlisle during his leaves of absence from Crow Creek.
7. Jones to J. M. Greene, Oct. 15, 1900, Selected Documents from the Records of the Office of the Commissioner of Indian Affairs, the Chief Clerk and the Assistant Commissioner of Indian Affairs, Microfilm, Reel 795, Doris Duke Oral History Project, University of New Mexico.
8. *The Red Man*, Sept. 23, 1900; Eastman to Jones, Oct. 2, 1900, BIA, RG 75, LR, NA.
9. James H. Stephens to CIA, Dec. 1, 1900, BIA, RG 75, Crow Creek Agency, Box 5, vol. 16, 1900–1901, LS, KC; *The Red Man*, Mar. 1, 1901; Stephens to CIA, Apr. 6, 1901, BIA, RG 75, Crow Creek Agency, Box 5, vol. 16, 1900–1901, LS, KC; Harry D. Chamberlain to J. Thomas Hall, Oct. 21, 1902, ibid., vol. 17, 1902–3, LS, KC; Chamberlain to CIA, May 23, 1903, ibid., Box 6, vol. 19, 1903–4, LS, KC.
10. Eastman to Chamberlain, July 13, 1901, BIA, RG 75, Crow Creek Agency, Box 6, vol. 17, 1901–2, LS, KC.
11. Eastman to Chamberlain, Dec. 14, 1901, BIA, RG 75, LR, NA; Chamberlain to Eastman, Sept. 6, 1902, BIA, RG 75, Crow Creek Agency, Box 5, vol. 17, 1902–3, LS, KC.
12. Stephens to CIA, Feb. 19, 1901, BIA, RG 75, Crow Creek Agency, Box 5, vol. 16, 1900–1901, LS, KC; *The Red Man*, Mar. 1, 1901; Eastman to Jones, June 21, 1901, BIA, RG 75, LR, NA.
13. Eastman to Jones, Dec. 28, 1901, BIA, RG 75, LR, NA.
14. Eastman to Jones, June 21, 1901, ibid.; Eastman to Jones, July 5, 1901, ibid.; Eastman to Jones, Dec. 28, 1901, ibid.
15. Eastman to Jones, July 5, 1901, ibid.

16. Eastman to Chamberlain, *ca.* July 1902, BIA, RG 75, Crow Creek Agency, Box 6, vol. 18, 1902–3, LS, KC.

17. J. E. Jenkins to Stephens, Dec. 18, 1899, ibid., Box 5, vol. 15, 1899–1900, LS, KC; Stephens to CIA, Dec. 21, 1899, ibid.; Matthew K. Sniffen to Hachaliah Burt, May 3, 1901, Indian Rights Association Papers, 1868–1968, Microfilm, Reel 75, Historical Society of Pennsylvania, Philadelphia, Penn., Microfilming Corporation of America. Hereafter cited as IRA-MCA. Ironically, Eastman served as an interpreter at the investigation. At Crow Creek in his official role as outing agent, he probably took the assignment for monetary reasons. See testimony of Comes Flying et al., Dec. 20, 1899, BIA, RG 75, Crow Creek Agency, Box 5, vol. 15, 1899–1900, LS, KC.

18. White Ghost to Secretary of the Interior, May 1, 1900, IRA-MCA, Reel 15; Welsh to Ethan A. Hitchcock, May 7, 1900, ibid., Reel 75; William H. Hare to Welsh, May 15, 1900, ibid., Reel 15; Burt to S. M. Brosius, June 30, 1900, ibid.

19. Eastman to Jones, June 21, 1901, BIA, RG 75, LR, NA.

20. Eastman to Jones, July 5, 1901, ibid.

21. Chamberlain to CIA, July 12, 1902, BIA, RG 75, Crow Creek Agency, Box 6, vol. 18, 1902–3, LS, KC.

22. Ibid. See White Ghost to Welsh, Nov. 20, 1902, IRA-MCA, Reel 16 for examples of his complaints.

23. Chamberlain to Jones, July 19, 1902, BIA, RG 75, Crow Creek Agency, Box 6, vol. 18, 1902–3, LS, KC.

24. Robert J. Gamble and Alfred B. Kittredge to Jones, July 24, 1902, BIA, RG 75, LR, NA. Jones notified the senators that Eastman would be offered a transfer. Kittredge to Jones, Aug. 18, 1902, ibid.; Gamble to Jones, Aug. 23, 1902, ibid.

25. Tonner to Secretary of the Interior, Aug. 2, 1902, BIA, RG 75, LS, NA.

26. Chamberlain to CIA, Aug. 7, 1902, BIA, RG 75, Crow Creek Agency, Box 6, vol. 18, 1902–3, LS, KC.

27. Ibid.

28. Eastman to CIA, Aug. 9, 1902, BIA, RG 75, LR, NA.

29. Ibid.

30. Ibid.

31. J. E. Edwards to Secretary of the Interior, Sept. 5, 1902, BIA, RG 75, LR, NA.

32. Jones to Secretary of the Interior, Sept. 13, 1902, ibid.; Chamberlain to CIA, Sept. 13, 1902, ibid.

33. Edwards to Secretary of the Interior, Sept. 29, 1902, ibid.; Hall to Welsh, Nov. 29, 1902, IRA-MCA, Reel 16.
34. See affidavit of Homer Clark, White Ghost, and E. P. H. Ashley, Oct. 4, 1902, BIA, RG 75, LR, NA; affidavit of Charles A. Eastman, Oct. 7, 1902, ibid.; affidavit of Mr. and Mrs. Andrew Lone Bull, Oct. 13, 1902, ibid.
35. Eastman to Jones, Oct. 7, 1902, ibid.
36. Eastman to CIA, Oct. 20, 1902, enclosure, ibid. The Reverend Burt also expressed his confidence on Eastman's behalf and was indignant when he learned that Edwards had apparently misconstrued his statements. Burt to Jones, Nov. 14, 1902, ibid.
37. Edwards to Secretary of the Interior, Oct. 13, 1902, ibid.
38. Edwards to Secretary of the Interior, Oct. 22, 1902, ibid.
39. Edwards to Secretary of the Interior, Oct. 22, 1902, ibid.
40. Augusta Hultman to A. O. Wright, Nov. 5, 1902, ibid.; Jones to Secretary of the Interior, Nov. 28, 1902, BIA, RG 75, LS, NA.
41. Frank C. Churchill to Hitchcock, Dec. 23, 1902, BIA, RG 75, LR, NA. For Hultman's and Freemont's reports on the incident see Chamberlain to CIA, Dec. 22, 1902, enclosure, BIA, RG 75, Crow Creek Agency, Box 6, vol. 18, 1902–3, LS, KC; Henrietta Freemont to CIA, Dec. 23, 1902, ibid. Eastman made an oral report to Churchill.
42. Churchill to Hitchcock, Dec. 23, 1902, BIA, RG 75, LR, NA; Chamberlain to CIA, Dec. 26, 1902, BIA, RG 75, Crow Creek Agency, Box 6, vol. 18, 1902–3, LS, KC.
43. Churchill to Hitchcock, Dec. 23, 1902. BIA, RG 75, LR, NA.
44. Churchill to Hitchcock, Jan. 7, 1903, ibid.
45. See *Sioux Falls Daily Press*, Apr. 2, 1903.
46. Eastman to Jones, Dec. 22, 1902, BIA, RG 75, LR, NA; Chamberlain to CIA, Dec. 26, 1902, BIA, RG 75, Crow Creek Agency, Box 6, vol. 18, 1902–3, LS, KC; Chamberlain to CIA, Mar. 7, 1903, ibid.
47. Jones to Eastman, Mar. 5, 1903, BIA, RG 75, Crow Creek Agency, Box 5, vol. 18, 1903, LS, KC; Eastman to Jones, Mar. 11, 1903, BIA, RG 75, LR, NA; Chamberlain to Jones, Mar. 11, 1903, BIA, RG 75, Crow Creek Agency, Box 6, vol. 18, 1902–3, LS, KC; Eastman to Jones, Mar. 12, 1903, telegram, BIA, RG 75, LR, NA.
48. Chamberlain to Freemont, Mar. 13, 1903, BIA, RG 75, Crow Creek Agency, Box 5, vol. 18, 1903, LS, KC.

CHAPTER 8

RENAMING THE SIOUX, 1903-09

THE PROJECT TO RENAME the American Indians origi-
nated in the 1890s as a result of the General Allotment Act of 1887
(Dawes Severalty Act), which granted to Indians allotments of
reservation land in severalty. Because Indians did not follow the
dominant American pattern of using surnames, something had to
be done to protect their newly acquired property rights and the future claims of heirs. Indeed, Indians often had throughout their
lives more than one name. Indian names, often symbolic, were
chosen from a variety of sources: revered animals, unique personal
characteristics, names of past ancestors, extraordinary achievements
of the individuals, or by just being selected to have a name bestowed
on them because of a special event. Commissioner of Indian Affairs
Thomas J. Morgan in the early 1890s realized the potential legal complications of the absence of surnames and ordered Indian agents and
superintendents of Indian schools to develop systems whereby Indians would receive new names compatible with dominant American
standards. Little was accomplished, however, and the project remained dormant until the early 1900s, when new and more successful
measures were undertaken.[1]

Through the efforts of Hamlin Garland, novelist, short-story
writer, and Indian reformer, the project received further attention.
Garland, known for his realistic portrayal of agrarian life in mid-
western America, also had a profound interest in Indians. Though he
has only recently received attention as an Indian reformer, he was an
early advocate of abolishing the allotment system and also believed
in the restoration and encouragement of Native American art and

religion, reforms which would be implemented during the 1930s. Garland became interested in the renaming project while on a literary research visit to the Cheyenne and Arapaho Indians residing at Darlington Agency, Indian Territory, in April, 1900, where he learned of the difficulties Indians were having with land claims and related matters from Chester Poe Cornelius, an Indian lawyer. Only by possessing proper last names, concluded Garland, could Indians operate as landowners and avoid legal squabbles. For the next two and one-half years he studied the feasibility of such a plan, soliciting aid from such individuals as Dr. George Bird Grinnell, noted author and Indian expert, Dr. C. Hart Merriam, magazine editor and head of the Division of Ornithology and Mammalogy of the U.S. Department of Agriculture, and W J McGee, head of the Smithsonian Institution's Bureau of American Ethnology. Support for the program came from President Theodore Roosevelt, Indian Commissioner William A. Jones, and Secretary of the Interior Ethan A. Hitchcock. Because of Garland's intense interest, he was made director of the renaming project.[2]

On December 1, 1902, a circular written by Garland was issued by the Indian bureau outlining the procedures to follow in renaming Indians. Included among the guidelines were the need to have names which could be easily pronounced, the abandonment, according to non-Indian standards of taste, of degrading and unpleasant names, and the retention of the original meaning of the names whenever possible and whenever felicitous. Garland selected the Cheyenne and Arapaho Indians at Darlington Agency and the Sioux at Crow Creek Agency as the initial tribes to be renamed. He had also explored the possibilities of including the Pueblo Indians in the project but discarded the idea on the advice of Charles F. Lummis, editor of Out West magazine, who had written to Garland that it would be extremely impractical to change the Hispanic baptismal names which most Pueblo Indians as well as mission Indians in southern California possessed. The extension of the renaming project to additional tribes, other than the Sioux, proved disappointing.[3] Garland attributed the failure to "half-hearted support on the part of the officials in the field."[4] Yet, the project was very successful among the Sioux, due mainly to Garland's selection of Eastman to conduct the work. Just exactly how Garland and Eastman became acquainted remains un-

clear. Garland most likely knew of Eastman's educational achievements and perhaps had even read some of Eastman's articles, which
proposed views similar to his own on Indian reform.

Toward the end of 1902, when Eastman was still embroiled in controversy at Crow Creek, he received a letter from Garland, asking him
for his views on the renaming program. Eastman reminded Garland
of Commissioner Morgan's futile attempts of the preceding decade
but believed the plan worthwhile, though he expressed concern over
the extra problems and work involved in renaming Indians who had
already accepted allotments. Nevertheless, Eastman believed that the
Sioux were, on their own initiative, attempting to adopt family
names. Asked if he would experiment with revising a few pages of
the Crow Creek rolls in order to establish permanent Sioux names,
Eastman accepted the temporary assignment.[5]

Because of Eastman's success in revising these sample pages, and
also because Commissioner Jones most likely wanted to ease the tensions and to solve the problems involving Eastman and others at
Crow Creek, he recommended to Secretary Hitchcock that Eastman
be employed full-time for the rest of the fiscal year on the renaming
project. By the end of that time, wrote Jones, "the character, value,
extent and practicability of such work can be determined."[6] Garland
also wrote to President Roosevelt, at the request of Eastman, concerning the position.[7] On March 5, 1903, Jones notified Eastman of
his appointment as clerk of the revision of the Sioux allotment rolls,
with a salary of $100 a month.[8]

Eastman had planned to continue revising the Crow Creek rolls
and to begin working on the Lower Brule rolls. However, because his
termination as government physician took effect sooner than Eastman had expected, he was forced to leave Crow Creek. He moved
back to Minnesota, establishing his residence at White Bear, a sub-
urb of St. Paul, and informed Garland and Jones that because of
his new locale he would begin with the Sisseton Agency in South
Dakota.[9]

Before going to Sisseton and other agencies, Eastman requested
that a copy of the allotment rolls be sent to him so that he could become acquainted with the names, arrange them in alphabetical order,
and check for misspellings and other errors. He also hoped that In-

dian agents would be notified of his coming and that office space would be provided at the agencies for his work.[10]

He reported early from Sisseton Agency that the Indians generally approved and understood the importance of revising their names, though he encountered several problems which plagued him throughout the renaming project. Eastman soon discovered that the work was more tedious and complicated than he had originally anticipated, due to the problem of tracking down all the distant relatives as well as grouping all the offspring of older Indians under one family name. Other obstacles were: plural marriages; separations and remarriages; legitimate and illegitimate children with incorrect surnames; mistranslated names; inconsistent family names among fathers, brothers, and sisters; wives not having their husbands' last names; and cumbersome, ridiculous, and perverted names. Examples of the latter were such names as Let-them-have-enough, Old-woman-butte, Red-nose-mother, and Skunk's-father.[11]

As before, he was ever sensitive to what he perceived as injustice done to his people. Eastman reported from Sisseton that he had conducted a personal investigation and discovered that many Indians were being swindled by shrewd lawyers and unprincipled land speculators. Commissioner Jones, commenting on Eastman's allegations, warned him that his statements were based on generalities and were not specific enough. If he wanted the matter pursued, wrote Jones, Eastman must supply names and more factual data. No additional letters were located showing that Eastman continued to press the issue.[12] Perhaps Eastman felt that he would again become involved in another long, complicated controversy, or reading Jones's letter closely, Eastman may have realized that the commissioner's tone was less than encouraging. If the Indians were being defrauded, as was the case in many instances, they probably voiced their complaints to other sympathetic individuals more readily available to aid them.

Eastman returned to White Bear to finish the name revisions after completion of his fieldwork among the Sissetons. He wrote to Jones that despite the more tedious aspects, he enjoyed the work and hoped that he would be reappointed to rename the rest of the Sioux. Eastman suggested that Indians who had not yet received allotments should also be renamed to avoid any possible future difficulties. Jones agreed and notified Eastman in July of his reappointment for the following year. Eastman continued to receive yearly appointments for six more years. On August 3, 1903, he sent to Washington a finished copy of the revised names of the Sissetons.[13]

Almost from the very beginning of his work, Eastman worried about how his traveling expenses would be met. He stated that it cost him between $30 and $40 to visit the Sisseton Agency and had received no compensation from Washington. "It will be impossible," Eastman wrote, "for me to continue paying travelling expenses out of my salary."[14] Garland suggested to Jones that Eastman get additional compensation or a raise in salary. Jones, after obtaining approval from Secretary Hitchcock, wrote to Eastman on November 5 that his salary was raised to $1,500 a year, but his previous claims for travel expenses were canceled.[15]

Eastman next turned attention toward renaming the Rosebud Sioux. He spent three months among them and said he met little resistance, but he wrote that it would take him several months to finish the work because of the larger tribe. Eastman further informed the commissioner that he had moved his family to Amherst, Massachusetts, for the winter.[16]

Jones, angry and puzzled over why he had moved, wrote to Eastman a piercing letter. "I am at a loss to understand," the commissioner declared, "what particular phase of the work requires your presence in Amherst and why you should have gone there without authority, with the expectation of remaining throughout the winter." He reminded Eastman that he was subject to the rules, regulations, and orders of the Interior Department and was expected to devote his "entire time and attention" to his duties, which, in Jones's view, "can better be performed upon the Indian reservations than elsewhere." Because Eastman was becoming a popular writer and lecturer, Jones advised him that he was not to make any public lectures or engage in other personal business while drawing his salary as a government employee. In his concluding remarks, Jones demanded that Eastman immediately submit a full report detailing the rationale for his change of residence, warning Eastman that if his reasons were unacceptable, he would not receive any monies due him "after the date of your departure from the Indian country."[17]

Eastman apologized for his inadvertence in not asking for specific authority to relocate. In explaining his reasons for moving, Eastman respectfully reminded Jones that according to his instructions he had "the privilege of selecting his own residence or headquarters" as well as permission to do his work "at home, or so much of it as could conveniently be done there." He said that he had rented a little cottage for the summer at White Bear, but as the winter months approached, he had to make new arrangements. He had looked for new accommodations but had been unable to find "a suitable house within our means." After hearing of his dilemma, Eastman's friends told him of an unexpected opportunity to purchase a home in Amherst on very favorable terms. He further stated that his wife desired to return to the East for personal reasons, upon which he did not elaborate.[18]

Eastman explained that his fieldwork at Rosebud was finished, and the completion of the revisions of over 5,000 names could be done as easily in Amherst as anywhere else. He stated that he did not expect the government to pay for his move to Amherst nor for his return to the Sioux reservations. Finally, Eastman wrote that he would present lectures on his own time and make sure that his nongovernment activities would not encroach upon his duties as renaming clerk. "I shall endeavor to comply," concluded Eastman, "with all the requirements of my position, and to satisfy your office as to the amount and quality of my work under my present appointment."[19]

Garland also wrote to Jones in support of Eastman, explaining that Eastman could do the final work equally as well in Amherst as elsewhere. Besides, opined Garland, by being in Amherst Eastman would not only be closer to New York where Garland resided, but also nearer to Jones in Washington. Garland lauded Eastman's qualities in performing his tasks, believed him to be the best man around to do such work, and even suggested that after Eastman completed renaming the Sioux, he could begin the revision of names for the Assiniboins, Crows, Northern Cheyennes, and possibly the Gros Ventres and Blackfeet. If Jones thought it wise, Garland proposed that Jones might make special arrangements with Eastman concerning his salary, although Garland said it would be extremely difficult and probably best not to do such a thing. He felt that Eastman would not let his lecturing and private business interests interfere with his government duties because he was not the type of person to abuse privileges or neglect responsibilities. "Let us cooperate," suggested Garland, "in every reasonable way with him."[20]

Jones, persuaded by these letters of explanation, changed his mind and wrote to Garland that he was personally "willing to have the Doctor continue his work in the East." He feared, however, that Secretary Hitchcock might cause problems because Hitchcock "does not think well of the work that is now being conducted by him" nor "does he feel very friendly toward Doctor Eastman personally for some reason or other." Since the secretary did not know that Eastman moved, Jones advised Garland to inform Eastman "unofficially" not to write any more letters regarding this matter.[21]

Eastman acquiesced once contacted by Garland and also said he would deduct from his salary claims "all time spent in lecture trips or any outside work."[22] No opposition ever came from Hitchcock. Reasons for his supposed disdain for Eastman remain unknown. Perhaps he disliked Eastman because of previous controversies, although no evidence of this has been found. As for the Eastmans, they lived in Amherst until 1919.[23]

Eastman continued to work on the Rosebud names, and by the first week of February he had completed revising the names of the first of the seven Rosebud districts.[24] His work was interrupted, however, by a severe illness when he became bedridden for two weeks, suffering from erysipelas, a skin infection, and also an abscess in his ear. It took him a month to recover, and by the end of April he was back to work.[25] On May 27, he completed the first copy of all the Rosebud districts. Additional copies were made and sent to Washington and the agency.[26]

Eastman visited other reservations and by 1906 had renamed the Sioux at Santee, Yankton, Standing Rock, and Devil's Lake. He worked for three more years until he had bestowed names on the entire Sioux nation.[27] Indians dubbed him the Name Giver, and in describing the manner in which he selected names, he wrote:

> It was my duty to group the various members of one family under a permanent name, selected for its euphony and appropriateness from among the various cognomens in use among them, of course suppressing mistranslations and grotesque or coarse nicknames calculated to embarrass the educated Indian. My instructions were that

the original native name was to be given the preference, if it were short enough and easily pronounced by Americans. If not, a translation or abbreviation might be arbitrarily given, but such as were already well established might be retained if the owner so desired.[28]

Many male Indians bore the names of animals, while female names often reflected some aspect of their appearance. Eastman strove to retain their original meanings as much as possible. He appreciated the poetry and the tradition embodied in many Indian names. A name such as Matoska (White Bear) was preserved. The complimentary women's name of Tateyohnakewastewin, which was difficult to pronounce and meant She-Who-Has-A-Beautiful-House, was changed by him to Goodhouse. Names such as High Eagle, Bobtailed Coyote, and Rotten Pumpkin became Higheagle, Robert T. Wolf, and Robert Pumpian.[29] Eastman observed that in one family he found Indian children named George Washington, Daniel Webster, and Patrick Henry.[30] In cases such as these he most probably selected the surname of the father or eldest male.

Although he encountered little resistance from the majority of Indians he renamed, there were some skeptics, whom he attempted to convince of the merits of the project and the need to adopt, in some instances, better names. "In a few cases," wrote Eastman, "when a man would not consent to give up an apparently undesirable name, I have done the best I could with it."[31] Yet, Eastman expressed sympathy for these doubting and suspicious Indians, who viewed the renaming project as still another scheme by Whites to take more land, but by having one of their own explain the program to them, many problems were averted. On more than one occasion, Indians said to Eastman that "because my brother tells me it is good to take a new name, I take it."[32]

Eastman originally accepted the renaming assignment after having another unpleasant experience as a government physician. Garland's initial selection of him to experiment with revising a few pages of the Crow Creek rolls resulted in the most successful revision of names project ever attempted for an entire Indian nation. Eastman anxiously wanted the position on a permanent basis and through Garland's influence with President Roosevelt and others, he received the appointment. It is somewhat ironic that he was supported by Roosevelt, who had earlier in his career staunchly opposed Eastman during the Pine Ridge controversy. Perhaps the President carried no grudges or more likely had complete faith in Garland's expertise on the subject and his choice of Eastman.

Eastman labored on the project from 1903 to 1909, revising names for approximately 25,000 Sioux. As an Indian, he moved more freely among his race than could a white man trying to do the same work. Although the renaming project can be viewed as part of the overall assimilation programs of the late nineteenth and early twentieth centuries, it was more than just a blatant assault on Indian naming practices, especially in regards to Eastman's participation. Of course, some beautiful Indian names were drastically altered, but, in most cases, Eastman tried to preserve the initial meaning of the original names. Those Indians possessing absurd or derogatory names benefited as well by receiving proper names.

Reported results of the renaming project showed a marked reduction in property title conflicts.[33] Unfortunately, government interest in the renaming of Indians waned, and Garland's pleas for extending the program to other tribes fell on deaf ears. Whether or not Eastman would have been reappointed to revise their names or, for that matter, if he truly wanted to continue the project remains uncertain. By 1909 he was a well-known author and was in demand as a lecturer, and for the next several years these became his primary occupations.

NOTES

1. See Daniel F. Littlefield, Jr., and Lonnie E. Underhill, "Renaming the American Indian: 1890–1913," *American Studies* 12 (Fall, 1971): 33–45. In this article the authors discuss how the renaming attacked Indian identity and culture.
2. Ibid., pp. 37–38; See Lonnie E. Underhill and Daniel F. Littlefield, Jr., eds., *Hamlin Garland's Observations on the American Indian, 1895–1905* (Tucson: University of Arizona Press, 1976).
3. Littlefield and Underhill, "Renaming the American Indian," pp. 39, 41.
4. Ibid., p. 41; Hamlin Garland, *Companions on the Trail* (New York: Macmillan, 1931), p. 139.
5. Eastman to Hamlin Garland, Dec. 3, 1902, Hamlin Garland Collec-

tion, University of Southern California Library, Los Angeles, California. Hereafter cited HGC. Jones to Garland, Jan. 2, 1903, HGC.

6. Jones to Secretary of the Interior, Feb. 18, 1903, ibid.

7. Donald Pizer, ed., *Hamlin Garland's Diaries* (San Marino: Huntington Library, 1968), pp. 204–5.

8. Jones to Eastman, Mar. 5, 1903, HGC; Eastman to Garland, Mar. 7, 1903, ibid.; Garland to Jones, July 20, 1903, BIA, RG 75, LR, NA.

9. Eastman to Garland, Mar. 7, 1903, BIA, RG 75, LR, NA; Eastman to Garland, Apr. 9, 1903, ibid.; Eastman to CIA, Apr. 16, 1903, ibid.

10. Eastman to Garland, Apr. 9, 1903, ibid.; Eastman to CIA, Apr. 16, 1903, ibid.; Eastman to CIA, July 11, 1903, ibid.

11. Eastman to Jones, May 12, 1903, ibid.; Eastman to Garland, Nov. 12, 1903, HGC.

12. Eastman to Jones, June 12, 1903, BIA, RG 75, LR, NA; Jones to Eastman, July 21, 1903, BIA, RG 75, LS, NA.

13. Eastman to Jones, June 12, 1903, BIA, RG 75, LR, NA; Eastman to CIA, Aug. 3, 1903, ibid.

14. Eastman to CIA, Apr. 16, 1903, ibid.; Eastman to CIA, July 11, 1903, ibid.

15. Garland to Jones, July 20, 1903, ibid.; Jones to Secretary of the Interior, Oct. 23, 1903, BIA, RG 75, LS, NA; Jones to Eastman, Nov. 5, 1903, HGC.

16. Eastman to CIA, July 11, 1903, BIA, RG 75, LR, NA; Eastman to CIA, Nov. 7, 1903, ibid.

17. Jones to Eastman, Nov. 25, 1903, ibid.

18. Eastman to CIA, Nov. 20, 1903, HGC.

19. Ibid.

20. Garland to Jones, Dec. 7, 1903, Letter-Book 1901–4, HGC.

21. Eastman to Garland, Dec. 22, 1903, HGC.

22. Eastman to Garland, Dec. 31, 1903, ibid.

23. Elaine G. Eastman to Charles R. Green, Feb. 3, 1927, Elaine Goodale Eastman Folder, Jones Public Library, Amherst, Massachusetts.

24. Eastman to Garland, Feb. 1, 1904, BIA, RG 75, LR, NA; Eastman to CIA, Feb. 2, 1904, ibid.

25. Eastman to Garland, Apr. 1, 1904, ibid.; Eastman to Garland, Apr. 7, 1904, ibid.; Eastman to CIA, Apr. 26, 1904, ibid.

26. Eastman to CIA, May 27, 1904, ibid.; Eastman to Garland, June 6, 1904, HGC; Eastman to CIA, July 21, 1904, ibid.

27. Eastman to CIA, July 21, 1904, BIA, RG 75, LR, NA; Eastman to CIA, Apr. 26, 1905, ibid.; Eastman to CIA, July 6, 1905, ibid.; East-

man to CIA, Oct. 10, 1905, ibid.; Eastman to Francis E. Leupp, Aug. 30, 1906, ibid.; Edgar B. Meritt to Eastman, Aug. 11, 1909, BIA, RG 75, CF, NA.

28. Eastman, *The Indian Today*, p. 109.
29. Forrest Crissey, "Renaming the Indians," *World Today* 10 (Jan., 1906): 87; *Guymon Herald* (Oklahoma), July 19, 1906.
30. Eastman, *The Indian Today*, pp. 109–10.
31. Eastman to CIA, July 21, 1904, BIA, RG 75, LR, NA.
32. Crissey, "Renaming the Indians," p. 85; Eastman, *From the Deep Woods*, p. 183.
33. *Guymon Herald*, July 19, 1906.

CHAPTER 9

WRITING AND LECTURING

CHARLES EASTMAN MADE his greatest impact on society as a writer and lecturer. He originally intended to preserve a written record of his Indian childhood for his children. After moving his burgeoning family to St. Paul in 1893, Eastman began to record his thoughts and recollections. Elaine read what her husband had written and persuaded him to send these earliest sketches of his childhood to *St. Nicholas: An Illustrated Magazine for Young Folks* for possible publication. They were immediately accepted and were serialized in six installments. These articles would later be incorporated in his first book, *Indian Boyhood*, published in 1902.[1] The six serialized articles were his first publications. In years to come he wrote many additional articles and eleven books (two of which were combinations of others and were published as special school editions).

Although all of these books except *Wigwam Evenings: Sioux Folk Tales Retold* (1909) and *Smoky Day's Wigwam Evenings: Indian Stories Retold* (1910) bore only Eastman's name, he acknowledged his wife's collaboration. Indeed, she served as his principal editor. "Dr. Eastman's books left his hand," Elaine later wrote, "as a rough draft in pencil, on scratch paper." From these, she would then type copies, "revising, omitting, and re-writing as necessary,"[2] the same procedure undoubtedly employed in getting his articles ready for publication.

The subjects of Eastman's books and articles can be grouped into three general categories: autobiography; information concerning Indian life, customs, and religion; and information dealing with Indian and White relations. Two of his books which are specifically autobiographical in nature are integral to an understanding of the mental, spiritual, and attitudinal stages of development of Eastman's life. Although Eastman apparently planned to write a third book, concerned exclusively with the last years of his life, the book was never published.

His first book, *Indian Boyhood* (1902), dealt with his reminiscences of his first fifteen years of life as an Indian in the wilds of Minnesota and Canada. In *From the Deep Woods to Civilization: Chapters in the Autobiography of an Indian*, published in 1916, he continued the story of his life, emphasizing his schooling and subsequent work in white civilization up to about 1915. Both books contain material which Eastman had previously published in article form.

Written mainly for children, *Indian Boyhood* depicts the idyllic existence Indians once enjoyed. Eastman did not ignore the harsh realities associated with the type of life he led as a youth. He referred briefly to famine, disease, confrontations with other Indian bands, and intermittent conflicts with the white man, but he devoted greater attention to the more gratifying aspects of his childhood, idealizing and romanticizing his past and associating it with an atmosphere of childlike simplicity. In an informal and at times intimate tone, Eastman conveyed an unconscious longing to return to a world he viewed as naturally good. Even in the final chapter, in recounting what must have been a personal and emotional trauma at his father's request that he live in the white world, Eastman never revealed his true feelings about his displacement. Rather, he assumed an optimistic tone as he, his father, and his grandmother began their journey into white society.

The youthful optimism and idealism which Eastman possessed when he began his passage into an alien culture soon diminished with the sobering experiences of adulthood. As Eastman related in his second autobiographical work, *From the Deep Woods to Civilization*, his varied experiences in white society gave him a more realistic perspective of that society. Eastman presented a more candid and critical opinion of the white world, openly attacking the evils of white society and lamenting the sorrows Indians encountered as a result of cultural contact, yet never completely turning his back on the positive aspects of the dominant society but only exposing the wrongs which certain Whites perpetrated on Indians.

Certain omissions in *From the Deep Woods to Civilization* are noteworthy. Eastman's presentation of the facts regarding the Pine Ridge controversy is entirely one-sided. Although he did not present false information, he was guilty of neglecting all data which would cast doubt on his arguments.[3] He also did not discuss the turmoil-filled years he spent as government physician at Crow Creek, possibly because of inherent fears that his readers would question his ability to get along with Indian agents and other government officials. He should have detailed thoroughly both incidents, letting his readers make the ultimate decision as to who was to blame.

Eastman's writings regarding Indian life, customs, and religion included many stories containing factual information about Indian culture, some of which were written especially for children. He heard many of these stories as a youth sitting around a campfire with other boys and listening to elders relate Indian tradition and history. In *Old Indian Days* (1907), Eastman presented fifteen stories—seven about Indian warriors and eight about Indian women. While all contained information about Indian customs, some stories were written far better than others. For example, one of the best stories on warriors, "The Love of Antelope," concerned an Indian named Antelope and his love for Taluta. Besides presenting information on courtship, marriage, and the role of women in Sioux society, Eastman discussed the Indians' practice of counting coup—the way in which warriors received honor and eagle feathers for extraordinary feats, usually in battle. In turn, one of the most poorly written stories on warriors was "The Madness of Bald Eagle," which contained information on the practice of accepting dares and explained the custom of redeeming peer approval through acts of bravery, but was sketchy and lacked character development.[4]

His stories on women stressed their importance and function in Indian society. Two of his best were "Winoa, The Woman-Child" and "Winoa, The Child-Woman," in which Eastman excellently portrayed the life and training of an Indian girl, from birth taught to accept her role in society: "to serve and to do for others." In "The War Maiden" Eastman wrote about the rather unusual practice of a woman going to war. She was not only accepted by the Indian men, but she also proved herself worthy in battle.[5]

Other books containing accounts on Indian life included some written for children, in which Eastman explained the Indians' concept of creation and their close relationship to nature and animals. In several of these stories animals represented Indians as leading characters, and the tales ended with a moral similar to the Aesop Fables. For instance, in one story concerning a drake outwitting a falcon, the drake believed that the falcon was dead, and later, while he was boasting of this feat to others, he was overtaken and killed by the falcon. The moral was "Do not exult too soon; nor is it wise to tell of your brave deeds within the hearing of your enemy."[6]

Another story concerned a turtle who had been captured by his enemies. In contemplating a manner of death, they suggested burning him, but the turtle replied that he would scatter the burning coals and kill them all. Next, they considered boiling him, to which the turtle said that he would dance in the boiling kettle and the steam would blind them forever. Finally, the turtle's captors suggested drowning. To this form of death the turtle remained silent, and his enemies suspected that this was the best way of disposing of him. After being thrown into the water, the turtle, of course, escaped. Eastman moralized that "patience and quick wit are better than speed."[7]

One of his best books containing stories about Indian life was *Red Hunters and the Animal People* (1904), in which Eastman stressed the honor and closeness that Indians felt for animals. The twelve excellent pieces in this book ranged from how hunters learned from animals in hope of acquiring their resourceful ways, to the Indians' view that animals were placed on the earth as a means of a life line for them.[8]

Eastman wrote many straightforward accounts about Indian customs and religion. To Eastman Indians lived the "freest life in the world," and their handicrafts, their rudimentary technology, and their medicine were indeed significant because many were adopted by or influenced white civilization. He described how Indians made bows and arrows, canoes, pottery, and pipes; discussed at length the work Indians did with leather and hides; and detailed information on such political and social subjects as Indian government, humor, and burial. From Indians, white men learned new agricultural methods for growing vegetables and fruits, and even borrowed the national emblem of the United States, the American eagle, from them.[9]

Eastman also stressed the healthier aspects of Indian living over white living. He encouraged white parents to involve their children in more outdoor activities because fresh air and nature were God's gifts and should be utilized. In one book, written specifically for the Boys Scouts and the Campfire Girls, he used the Indian as the prototype of these organizations and presented useful information that these youths could employ in their activities, such as outdoor survival techniques. In addition, he suggested special and honored Indian names and secret signals that they could adopt.[10]

Many of these books and articles brought out his belief in the compatibility between certain aspects of Indian worship and Christianity. Eastman syncretized his beliefs to a certain extent, yet spiritually he maintained an affinity with his past. His Indian religion seemed to be the source from which he maintained his identity, an aspect which he covered more thoroughly in *The Soul of the Indian*, published in 1911. The purpose, as he stated in the Foreword of the book, was "to paint the religious life of the typical American Indian as it was before he knew the white man." He presented his recollections knowing that "the religion of the Indian is the last thing about him that the man of another race will ever understand." His purpose for writing the book appears to have been his need to reaffirm his identity with the past rather than to explain that past to white society. Eastman let his readers know that he was proud to be an Indian and was proud of his ancestral religious beliefs, which seemed to give meaning and perspective to his life.

In the Foreword of this book, Eastman explained the sources of his religious knowledge. "It is as true as I can make it to my childhood teaching and ancestral ideals, but from the human, not the ethnological standpoint." He used the term the Great Mystery (Wakan Tanka) to explain the Indians' concept of God and His creation. They worshipped this all-powerful force in silence and solitude. The responsibility for religious instruction was given to the woman, who from the time the baby was conceived practiced a sort of spiritual training, praying and meditating "to instill into the receptive soul of the unborn child the love of the 'Great Mystery' and a sense of brotherhood with all creation." After birth, she began pointing out and explaining nature to her newborn baby.[11] Eastman recalled his own surrogate mother, Uncheedah, through whose guidance he was taught to pray in silence, was told the history of his people, and was instructed in the art of storytelling.

An integral part of the ritual of passage in which a boy became a man was the first offering, which required that the Indian child sacrifice the thing most dear to him to the Great Mystery. Such a sacrifice instilled in the child an appreciation of others' needs. Eastman decided to sacrifice his beloved dog because it was the thing he most cherished.[12] When detailing the procedure, he failed to mention to his readers, however, that he probably ate some of the dog's remains, most likely feeling that his white audience might be offended by this part of the ceremony.[13]

In sum, Eastman described the Indians' concept of religion as recognizing "a power behind every natural force. He saw God, not only in the sky, but in every creation. All Nature sang his praises— birds, waterfalls, tree tops—everything whispered the name of the mysterious God."[14] To Indians the supernatural was commonplace. "The virgin birth would appear," wrote Eastman, "scarcely more miraculous than is the birth of every child that comes into the world, or the miracle of the loaves and fishes excite more wonder than the harvest that springs from a single ear of corn."[15]

He commented on white missionaries and their frequent attacks on Indian beliefs. He thought that their methods were unjust, characterizing them as "good men imbued with the narrowness of their age" and chastising their practice of classifying Indians as pagans because they followed a different religion. To substantiate this view, Eastman told about a group of Indians listening to a missionary tell about the creation and the fall of Adam and Eve. After he finished his account, the Indians, in turn, told him about their belief of how maize originated. When the missionary became outraged and discounted their story as false, the Indians calmly replied that they believed his stories, so why did he not believe theirs?[16]

The most significant topics to Eastman were perhaps the ones concerning Indian and White relations, especially during the reservation period. In Eastman's opinion the coming of the white men destroyed forever the Indian's way of life. Labeling Indian and White contact as the Transition Period—a movement from the natural life to an artificial existence—Eastman declared that the two greatest white civilizers were whiskey and gunpowder. Contact with Whites forced Indian women into prostitution, altered or perverted Indian customs and manners, and caused divisions within tribes. He speculated that the mass killing of buffalo was a conspiracy by Whites to conquer the Plains Indians because it was less expensive to attack them economically than militarily.[17]

Warfare between Indians and Whites was, according to Eastman, the usual and gravest result of contact. Originally, war among Indians was regarded as part of their life. "It was held to develop," wrote Eastman, "the quality of manliness, and its motive was chivalric or patriotic." He suggested incorrectly that these tribal wars were little more than tournaments and compared them to the white man's football games. "It was common, in early times, for a battle or skirmish to last all day, with great display of daring and horsemanship, but with scarcely more killed and wounded than may be carried from the field during a university game of football."[18]

Eastman described how Indians revered a brave enemy in mourning by scalping him and holding a ceremony to honor his departed spirit.[19] Warfare with Whites, however, was different. Eastman believed that all major Indian wars were caused by land-hungry Whites and broken treaties.[20] He declared that "wanton cruelties and the more barbarous customs of war were greatly intensified with the coming of white men, who brought with them fiery liquor and deadly weapons, aroused the Indian's worst passions, provoking in him revenge and cupidity, and even offered bounties for the scalps of innocent men, women, and children."[21]

Eastman had the opportunity to interview several famous Indian leaders and to write accounts of their lives and battles. Such prestigious individuals as Sitting Bull, Red Cloud, and Chief Joseph were included in a book entitled *Indian Heroes and Great Chieftains* (1918), which also contained excellent photographs of many famous Indians. His vivid portrayal of these Indians and other leading figures, as well as battles between Indians and Whites, appears, in the main, accurate in detail and sympathetic in tone.[22]

He used the Battle of the Little Big Horn as an example of the consequence of broken treaties. In no uncertain terms he condemned historians and military personnel for inflating the number of Indians engaged in this encounter and for underestimating the Indians' military genius. In summing up the battle Eastman wrote, "The simple truth is that Custer met the combined forces of the hostiles, which were greater than his own, and that he had not so much underestimated their numbers as their ability." He stated, however, that this victory was short-lived, and the result of this war and most Indian wars with Whites was imprisonment on reservations.[23]

Eastman sharply criticized the Indian bureau's responsibility for the wretched conditions on reservations, basing his observations on his own experiences as a government physician on reservations and as a visitor to several reserves. Commenting that many of the reservations were located in dry places and were unfit for agriculture except with proper irrigation, he complained that Indians were forced to eat unhealthful food. "In a word," wrote Eastman, "he lived a squalid life, unclean and apathetic physically, mentally, and spiritually."[24]

Eastman held the Indian bureau and its system responsible, because though the bureau was set up to serve Indians, instead it became an autocracy over them. Furthermore, he believed that many Indian agents were "nothing more than a ward politician of the commonest stamp, whose main purpose is to get all that is coming to him. His salary is small, but there are endless opportunities for graft." Eastman recognized that there were good men in the Indian bureau, but their numbers were few and they were not in positions of authority to implement their views.[25]

To rectify matters, he called for the abolition of the Indian bureau, whose political interests appalled him. He blamed it "for all the ills of our Indian civilization."[26] He thought that the bureau had outlived its usefulness and was too paternalistic toward Indians, but he was not, however, in favor of complete termination of government services and aid. Indeed, he wanted the machinery updated possibly in the form of a commission that would serve as a guardian over Indians. He specifically stressed that at least half the members on the commission should be Indians, that it should be as free as possible from political pressures, and that it should have direct authority to handle Indian affairs without going through other departments for approval.[27] Such a commission or program was never established.

Eastman also expressed his views about Indian policies and humanitarian organizations. He generally condemned Republican administration during the early 1860s for its extreme corruption in the handling of Indian affairs; but, in turn, he applauded President Abraham Lincoln's courage in pardoning hundreds of Indians held responsible for the 1862 Sioux Uprising in Minnesota. In addition, he praised Indian reform measures enacted under President Ulysses S. Grant, especially the upgrading of agency officials in order to curb graft and corruption on reservations. He expressed anger at the abandonment of the policy as partisan politics again dictated the selection of Indian agents.[28]

Eastman, along with many other reform-minded individuals and organizations, supported the Dawes Severalty Act of 1887, which provided for allotments in severalty and the breakup of reservations. He called it the Emancipation Act of the Indian and praised such organizations as the Board of Indian Commissioners, the Indian Rights Association, and the Lake Mohonk Conference of Friends of the Indian, not only for their support of this act, but also for their work on behalf of Indians.[29] Eastman supported the Dawes Act primarily because it granted citizenship to Indians who accepted allotments. By becoming citizens Indians could obtain rights of the dominant Americans, particularly the suffrage, which he hoped would give Indians a voice in decisions affecting their lives. His later publications, however, contain little praise and minimal mention of the Dawes Act but do contain criticism of the Burke Act of 1906, which dealt with Indian allotment fees, patents, and citizenship. Most reformers condemned the Burke Act, especially the provisions making it more difficult for Indians to acquire citizenship. Eastman chastised the framers of the act as interested only in graft and believed that such a law would confuse the status of Indians.[30] Eastman can certainly be criticized for supporting the Dawes Act, especially by citing the devastating results of the act. The Dawes Act and related pieces of legislation operated for nearly fifty years, during which time Indians lost over 85 million acres. Yet, in his defense, most well-meaning reformers supported the Dawes Act, sincerely believing that it would bring the two races closer together. Perhaps Eastman was too naive and put too much faith in the Dawes Act as a means to achieve harmony between Indians and Whites.

Many of his later publications, written between 1910 and 1919, dealt with the contributions and needs of Indians. He wrote that Indians were no longer regarded as "bloody savages," and white civilization was finally recognizing their worth. He cited, for example, their native arts and crafts as much in demand, and he ridiculed the use of machine-made products in the place of handmade items. Furthermore, non-Indian painters, sculptors, authors, and other patrons were honoring and praising Indians for their achievements.[31]

Even though Indians were at last being recognized, they still suffered from unhealthful living conditions and inadequate educational facilities. Eastman lamented that the annual death rate of Indians was alarming in comparison to the death rate of Whites, and he stated that tuberculosis and trachoma, an eye disease, were among the major diseases that attacked Indians. He believed that Indians were receiving better care and treatment than in previous years, but that there was still a need for more services. In addition, educational facilities for Indians were often overcrowded, unsanitary, and breeding grounds for disease. He called for the support of programs that directed more appropriations to improve Indian health and to teach Indians about proper hygiene.[32]

Eastman continually stressed the need for Indians to obtain a proper education, believing that this was the best way for Indians to contribute to their people and to white society. He offered himself as an example of what an Indian could attain. Though he recognized that many schools were inadequate, he stated, "I would give up anything rather than the schools, unmoral [sic] as many of them are."[33] He suggested that more qualified teachers and improved facilities were needed to eradicate the deficiencies, praising the Hampton Institute in Virginia and Carlisle School in Pennsylvania, two institutions attended by Indians, because they showed that Indians could be properly educated. He also remarked that more and more educated Indians were being accepted by their fellow tribesmen upon returning to the reservation.[34]

The granting of citizenship to Indians continued to be, in Eastman's opinion, their most pressing need, particularly following World War I. He regarded Indian status in the United States as extremely confusing. "I do not believe," he wrote, "there is a learned judge in these United States who can tell an Indian's exact status without a great deal of study, and even then he may be in doubt."[35] Eastman used Indian involvement in World War I and the goals of peace after the war as reasons for granting citizenship. Emphasizing the way they were actively involved in the defense of liberty and their need to be adequately compensated, he used President Wood-row Wilson's goals of peace for European countries as a premise to what should be applied at home for Indians. He wrote, "We ask nothing unreasonable—only the freedom and privileges for which your boy and mine have fought."[36] Indians had to wait for several more years, however, before receiving such a privilege.

Lucrative lecture engagements resulted from his writings. Address-ing audiences was nothing new to Eastman, who during his college days had given speeches before groups and later spoke at the Lake Mohonk Conference of Friends of the Indian.[37] After publication of *Indian Boyhood* he accepted a lecture invitation from the Twentieth Century Club in Brooklyn, New York, for which he received $100. While there, he met Major James B. Pond, a lyceum manager, who asked Eastman if he wanted "to go on the lecture platform under his management." Eastman found the arrangements satisfactory and accepted his offer. The two men developed a good rapport and worked together until Pond's untimely death. Because of the initial success of this first venture and a growing demand for more personal appearances. Eastman continued to give lectures.[38] His wife took over the duties of handling all of his correspondence and publicity.[39]

Eastman wrote that he could lecture on any general or specific Indian topic. The subjects of his talks ranged from "The School of Savagery," "The Real Indian," "The Story of the Little Big Horn," to aesthetic topics such as, "Indian Wit, Music, Poetry and Elo-quence."[40] Frequently Eastman would be attired in full Sioux re-galia while presenting these lectures. He must have cast a striking pose, wearing such items as an eagle-feathered war bonnet, a beau-tifully beaded tan costume made from animal skins, and carrying a tomahawk/peacepipe.[41] His stage presence and commanding voice must have been overwhelming.

Response to Eastman's writings and lectures was phenomenal. Almost every review of his books contained both laudatory remarks of their contents and high praise of the author. For example, *The Soul of the Indian* and *The Indian Today* (1915), two of his most profound books, received good reviews. In the case of the former, one reviewer wrote, "Not being influenced by the prejudices and legends which prevail in the mind of most white men concerning the Indian, Dr. Eastman is able to give us a clear idea of what the red man really thinks and feels."[42] Regarding the latter book, several reviewers believed that it was well written, forceful, and most enlightening.[43]

In evaluating Eastman's expertise as a writer, several observations are in order. One of the major criticisms of his works is his neglect, at times, to make it clear to the reader whether he is discussing particular traits of all Indians or of just the Sioux, though most of what he wrote applied to his kinsmen. Because he seemed to draw little distinction between being an Indian and being a Sioux, his works tend to emphasize the similarities rather than the marked differences among Indian cultures. He helped to influence the contemporary stereotyped image of Native Americans. Today, non-Indians the world over have painted a mental picture of what an Indian is: a Plains Indian—more specifically, a Sioux.

In general, Eastman's depiction of Indian life and subsequent white contact is reinforced by several of his contemporaries, two of whom were Zitkala-Sa (Gertrude Bonnin), a writer, poet, and lecturer, and Luther Standing Bear, a noted Sioux author. In comparing Eastman to these writers, interesting and important distinctions emerge. Gertrude Bonnin, born in 1876 at Yankton Reservation, South Dakota, learned quickly from her mother to distrust and resent the white man. She sought a formal education despite her mother's wishes and later attended Earlham College in Indiana. A few years later, she studied at the Boston Conservatory of Music, when she began to write. Some of her articles were published in the *Atlantic Monthly* and in *Harper's Monthly*. Her most memorable book was *American Indian Stories*, published in 1921, in which she depicted her childhood, her initial rejection and eventual acceptance of Christianity, and her changing attitudes toward the white man. Like Eastman, her autobiography is romantic in scope and viewed the Indian way of life as a state of grace eventually corrupted by the coming of the white man. Bonnin's account, however, was less detailed on Sioux customs and more resentful toward the white man.[44]

Luther Standing Bear, born in the 1860s, unlike Eastman, who was a Santee, or Eastern, Sioux, was a Teton, or Western, Sioux. Standing Bear attended Carlisle Indian School, where he acquired a trade, tinsmithing, which proved to be impractical on the reservation, and as a result, he undertook various jobs ranging from an assistant teacher at a reservation school to an agency clerk and storekeeper. He eventually became involved in show business. Later in his life he wrote four books, a noteworthy accomplishment for someone with only a rudimentary education as Carlisle provided. Two of his best works are *My People the Sioux* (1928) and *Land of the Spotted Eagle* (1933).

Standing Bear was not as prolific a writer as Eastman, but they wrote about many of the same topics. Although they expressed similar points of view regarding Indian and White relations, reservation life, and the role of women, Standing Bear tended to give a more elaborate account of certain events than did Eastman. Their descriptions of the Sun Dance, for example, reflect their different viewpoints. According to Eastman, the Sun Dance occurred when a Sioux warrior wanted to fulfill a vow made to the Sun for prolonging his life. Standing Bear, on the other hand, remembered the Sun Dance as a sacrificial rite which was fulfilled every year. Both writers had similar accounts of the elaborate selection and importance of the pole to the ceremony and also agreed on the symbolic importance of the figures which hung from the pole, but differed in their accounts of the final stage of the Sun Dance. Standing Bear recalled, in detail, the brutal aspects of the ceremony, from the piercing of the participant's breast, through which a wooden pin was inserted, to the ensuing results. Eastman, however, did not emphasize these points. The cut made, according to Eastman, was just deep enough to draw blood. The rawhide was then attached to the shoulders of the participant rather than the breast. In fairness to both writers, there are two rites of sacrifice of the Sun Dance—one which pierces the breast, and the other which pierces the shoulders. The lodge ceremony (breast) is the more spectacular. Unlike his conscious omission in *Indian Boyhood* regarding his consumption of his favorite dog, Eastman did not avoid the gruesome aspects of the Sun Dance to appease the sensibilities of the white audience. Rather, he paralleled the increase of cruelty in the event to the Indians' contact with white men. He declared, "The Sun Dance of the Plains Indians, the most important of their public ceremonies, was abused and perverted until it became a horrible exhibition of barbarism."[45] The amount of brutality involved in the Sun Dance and aspects of the ceremony still remain matters of controversy.

The diversity in the writing styles and content of Standing Bear and Eastman can be attributed to many factors. Because they were from different bands, they probably had different versions of particular events. Standing Bear's tendency to write more detailed accounts than Eastman could be explained by having people like E. A. Brininstool, author of several books on western history, and Dr. Melvin R. Gilmore, an ethnologist, serve as collaborators on his books. Eastman, on the other hand, relied primarily on his own expertise and his wife's knowledge and editorial skills.

Eastman's books were so popular that some were translated into different languages. Even today, Eastman's works continue to be in vogue. Recently published anthologies contain selections from his works, and some of his books are still being reprinted. The *Wassaja/ The Indian Historian*, a national Indian magazine, frequently cites and praises Eastman's works. As a source for Indian topics, Eastman's writings have been employed by several historians of the past and of the present.[46] Indeed, Eastman's knowledge of historical data regarding Indian and White relations are quite accurate. For example, his views on the Custer debacle and on the Wounded Knee tragedy parallel most of the major accounts of these confrontations. In addition, the information he presented on Indian customs, the different ways in which Indians and Whites conducted warfare, the lack of respect most missionaries had toward Indian beliefs, and the deplorable conditions on reservations are valid and, in most cases, accurate observations. His interpretation that the mass slaughter of the buffalo—the Indians' lifeline—was a plot conceived by Whites to defeat economically the Plains Indians because it would be less costly to engage in economic warfare than major military operations is a view still held by many contemporary writers.

His statements on the corruption, graft, and inefficiency of the Bureau of Indian Affairs primarily surfaced after 1910. By that date, Eastman had had two bitter confrontations with white agents while serving under them as a government physician. Ironically, by criticizing the bureau, Eastman was demeaning the vehicle through which he pursued his original goal as a physician to his people. Failing in this role, he engaged in other pursuits, specifically writing and lecturing. Although certainly his criticism of the bureau was tempered by the unpleasant episodes he had encountered at Pine Ridge and at Crow Creek, he justifiably condemned the wretched conditions on reservations and called for desperately needed reforms.

Eastman received equal praise as a lecturer. The popularity of his books made him a sought after speaker in many cities throughout the United States and in England. People who heard his lectures found him to be a knowledgeable, dignified, and an attractive speaker.[47]

Through his writing and lecturing, Eastman hoped to influence Whites, to make them aware of the "Indian problem" from an Indian point of view, and to spur them to the cause of reform. On some occasions he used powerful language to make a point, and at other times, his audience had to read between the lines to get his message. One of his nephews, Oliver Eastman, a Flandreau Sioux, believed that his uncle's books were popular because of their truthfulness. However, he thought that Eastman was forced to choose his words carefully in order not to offend his white readers.[48] Although this may be true, he did, nevertheless, make some bold and valid statements regarding reform of Indian policy.

There is little doubt that Eastman believed Indians should adopt white ways; however, he did not favor total rejection of past customs and traditions. He supported many of the old customs but realized that Indians were doomed if they clung to the past and did not alter their ways. As a subjugated people, Indians had to acquire the more advanced aspects of white civilization to survive and then to compete in white society.

Eastman's writings are important to historians not only because he interviewed several famous Indians and recorded their views but also because he was writing about Indian history from his own perspective as an Indian—an uncommon perspective in the early twentieth century. Through his works he hoped to bring Indians and Whites closer together in an effort to break down the wall of prejudice which existed. That was his greatest contribution as author and lecturer. Indeed, commenting on the primary purpose of his lectures, which can also be applied to his writings as well, Eastman wrote:

> My chief object has been, not to entertain, but to present the American Indian in his true character before Americans. The barbarous and atrocious character commonly attributed to him has dated from the transition period, when the strong drink, powerful temptations, and

commercialism of the white man led to deep demoralization. Really
it was a campaign of education on the Indian and his true place in
American history.[49]

That his books are still widely read is testimony to his success.

NOTES

1. Eastman, *From the Deep Woods*, p. 139; Charles A. Eastman,
   "Recollections of the Wild Life," *St. Nicholas: An Illustrated Maga-*
   zine for Young Folks 21 (Dec., 1893–May, 1894): 129–31, 226–28,
   306–8, 437–40, 513–15, 607–11.
2. Eastman, *From the Deep Woods*, pp. 185–86; Elaine G. Eastman to
   Harold G. Rugg, Apr. 19, 1939, Charles A. Eastman Folder, Baker
   Library.
3. See Eastman, *From the Deep Woods*, pp. 116–35.
4. Charles A. Eastman, *Old Indian Days* (New York: McClure, 1907),
   pp. 3–67, 68–75.
5. Ibid., pp. 169–95, 260–75; see also Charles A. Eastman, "The War
   Maiden of the Sioux," *Ladies' Home Journal* 23 (Aug., 1906): 14;
   Charles A. Eastman, "The Song of the Birch Canoe," *The Craftsman*
   23 (Oct., 1912): 3–11.
6. Charles A. Eastman and Elaine Goodale Eastman, *Wigwam Eve-*
   nings: Sioux Folk Tales Retold (Boston: Little, Brown, 1909), pp.
   41–47.
7. Ibid., pp. 34–37.
8. See Charles A. Eastman, *Red Hunters and the Animal People* (New
   York: Harper & Brothers, 1904); Charles A. Eastman, "The Gray
   Chieftain," *Harpers Magazine* 108 (May, 1904): 882–87. See Marion
   W. Copeland, *Charles Alexander Eastman* (Caldwell: Caxton Printers, 1978) for a symbolic analysis of Eastman's works, especially his
   legends and folk tales. Her pamphlet is part of the Western Writers
   Series directed by Boise State University.
9. Eastman, *Indian Boyhood*, pp. 3, 192, 220–21, 229; Eastman, *The*
   Indian Today, p. 163; Charles A. Eastman, "Indian Handicrafts,"
   The Craftsman 8 (Aug., 1905): 658–62; Charles A. Eastman, "The
   American Eagle: An Indian Symbol," *American Indian Magazine* 7
   (Summer, 1919): 89–92.
10. See Charles A. Eastman, *Indian Scout Talks: A Guide for Boy Scouts*
   and Camp Fire Girls (Boston: Little, Brown, 1914); Charles A. East-

man, "The Language of Footprints," *St. Nicholas* 44 (Jan., 1917):
267–69; Charles A. Eastman, "What Can the Out-of-Doors Do for
Our Children?" *Education* 41 (1920–21): 599–605.

11. Eastman, *The Soul of the Indian*, pp. ix–x, xii, 4, 28–31; Eastman,
Indian Boyhood, p. 18; Charles A. Eastman, "Education without
Books," *The Craftsman* 21 (Jan., 1912): 373; see also Charles A.
Eastman, "The Sioux Mythology," *Popular Science Monthly* 46
(Nov., 1894): 88–91; Eastman, "Great Spirit," pp. 3–4.

12. See Eastman, *Indian Boyhood*, pp. 87–96; Charles A. Eastman,
"Hakadah's First Offering," *Current Literature* 34 (Jan., 1903):
29–32.

13. Ethel Nurge, ed., *The Modern Sioux: Social Systems and Reservation
Culture* (Lincoln: University of Nebraska Press, 1970), p. 37.

14. Eastman, "The Sioux Mythology," p. 88.

15. Eastman, *The Soul of the Indian*, pp. 16–17.

16. Ibid., pp. xiii, 119–20.

17. Ibid., pp. 42, 53–63, 73–74; Eastman, *The Indian Today*, pp. 13, 15,
32; Eastman, *Pratt*, p. 190.

18. Eastman, *The Soul of the Indian*, p. 106; Charles A. Eastman, "The
Indian and the Moral Code," *The Outlook* 97 (Jan. 7, 1911): 32–33.

19. Ibid.

20. Eastman, *The Indian Today*, p. 28; Charles A. Eastman, *Indian
Heroes and Great Chieftains* (Boston: Little, Brown, 1918), p. 184.

21. Eastman, *The Soul of the Indian*, p. 108.

22. See Eastman, *Indian Heroes and Great Chieftains*; Charles A. Eastman, "Rain-in-the-Face, The Story of a Sioux Warrior," *The Outlook* 84 (Oct. 27, 1906): 507–12; Charles A. Eastman, "A Half-
Forgotten Lincoln Story," *The Rotarian* 76 (Feb., 1950): 34. For
criticism of Eastman's account of Spotted Tail, see George E. Hyde,
Spotted Tail's Folk: A History of the Brule Sioux (Norman: University of Oklahoma Press, 1961), pp. 13, 15, 20, 33, 35, 39–40.

23. Charles A. Eastman, "The Story of the Little Big Horn," *The Chautauquan* 31 (July, 1900): 353–58; Charles A. Eastman, "The Sioux of
Yesterday and Today," *American Indian Magazine* 5 (Winter,
1917): 235–37; Warren K. Moorehead, *The American Indian in the
United States* (Andover: Andover Press, 1914), p. 199.

24. Eastman, *The Indian Today*, pp. 81–82, 136.

25. Ibid., pp. 42–43.

26. Charles A. Eastman, "Justice for the Sioux," *American Indian Magazine* 7 (Summer, 1919): 80.

27. Eastman, *The Indian Today*, pp. 43, 113–14; Charles A. Eastman,

"The Indian's Plea for Freedom," *American Indian Magazine* 6 (Winter, 1919): 164.

28. Eastman, *Indian Heroes and Great Chieftains*, p. 237; Eastman, *The Indian Today*, pp. 49–55; Eastman, *Pratt*, p. 102; Eastman, "A Half-Forgotten Lincoln Story," p. 34.

29. Eastman, *The Indian Today*, pp. 58–61; Charles A. Eastman, "The Indian as a Citizen," *Lippincott's Magazine* 95 (Jan., 1915): 72.

30. Eastman, *The Indian Today*, p. 103; Eastman, *From the Deep Woods*, pp. 163–64.

31. Eastman, *The Indian Today*, pp. 152–57; Charles A. Eastman, "My People: The Indian's Contribution to the Art of America," *The Red Man* (Dec., 1914): 133–40, and in *The Craftsman* 27 (Nov., 1914): 179–86; Charles A. Eastman, "The Indian's Gift to the Nation," *Quarterly Journal of The Society of American Indians* 3 (Jan.–Mar., 1915): 17–23. Hereafter cited as *Quarterly Journal*.

32. Eastman, *The Indian Today*, pp. 135–36, 143–46; Charles A. Eastman, "The Indian's Health Problem," *Popular Science Monthly* 86 (Jan., 1915): 49–54 and in *American Indian Magazine* 4 (Apr.–June, 1916): 139–45.

33. Eastman, *The Indian Today*, p. 80.

34. Ibid., pp. 69–74, 100, 115–17.

35. Eastman, "The Indian's Plea for Freedom," p. 164.

36. Ibid., pp. 162–63, 165; Eastman, "Justice for the Sioux," p. 81; see also Eastman, "The Sioux of Yesterday and Today," pp. 233–39; Charles A. Eastman, "A Review of the Indian Citizenship Bills," *American Indian Magazine* 6 (Winter, 1919): 181–83.

37. Eastman, *From the Deep Woods*, p. 72; LMC, 8th sess., 1890, p. 46.

38. Eastman, *From the Deep Woods*, pp. 186–87; Eastman to Garland, Dec. 3, 1902, HGC.

39. Eastman, "All the Days of My Life," p. 182.

40. Eastman to Garland, Dec. 3, 1902, HGC; Charles A. Eastman Folder, Jones Public Library.

41. Charles A. Eastman Folder, Baker Library.

42. *American Review of Reviews* 43 (Jan.–June, 1911): 508–9.

43. *Quarterly Journal* 3 (July–Sept., 1915): 216–17; *American Review of Reviews* 52 (July–Dec., 1915): 116–17; *ALA Booklist* 12 (Oct.–July, 1915–16): 24; *The Nation* 101 (July–Dec., 1915): 206–7.

44. See Zitkala-Sa (Gertrude Bonnin), *American Indian Stories* (Glorieta, N.M.: Rio Grande Press, 1976).

45. Eastman, *The Soul of the Indian*, pp. 55–62; Luther Standing Bear,

My People the Sioux (Lincoln: University of Nebraska Press, 1975), pp. 113–22.

46. See Elaine G. Eastman, "Tales of the Indian Life," *Nebraska History* 21 (Apr.–June, 1940): 126; Natachee Scott Momaday, *American Indian Authors* (Boston: Houghton Mifflin, 1972); Moorehead, *The American Indian in the United States*; Utley, *The Last Days of the Sioux Nation.* To date, *From the Deep Woods, Indian Boyhood, Indian Scout Talks, Old Indian Days,* and *The Soul of the Indian* have been reprinted.

47. Charles A. Eastman Folder, Jones Public Library; Charles A. Eastman Folder, Baker Library.

48. Oliver Eastman, MS 768, Doris Duke Oral History Project, History Department, University of South Dakota, Vermillion, S.D.

49. Eastman, *From the Deep Woods,* p. 187.

CHAPTER 10

PROMOTING THE AMERICAN INDIAN

CHARLES A. EASTMAN was the foremost educated Indian in the United States. By the first decade of the twentieth century his national reputation was secure. His books, articles, and lecture engagements continued to bring him greater recognition, even beyond the United States. Because of the popularity of his works, he was one of the authors invited to Mark Twain's seventieth anniversary dinner held at the exclusive Delmonico's in New York City on December 5, 1905. A photograph of the occasion shows Eastman in formal dress occupying one of the twenty tables of dignitaries.[1] His fame grew and from 1910 to 1921 Eastman was at the peak of his career.

After leaving the Indian service in December, 1909, Eastman devoted much of his time to writing and lecturing. He also became associated with several activities and movements which directly involved Native American culture. For example, during the summer of 1910, Eastman went to northern Minnesota and Ontario, Canada, to collect items from the Ojibways, traditional enemies of the Sioux, for the University of Pennsylvania Museum. Details regarding how Eastman secured this summer employment have not been located. The Ojibways welcomed Eastman in their camps and exchanged stories with him. Eastman thoroughly enjoyed the time he spent with these people. In his leisure hours, he hunted and fished, on one occasion catching a 150-pound sturgeon. Eastman's close rapport with the Ojibways enabled him to bring back some rare and curious items.[2]

In 1910, Eastman began his long association with the Boy Scouts of America, an organization which used the American Indian as its prototype. A need to return to nature and a reaction to the increased urbanization in the United States help explain the broad appeal of the Boy Scout movement in America. Frederick Jackson Turner's famous paper on the significance of the frontier in American history in 1893 and subsequent works by others convinced many people of the necessity to retain in some way those noble outdoor experiences that made Americans great. Ernest Thompson Seton, founder of the movement in America, held Eastman and his works in high esteem.[3] Seton was extremely happy at having a national figure like Eastman participating in the movement. Eastman wrote articles for *Boys' Life*, the organization's magazine, and wrote a book entitled *Indian Scout Talks* (1914), which became a useful guide and reference for Boy Scouts and their sister organization, the Campfire Girls of America, to employ in their activities and programs. He also spoke to several scout troops and served as a camp director and National Councilman.[4]

Undoubtedly influenced by the way American families accepted the Boy Scout movement and also by the prospects of achieving financial rewards, the Eastmans decided to start their own summer camp. Again, returning to the wilderness and learning from that experience were manifested in the growing summer camp programs that swept America during this period, and the Eastmans' camp was part of that phenomenon. They named their camp the School of the Woods, and billed it as "The Summer Camp with a Difference." The Eastmans pointed out that their summer program offered land and water sports and included genuine Indian activities and instruction conducted by a "Real Indian." Located at Granite Lake, near Munsonville, New Hampshire, a well-known recreation area, the camp opened on July 1, 1915. This first camp was restricted only to girls, who had to pay $200 for the two-month season and had to supply most of their own equipment and clothing, including their own camp outfits, which consisted of middy blouses and bloomers.

The entire Eastman family worked at the camp Elaine and her three eldest daughters—Dora Winona, a graduate of Mount Holyoke College in South Hadley, Massachusetts; Irene Taluta, on her way to becoming a well-known concert soprano; and Virginia, attending Wellesley College in Wellesley, Massachusetts—acted as counselors.

The other three children, Ohiyesa II, Eleanor, and Florence, the youngest, helped with other camp functions.[5]

Pleased with the success and income from their first season, they enlarged their operation to include boys in 1916 and changed the name of the camp to Camp Oahe for girls and Camp Ohiyesa for boys. They printed elaborate promotional brochures that contained pictures of campers engaged in activities and information about their program. In his campaign to promote the camps, Eastman announced, "We will follow the Indian method, for the American Indian is the only man I know who accepts natural things as lessons in themselves, direct from the Great Giver of life. Let us return to the normal attitude of trust in our surroundings for the laws of the wilderness must necessarily be just, and man is almost universally respected by the animals, unless he is himself the aggressor."[6] The Eastmans continued to attract eager campers for the next several summers.

During these prewar years, Eastman continued to receive invitations annually from Albert K. Smiley to participate in the Lake Mohonk Conference of Friends of the Indian and to correspond with leading figures involved with Indian reform.[7] He also became active in several other projects which attempted to help white Americans gain a deeper appreciation of Native Americans. Eastman was especially proud of having been selected to represent the North American Indian at the First Universal Races Congress held in London, England, on July 26–29, 1911. Representatives of fifty-three different nationalities participated in this affair, which had as its objectives the promotion of interracial harmony and world peace. The First Universal Races Congress was an outgrowth of an ethnic studies conference held in Eisenach, Germany, in 1906. The need to promote world interracial concord and to avert the ever-present danger of war was on the minds of many during the first decade of the twentieth century, and the First Universal Races Congress was one of several efforts to achieve such harmony.[8]

Eastman wrote to his old friend Pratt, who had by 1910 retired from active duty, and to Dr. Carlos Montezuma, the educated Yavapai physician, telling them of his willingness to participate at the meeting. Because he had been asked to supply photographs of leading American Indians and names of university graduates, Eastman requested one from Montezuma, who had obtained a medical degree from Chicago Medical College in 1889, and asked Pratt about others. Eastman also informed the general that his address would contain praise of Pratt's work with the Indians at Carlisle.[9] After Elaine had gone over the final draft of his paper, Eastman anxiously prepared for his first voyage abroad.[10]

On Friday afternoon, July 28, 1911, Eastman presented his paper on the North American Indian at the University of London, the institution hosting the conference. Incidentally, at the same session, another famous American, Dr. W. E. B. DuBois, representing the American Negro, also spoke. Eastman's speech, a broad historical and sociological overview of Native American culture before and after European contact, stressed the need to incorporate Indians into the mainstream of American society and once again took the opportunity to criticize and condemn the Indian bureau for perpetuating paternalism and dependency. His remarks were warmly received. He also apparently settled a disagreement between Christian and non-Christian delegates. The latter group objected to the frequent use of the word Christianity in the Congress's platform, and Eastman's suggestion of substituting the term universal brotherhood met with instant approval.[11]

It was hoped that this interracial conference would be held annually, but the aspirations of its organizers diminished when war clouds gathered over Europe, and no other conferences were ever held. Nevertheless, Eastman's participation in such a noble and humanitarian meeting displayed his lifelong goal of promoting interracial concord.

Eastman apparently did not make enough money from his book royalties and lecture engagements to support his large family despite his growing recognition and fame during the years preceding World War I. Deeply concerned about his financial inability to send his children to college, he detailed his financial worries in correspondence to Pratt in January, 1911, wherein he proposed a possible solution. If John Wanamaker, a wealthy businessman and philanthropist interested in Indians, would give him money to write a history of the Sioux, Eastman reasoned that his monetary problems would be solved. By producing a valuable work, explained Eastman, his debt would be discharged. He asked Pratt to write to Wanamaker on his behalf.[12] Whether or not Wanamaker gave Eastman a cash advance was not revealed in the materials searched.

Eastman's financial misfortune was one of the several topics discussed by former Commissioner of Indian Affairs Francis E. Leupp in his controversial book, *The Indian and His Problem* (1910). Although not directly mentioning Eastman's name, Leupp referred to a debt an educated Indian, who moved from job to job after "failing at the one for which he was especially educated," owed to "a trustful landlady," and the troubles she had in trying to collect from him.[13] Eastman became infuriated with Leupp's criticism of educated Indians as well as many Whites involved in Indian reform, Eastman and others such as Herbert Welsh of the Indian Rights Association viewed the book as a personal attack against them. "It impresses me as superficial," declared Eastman, "written rather as a defense of his official acts and a means of paying off old grudges than for any other motive."[14] Welsh wrote that Leupp had been a disappointment as the IRA's agent in Washington from 1895 to 1898 and possessed "a narrow, extremely sensitive and vindictive spirit."[15] The IRA and Leupp also engaged in bitter disagreements when Leupp served as Commissioner of Indian Affairs from 1904 to 1909.

The publication of six books between 1911 and 1918 and the translation of some of Eastman's works into foreign editions apparently helped ease his monetary problems. Cash advances and royalties from these books and money made from lecture tours furnished enough capital to begin the summer camp in 1915, which afterward became a major source of revenue until 1921. He also continued to keep himself informed as to how the Santee claims case was progressing in Washington.[16]

Why Eastman did not return to the medical profession during these lean years remains a mystery. Perhaps he had lost confidence in his abilities as a physician, or the expenses of beginning a new practice were beyond his means. Unlike Dr. Carlos Montezuma, the Yavapai physician who secured employment at a good clinic in Chicago, Eastman did not return to medicine full-time. During the late 1920s and early 1930s, however, he occasionally helped other doctors with their patients.[17]

It was during the era of Progressivism, when many of the injustices in American society were under attack, that Eastman and others who comprised the small number of educated Indians in America met in an effort to form a Pan-Indian organization which would extend the ideals of change and progress to include improvements among their own race. As early as 1899, Eastman, his brother John, and the Reverend Sherman Coolidge, an Arapaho Episcopal minister, had discussed the possibilities of organizing such a group but decided against it because such a body might be misunderstood by Indians and Whites and would undoubtedly cause the Indian bureau to view as conspiratorial a meeting of educated Indians.[18] By 1911, however, these fears had vanished.

Dr. Fayette A. McKenzie, professor of economics and sociology at Ohio State University, was primarily responsible for this new attempt to form a national organization. McKenzie, a non-Indian, had studied and written on Indian and White relations, and he believed in the need for professional Indians to unite.[19] Eastman held similar views and observed "that a permanent organization of educated Indians, if such a one could be successfully launched, uniting the ablest and most progressive men of the different tribes for a common object, might be productive of much good."[20]

In response to McKenzie's invitation, Eastman and five other prominent Indians met at Columbus, Ohio, on April 3, 1911. Besides Eastman and Montezuma, the other four in attendance were Thomas L. Sloan, a lawyer from the Omaha tribe; Charles E. Daganett, a Peoria and supervisor of Employment for the Indian bureau; Laura M. Cornelius, an Oneida from Wisconsin; and Henry Standing Bear, a Sioux from Pine Ridge. They adopted the temporary name of the American Indian Association and formed an executive committee. The preamble of their constitution declared, "The time has come when the American Indian race should contribute, in a more united way, its influence and exertion with the rest of the citizens of the United States in all lines of progress and reform for the welfare of the Indian race in particular, and humanity in general."[21] Before adjourning their meeting, they decided to accept an invitation from the president of Ohio State University, the mayor of Columbus, and others to hold their first national conference in Columbus in October, 1911.[22]

Shortly after leaving Columbus, Eastman, Montezuma, and others had second thoughts about electing Daganett as temporary chairman. They feared that his effectiveness in the organization might be compromised because he was an Indian bureau employee. Pratt, who received information on the meeting from Montezuma, Sloan, and Eastman, agreed with his Indian friends, but believed that the others who served on the executive committee were excellent choices, especially Cornelius, Sloan, and Eastman. Pratt saw Sloan as the organization's legal authority and Eastman as the best vehicle to employ in informing the general public of the organization's goals and wholeheartedly pledged his support to the new body.[23]

Two months later the executive committee met again to prepare for its upcoming conference. Daganett remained as temporary chairman. The committee decided that only people of Indian blood could be active members, while non-Indians would be accepted as associate members and could attend meetings only as observers. They requested that tribes choose delegates, and only those with invitations from the executive committee would be accepted. Nontribal delegates could also participate if they secured approval from the committee. After resolving the questions of membership and delegates, the committee declared that the conference would convene on Columbus Day, October 12, 1911, as a symbolic gesture of their new beginning.[24]

Commissioner of Indian Affairs Robert G. Valentine welcomed the delegates to Columbus and presented the opening address. Valentine's hopes of having the body produce a united front with similar opinions on issues affecting Indians were commendable yet visionary. Factionalism, although at a minimum at the first conference, soon undermined the organization's purposes and goals. Other papers read at the meeting dealt with industrial, educational, legal, and political problems. Eastman was listed on the tentative program as delivering a paper on the North American Indian, probably the same one he had presented earlier in London, but whether or not he read this paper is unknown. He did, however, participate in the lively discussion sessions.[25]

At the business meeting, which only Indians could attend, the delegates changed the name of their organization to the Society of American Indians. Eastman, who had been nominated along with Sloan and Coolidge for chairman of the executive committee, withdrew his name because he became disenchanted with many of his

fellow delegates. Later explaining his discontent, he declared that the
SAI should stress and promote social and moral programs among
Indians instead of concentrating on governmental Indian affairs.
Since other Indian reform associations directed their efforts to influence federal Indian policy, Eastman envisioned the SAI as an
organization primarily rendering social services to less fortunate Indians who had not received the opportunities that he and other SAI
members had. This did not mean that Eastman advocated that the
SAI ignore legislation regarding Indians. Indeed, when Eastman was
later elected president of the SAI in 1918, he kept the membership
abreast of important bills affecting Indians. His strong belief in tribal
patriotism, part of his Sioux heritage, also explains Eastman's initial
dissatisfaction with the SAI. He wanted the SAI to become an elected
intertribal organization, sort of an Indian congress consisting of tribal
delegates, but the SAI never became such a body. After the votes
were counted at this first meeting, Sloan won the chairmanship, and
Daganett was elected secretary-treasurer.[26]

Arthur C. Parker, a Seneca ethnologist who had been elected to
the SAI executive committee, realized the importance of having
Eastman working with their movement and wrote a passionate letter
to Eastman praising his leadership. Parker tried to convince him not
to turn his back on the SAI, "I want to feel that your heart is still
with us in an active way."[27]

The selection of Sloan and Daganett as officers further disturbed
many of the SAI members, including Eastman. They criticized
Sloan's advocacy of the use of peyote, an issue which would later
divide the SAI leadership even more. Daganett, on the other hand,
began having second thoughts about his office and, when he asked
Eastman for advice, Eastman wrote to him that he should resign because he held an Indian bureau position which could, in the future,
prove embarrassing to himself and the SAI. At the January, 1912,
executive committee meeting both men resigned from their offices.[28]

Parker wrote to Eastman, who had not attended the meeting, and
informed him of the resignations. In their places, Coolidge was
elected president, and Parker became secretary-treasurer. Parker also
notified Eastman that he had been elected as chairman of the membership committee and vice-president. He hoped Eastman would
accept the positions.[29] Eastman declined the offices because other

work occupied his time, but he told Parker that he had spoken to
many of his friends about the SAI, and a number of them had joined.
"I wish you all success," concluded Eastman, "and shall do what I
can as a member."[30]

In September, 1912, Eastman learned that he was among the leading candidates being considered for the position of Commissioner of
Indian Affairs. The prospect of becoming commissioner must have
intrigued him, because as commissioner he could implement some of
his ideas and other innovative, constructive programs to improve
conditions among Indians. Eastman's major support for the office
came from Professor Warren K. Moorehead, a leading Indian reformer, curator and later director of the Department of Archaeology
at Phillips Academy in Andover, Massachusetts, whose life spanned
from 1866 to 1939. He was appointed a member of the Board of Indian Commissioners in 1908, serving until its demise in 1933. In their
correspondence on this matter, Eastman appeared anxious to obtain the appointment. He secured letters of recommendation from
influential friends, and several eastern newspapers gave him their
endorsements.[31]

Eastman's enthusiasm waned when he received news from Moorehead that Edgar B. Meritt and Frederick H. Abbott, two Indian
bureau employees, were the top contenders. Moorehead realized that
his friend no longer had a chance for the commissionership and
informed Eastman that he would support Meritt.[32] Moorehead's
sources of information, however, had not been very accurate, as
neither of these men became commissioner. The appointment went
to Cato Sells, who served as commissioner throughout President
Woodrow Wilson's two terms.

Although disappointed, Eastman apparently harbored no resentment toward Moorehead, for the two continued to correspond and
help each other whenever possible. In fact, Eastman agreed to help
Moorehead with sections of his forthcoming book, *The American
Indian in the United States*, published in 1914, and spent a considerable amount of time reading proofs and making corrections, for
which Moorehead promised to pay him $50 from the royalties.[33]
Eastman was generally pleased with the final product. His chief criticism was that non-Indian writers tended to interpret what nature
and religion meant to the Indian "too much in the light of his

present-day environment." Eastman also pointed out errors in dates, and Moorehead thanked him for his additional comments.[34]

Eastman did not attend the SAI meetings from 1912 through 1917 because of other commitments, but he remained a member. Parker, as usual, tried to persuade Eastman to become more active in the organization. "At any time you wish to advise us upon any subject or line of policy," wrote Parker, "I am sure that your counsel would be most gladly received."[35] In the official magazine of the SAI, the *Quarterly Journal of the Society of American Indians*, first published on April 15, 1913, and later renamed the *American Indian Magazine* in 1916, selections consistently contained quotations from Eastman or comments on his achievements.[36]

In 1915, Eastman began to contribute articles to the journal, the first of them entitled "The Indian's Gift to the Nation," a chapter from his new book, *The Indian Today*, in which he had devoted space to the work of the SAI and his personal view that the organization needed to get involved with social and moral work among Indians.[37] Professor McKenzie later wrote a favorable review of the book in the *Quarterly Journal*, no doubt to attract more participation from Eastman. Additional issues continued to carry laudatory comments on Eastman, and with the publication of a special Sioux edition in 1917, Eastman decided to become more active in the SAI.[38]

Unfortunately by 1918 the reform zeal which swept America during the Progressive Era began to disappear, and, simultaneously, factionalism intensified among the leaders of the SAI. According to Hazel W. Hertzberg, who has written the definitive study on modern Pan-Indian movements, issues such as the magazine supplanting the SAI as the major vehicle of the movement, the demand for a stronger denunciation of the Indian bureau, the organization of a separate Indian regiment in the U.S. Army, and the controversy over peyote divided and weakened the SAI. The latter issue is a prime example of this divisiveness.[39]

Both Indians and Whites fervently disagreed on the use of peyote in religious ceremonies. Among those favoring its usage were Sloan; Francis LaFlesche, an Omaha; Paul Boynton, a Cheyenne-Arapaho; Cleaver Warden, an Arapaho; and James Mooney of the Bureau of American Ethnology. Eastman, General Pratt, and Gertrude Bonnin, a Sioux, were among those contending that it was a highly harmful drug. All testified at the 1918 hearings on Arizona Congressman Carl M. Hayden's bill to suppress liquor traffic and peyote among Indians.[40]

Eastman stated in his testimony supporting the Hayden Bill that he had thoroughly studied the peyote question, and, drawing upon his medical training, considered peyote a dangerous drug, causing moral as well as physical decay. He strongly criticized peyote eating among educated Indians. Eastman also described three groups of Sioux who used peyote: one group foolishly believed it would relieve physical discomforts or injuries, while another consisted of Sioux who liked to experiment with drugs such as this, and a third used peyote because they opposed "the white man's religion." Eastman did believe, however, that Indians had a right to have their own church, but the taking of peyote as part of a religious ceremony was merely a "subterfuge."[41] Although the House passed the bill, it failed in the Senate, and the peyote controversy raged on.[42]

Unhappy with the failure of the Hayden Bill, Eastman turned his attention to the upcoming SAI meeting and helped Bonnin, who had earlier replaced Parker as secretary-treasurer, with the program. The conference, held in Pierre, South Dakota, on September 25–28, 1918, failed to attract a large audience. Parker, president of the SAI and editor of the journal, did not attend. His moderate views on the abolition of the Indian bureau and his hopes of having the journal become the main forum for Pan-Indianism, thus placing the SAI in a secondary role, had put him in disfavor, and, as a result, he left the organization. Ironically, Eastman, whom Parker had pleaded with for years to become more involved, replaced him as president. Montezuma, who differed with Parker on several issues, approved of Eastman's selection. He and Eastman were especially pleased with two resolutions adopted at the conference, one calling for the immediate abolition of the Indian bureau, and the other endorsing the war effort and Indian participation as American soldiers.[43]

Shortly after Eastman became president, personal tragedy struck his family when his second daughter, Irene Taluta, who had accompanied her father on several lecture tours, died on October 23, 1918, as a result of an influenza epidemic. Apparently his wife Elaine and two other daughters were also stricken, but they recovered. The Eastmans buried their daughter under a tree at their summer camp in New Hampshire.[44]

A saddened Eastman resumed his presidential duties. He sent letters to past, present, and future Indian and white members asking for their support, one such letter going to his old friend Hamlin Garland, who responded that he would be delighted to become an associate member.[45] By March 12, 1919, Secretary-Treasurer Bonnin boasted that the new membership drive had attracted approximately 300 Indian and 100 white members. Six months later, however, she complained that the SAI had suffered financial setbacks and had scarcely enough money to operate.[46]

Despite these monetary problems, Eastman worked hard at his new job. The war had ended, and the SAI hoped to profit from the heady idealism expressed by President Wilson, especially his pronouncements concerning self-determination. Eastman hoped that Wilson's pledges to the people of Europe would be extended to Native Americans, with a grant of American citizenship the first order of business. He kept readers of the SAI journal informed of pending legislation in Congress which would grant Indian citizenship. Eastman favored a bill introduced by Representative Charles Carter of Oklahoma, providing immediate citizenship for all Indians, but he criticized a section which individualized and removed "restrictions upon all property and moneys belonging to adult mixed blood Indians of less than one-half Indian blood," contending that this would "create a distinction between citizens, giving some a clear title, while the rights of others" would still be under the control of the Indian bureau.[47]

Eastman repeatedly pointed to the participation of approximately 10,000 Indians in the war, among them his own son, who had joined the U.S. Navy.[48] It is interesting to note that according to a letter written by Elaine in 1934, her husband had become "a citizen simply by leaving his tribe and adopting the habits of civilized life" and that to the best of her knowledge "none of his civic rights were ever questioned."[49]

During the spring of 1919, Eastman, Montezuma, and Father Phillip B. Gordon, a Chippewa and vice president of the SAI, spent three months on a lecture campaign promoting Indian citizenship

and the abolition of the Indian bureau. They were cordially welcomed everywhere except by the agent at the Menominee Reservation in Wisconsin. Unable to enter the reserve, they spoke at a
nearby Catholic school, and later held a meeting at a government
school in the vicinity.[50] After the tour, Bonnin thanked the three
men for their time and devotion and singled out Eastman for special
praise.[51]

The SAI held its eighth annual conference in Minneapolis, Minnesota, on October 2–4, 1919. In his welcoming address, Eastman gave
an extremely romantic presentation on Native Americans, their place
in history, and their contributions to America and presented a pag-
eant which he wrote entitled "The Conspiracy of Pontiac," with
himself playing the role of Pontiac. He concluded his address by
again calling for the abolition of the Indian bureau and immediate
citizenship.[52]

Eastman's expectations of having the SAI work as a cohesive body
and present a united front on these two issues diminished as the conference progressed. Sloan, the pro-peyote advocate, and his friends
caused so much dissension at the meeting that no conference platform ever appeared. Moreover, Sloan defeated Eastman and Captain
Raymond T. Bonnin, a Sioux and husband of Gertrude, for the office
of president. Unhappy with Sloan's new policy of making the SAI
"a political pressure group with patronage interests," Eastman refused to have anything more to do with the organization which he
helped create. The SAI steadily declined after the 1919 conference
and disappeared from the American scene during the mid-twenties.[53]

Another fraternal Pan-Indian organization to which Eastman belonged was the Teepee Order of America, founded around 1915 by
Red Fox St. James, an odd character who kept changing his name
and who claimed to be one-quarter blood Indian. Initially only
native-born Protestants between the ages of fifteen and thirty could
join the movement. Members participated in Indian activities and
studied aspects of Native American culture. Not much is known
about Eastman's role in the movement, only that he served as its first
head chief and helped organize a special set of rituals. Eastman also
had apparently some involvement with the Masons, but again, details on that relationship have not been discovered.[54]

Still another interesting but poorly documented event in Eastman's life during this period concerned a magnificent mahogany sculpture done of him by Eugenie F. Shonnard, who had studied sculpture and art under some of the foremost artists in the United States and in France. Eastman apparently sat for Shonnard sometime in 1920. The finished product, at the Museum of New Mexico in Santa Fe, shows a side profile of a seated Eastman, wearing his Sioux war bonnet and garments.[55]

Between 1910 and 1920 Eastman had been involved in a number of different pursuits, most of which were in one way or another connected with American Indians. Perhaps the most important of these was the possibility of his appointment as Commissioner of Indian Affairs under President Wilson. If Eastman had been appointed, he hoped to implement his ideas, reforming the bureaucratic machinery from within and expanding the number of Indian employees of the bureau so that the bureau would truly represent the interest of Indians. Yet as president of the SAI, Eastman campaigned for the abolition of the Bureau of Indian Affairs and the granting of immediate citizenship to Indians. Without himself or another Indian of his stature as commissioner, he saw no hope of reforming the bureau. His acceptance to head the SAI can be viewed as another example of his efforts to help Indian people become acculturated. Eastman believed that granting immediate citizenship to Indians would improve their status. He vaguely defined President Wilson's self-determination ideals as tribal patriotism and truly hoped that Indians would fully participate in the mainstream of the dominant society.

By 1920 financial problems again began to plague Eastman. Although the number of campers had been good during the war years, expenses and decreases in attendance after the 1919 season caused undue hardships. Equally as important were the mounting tensions between Eastman and his wife. As early as 1894, when Eastman was working for the YMCA, rumors spread of their incompatibility, and his prolonged absences from Elaine had not helped matters. The couple grew apart, and after thirty years of marriage, they finally separated by August, 1921.

Exact reasons for their separation remain shrouded in secrecy. The subject continues to be a delicate matter among most members of the family contacted. Several who are familiar with the causes steadfastly refuse to discuss the separation in any detail, but a few relatives did provide some significant information. Two of Eastman's nieces, still living in South Dakota today, had the opportunity as young girls to visit the Eastmans, one during the early 1900s when they lived at Bald Eagle Lake, Minnesota, the other at their summer camp in New Hampshire. They remembered their Uncle Charles spending many hours in his room writing. Both remarked that it appeared to them that Elaine tried to dominate Charles, and he resented her overbearing manner, but the two nieces did not exhibit any deep hostility toward their Aunt Elaine.

One of Eastman's grandsons, the late Dr. Herbert B. Fowler, a nationally known psychiatrist, stated that Eastman had always had "an eye for the ladies" and liked "stepping around." When a counselor at their summer camp became pregnant, Eastman left the camp and his marriage. Fowler claimed as did others that Eastman was not the father and that he used this as an excuse to leave Elaine. Another reason Fowler gave for the separation was that his grandfather deeply resented the way Elaine would rewrite and change the meaning of his manuscripts. Although Eastman apparently harbored resentment toward his wife's revisions of his manuscripts, without her editorial assistance he was never able to publish anything after their separation, even though he was working on several major projects. It is worth noting that Fowler's views on the separation are extremely biased against Elaine, and that Elaine Goodale Eastman was not his grandmother.[56]

Another reason given by an informant for the separation was that Elaine and Charles were growing intellectually further apart; she stressed total assimilation of Native Americans into the dominant society, while he favored a more selective process of acculturation. Indeed, Elaine was a staunch assimilationist. Addressing the Lake Mohonk Conference of Friends of the Indian in 1895, she savagely attacked the role the Indian grandmother played as a teacher of the old customs and traditions, depicting such women as tyrants and major obstacles to transforming the Indian into a carbon copy of his white breathren. Elaine declared, "It is the grandmother who almost invariably predicts an early death for the child who goes to school, and who prophesies every misfortune for those who accept the new way. She is invariably suspicious of the white man, and takes no pains to hide her dislike of him. She revives some of the worst features of the old Indian life in her songs, her death-dirges and songs upon every possible occasion." She hoped that younger Indian women, through proper training, would become more enlightened.[57] One wonders what Elaine's husband thought about his wife's speech, especially when one considers Eastman's deep love and respect for his Indian grandmother.

Whatever the reasons for the separation, Eastman and his wife apparently made a pact to keep it a secret. They never formally mentioned it in any of their correspondence after 1921. When Elaine did refer to her husband, she wrote that he lived with their son in Detroit.[58] Perhaps the Eastmans feared social stigma and the possible sensationalism of their estrangement. Their marriage had received national attention in 1891 and knowledge that it had failed would have been devastating to their future careers, let alone their pride and self-esteem.

After 1921 Eastman spent most of the winter months in Detroit with his son, Ohiyesa II, who later worked as a copywriter in the advertising department of the Kelvinator Company. Eastman continued to remain active, his final eighteen years filled with new experiences and achievements. He had become an Indian statesman, with much honor if limited influence.

NOTES

1. Charles A. Eastman Folder, Jones Public Library.
2. *Dartmouth Alumni Magazine*, Dec., 1910, Baker Library, Dartmouth College, Hanover, N.H.; Eastman, *From the Deep Woods*, pp. 166–81; Charles A. Eastman, "A Canoe Trip among the Northern Ojibways," *The Red Man* 3 (Feb., 1911): 236–44; Charles A. Eastman, "Camping with Indians," *The Teepee Book* I (Sept., 1915): 223–30.
3. Roderick Nash, *Wilderness and the American Mind* (New Haven: Yale University Press, 1973), pp. 147–48; see Ernest Thompson Seton's following books: *The Book of Woodcraft* (New York: Doubleday, Page, 1922); *The Gospel of the Red Man: An Indian Bible* (Garden City: Doubleday, Doran, 1936); *Trail of an Artist-Naturalist* (London: Hodder and Stoughton, 1951).
4. Charles A. Eastman, "How to Make Wigwams and Shelters," *Boys'*

Life (June, 1914): 18; Charles A. Eastman, "Stories Back of Indian Names," *Boys' Life* (Dec., 1914): 21; Eastman, *Indian Scout Talks*; Charles A. Eastman Folder, Baker Library.

5. Charles A. Eastman Folder, Baker Library.
6. Charles A. Eastman Folder, Jones Public Library.
7. See for example, Albert K. Smiley to Eastman, June 12, 1907, Smiley Family Papers, Box 16, Lake Mohonk Conferences, Quaker Collection, Haverford College, Haverford, Penn. This collection contains invitations and responses to them by the Eastmans. Because of his other commitments during the early 1900s, Eastman attended only the 1905, 1907, and 1910 meetings.
8. Eastman, *From the Deep Woods*, p. 189; *The Times* (London), Jan. 23, 1911; see also Gustav Spiller, ed., *Inter-Racial Problems: Papers from the First Universal Races Congress Held in London in 1911* (New York: Citadel Press, 1970).
9. Eastman to Carlos Montezuma, Jan. 27, 1911, Montezuma Papers, Correspondence, 1908–13, Reel 2; Eastman to Pratt, Dec. 27, 1910, Richard Henry Pratt Papers, Box 4, Beinecke Rare Book and Manuscript Library, Yale University, New Haven, Conn.; Eastman to Pratt, Jan. 27, 1911, ibid.
10. Elaine G. Eastman to Pratt, Dec. 16, 1910, Pratt Papers, Box 4.
11. Spiller, ed., *Inter-Racial Problems*, pp. 9–10; *Record of the First Universal Races Congress* (London: A. S. King & Son, 1911), pp. 367–76; Eastman, *From the Deep Woods*, pp. 189–90.
12. Eastman to Pratt, Jan. 20, 1911, Pratt Papers, Box 4; Eastman to Pratt, Jan. 27, 1911, ibid.
13. Francis E. Leupp, *The Indian and His Problem* (New York: Charles Scribner's Sons, 1910), pp. 116–17.
14. Eastman to Welsh, June 7, 1910, IRA-MCA, Reel 22.
15. Welsh to Eastman, June 9, 1910, ibid., Reel 79.
16. See Bibliography for Eastman's publications during these years and Chapter 6 for his participation in the Santee claims case.
17. Dr. Herbert B. Fowler, interview, Portland, Oregon, Oct. 21, 1976. Dr. Fowler, a psychiatrist, who died January 2, 1977, was Eastman's grandson.
18. Eastman, *The Indian Today*, pp. 130–31.
19. Hertzberg, *The Search for an American Indian Identity*, pp. 31–32.
20. Elaine G. Eastman to Pratt, Dec. 16, 1910, Pratt Papers, Box 4.
21. Hertzberg, *The Search for an American Indian Identity*, p. 36; Eastman to Montezuma, Feb. 9, 1911, Montezuma Papers, Correspondence, 1908–13, Reel 2.

22. Hertzberg, *The Search for an American Indian Identity*, p. 37.
23. Pratt to Montezuma, Apr. 14, 1911, Montezuma Papers, Correspondence, 1908–13, Reel 2; Pratt to Montezuma, Apr. 21, 1911, ibid.; Pratt to Thomas L. Sloan, Apr. 27, 1911, Pratt Papers, Box 14.
24. Hertzberg, *The Search for an American Indian Identity*, pp. 37–38, 59.
25. See ibid., pp. 60–71 for a thorough discussion of the papers presented and the responses to them; "Program, Oct. 12–16, 1911," Montezuma Papers, Correspondence, 1908–13, Reel 2.
26. Hertzberg, *The Search for an American Indian Identity*, pp. 71, 97, 132–33, 138, 180; Eastman, *The Indian Today*, pp. 132–33.
27. Arthur C. Parker to Eastman, Nov. 3, 1911, Arthur C. Parker Papers, Box 1, New York State Museum, Albany, New York.
28. Hertzberg, *The Search for an American Indian Identity*, pp. 75–76, 79, 82; Eastman to Parker, Dec. 13, 1911, Parker Papers, Box 1.
29. Parker to Eastman, Jan. 21, 1912, Parker Papers, Box 1.
30. Eastman to Parker, Feb. 2, 1912, ibid.
31. Eastman to Warren K. Moorehead, Sept. 19, 1912, Warren King Moorehead Papers, Box 27, Ohio State Historical Society, Columbus, Ohio; Eastman to Moorehead, Oct. 11, 1912, ibid.; Eastman to Moorehead, Feb. 12, 1913, ibid.; Charles A. Eastman Folder, Baker Library; Charles A. Eastman Folder, Jones Public Library. For information on Moorehead see John W. Weatherford, "Warren King Moorehead and His Papers," *Ohio Historical Quarterly* 65 (Apr., 1956): 179–90.
32. Moorehead to Eastman, Sept. 21, 1912, Moorehead Papers, Box 27; Moorehead to Eastman, Feb. 13, 1913, ibid.
33. Moorehead to Eastman, Sept. 9, 1914, ibid.; Eastman to Moorehead, Sept. 14, 1914, ibid.
34. Eastman to Moorehead, Mar. 30, 1915, ibid.; Moorehead to Eastman, Apr. 6, 1915, ibid.
35. Parker to Eastman, Aug. 15, 1913, Parker Papers, Box 1.
36. See *Quarterly Journal* 1 (Jan.–Apr., 1913): 6, 8, 18; ibid. 1 (Oct.–Dec., 1913): 371; ibid. 2 (July–Sept., 1914): 176, 186–87.
37. Charles A. Eastman, "The Indians' Gift to the Nation," ibid. 3 (Jan.–Mar., 1915), 17–23; Eastman, *The Indian Today*, pp. 130–32.
38. *Quarterly Journal* 3 (July–Sept., 1915): 216–17; Hertzberg, *The Search for an American Indian Identity*, pp. 132–33, 172–73; *American Indian Magazine* 4 (Jan.–Mar., 1916): 10–11, 64.
39. See Hertzberg, *The Search for an American Indian Identity*, pp. 167–74.

40. Ibid., pp. 173–74, 259–71.
41. U.S. Congress, House Subcommittee on Indian Affairs, *Peyote Hearings*, 65th Cong., 2d sess., Feb. 21, 1918, Part I, pp. 139–41, 164; Hertzberg, *The Search for an American Indian Identity*, pp. 263–64.
42. See Hertzberg, *The Search for an American Indian Identity*, pp. 271–84.
43. Ibid., pp. 173, 175–78.
44. *American Indian Magazine* 6 (July-Sept., 1918): 151–52; *New York Times*, Oct. 25, 1918; Gertrude Bonnin to Montezuma, Oct. 22, 1918, Montezuma Papers, Correspondence, 1913–18, Reel 3. For information on Irene's career see Irene Taluta Eastman Folder, Jones Public Library, Amherst, Mass.; *American Indian Magazine* 5 (Oct.–Dec., 1917): 263–64.
45. Eastman to Friend and Fellow-Indian, Jan. 11, 1919, Montezuma Papers, Correspondence, 1919–37, Reel 4; Eastman to Friend and Fellow-Member, ibid.; Eastman to Garland, Dec. 19, 1918, HGC; Garland to Eastman, Jan. 2, 1919, ibid.
46. Bonnin to Montezuma, Mar. 12, 1919, Montezuma Papers, Correspondence, 1919–37, Reel 4; Bonnin to Montezuma, Sept. 8, 1919, ibid.
47. See Charles A. Eastman, "A Review of the Indian Citizenship Bills," *American Indian Magazine* 6 (Winter, 1919): 181–83.
48. See *American Indian Magazine* 7 (Summer, 1919): 81, 94–95.
49. Elaine G. Eastman to Matthew K. Sniffen, Sept. 30, 1934, IRA-MCA, Reel 52.
50. Hertzberg, *The Search for an American Indian Identity*, pp. 182–83; *American Indian Magazine* 7 (Summer, 1919): 62–63.
51. Bonnin to Montezuma, June 27, 1919, Montezuma Papers, Correspondence, 1919–37, Reel 4.
52. Hertzberg, *The Search for an American Indian Identity*, pp. 184–86; "News and Comment," *Minnesota Historical Society Bulletin* 3 (Nov., 1919): 230.
53. Hertzberg, *The Search for an American Indian Identity*, pp. 187–88, 197, 199.
54. Ibid., pp. 213–18.
55. See Eugenie F. Shonnard Collection, History Library and Archives, Museum of New Mexico, Santa Fe, N.M.
56. Grace Moore, interview, May 14, 1978, Flandreau, S.D.; Bessie Jones, interview, May 14, 1978, Flandreau, S.D.; Dr. Herbert B. Fowler, interview, Oct. 14 and Oct. 21, 1976, Portland, Oregon; James D.

Ewing to author, May 3, 1976. Other informants contacted wished to remain anonymous.

57. LMC, 13th sess., 1895, p. 93.

58. See for example, Elaine G. Eastman to Mrs. Grace Moore, Feb. 24, 1936, Montezuma Papers, Correspondence, 1919–37, Reel 4.

CHAPTER 11

U.S. INDIAN INSPECTOR, 1923-25

DURING THE EARLY 1920s Eastman anxiously awaited the U.S. Court of Claims decision on the Santee claims. He expected a large sum of money, which would enable him to live a comfortable life, but as with many of his expectations, this one remained unrealized. He apparently received only $5,000, a sum considerably less than he expected, and his efforts to obtain congressional legislation granting him an additional $15,000 from the Santee claims settlement failed.[1] Eastman was further frustrated when the Commissioner of Indian Affairs refused his request to take a census among the Santees for the distribution of their settlement money. However, with the death of James McLaughlin, an Indian inspector since 1895, Eastman received that inspectorship on August 28, 1923, and completed the census.[2]

He reentered the Indian service for the fifth and final time, at a salary of $2,500 (later raised to $3,000 annually).[3] He had returned to the bureau solely for the money. Once the subject of investigations, he now traveled extensively as an Indian inspector, conducting inspections of general conditions and problems at reservations and investigating charges made against Indians and government employees.

Eastman was involved in a myriad of assignments and special duties during his nineteen months of service as an Indian inspector, but several examples serve to illustrate the type of work he performed. Shortly after his appointment Eastman received oral instructions to go to Chicago and observe the Illinois Indian Day Celebration, originally planned as a Society of American Indians conference by Carlos Montezuma, who became seriously ill and was forced to withdraw.

When Montezuma finally died on January 31, 1923, at the McDowell Reservation in Arizona, the affair fell under the sponsorship of local civic organizations in Chicago, who transformed the conference into a celebration consisting of a number of events with Indians serving as main attractions.[4] "The papers spoke of the Society of American Indians also to have a meeting," wrote a puzzled Eastman, "but I found no trace of one." Sloan, who still nominally led the SAI, attended the celebration, and Eastman correctly observed that Sloan's efforts "to revive that defunct society" had been unsuccessful. The unauthentic dances of the "Show Indians" disgusted Eastman. In his opinion, none of the Indians present at the celebration had "the respect of his race and people."[5]

Another special assignment Eastman received during his first few months as inspector required him to complete final preparations for a ceremony honoring Prime Minister David Lloyd George of Great Britain. The prime minister, who was visiting Canada, had expressed a desire to visit the United States and to meet some American Indians. Indian Commissioner Charles H. Burke directed Roscoe C. Craige, superintendent at Cheyenne River Agency, South Dakota, to select a delegation of Sioux as a welcoming committee and to bring a Sioux war bonnet for Lloyd George for a ceremony to take place at the Radisson Hotel in Minneapolis, Minnesota, on October 15, 1923.[6]

Eastman arrived in Minneapolis on October 12 to discuss last-minute details with the prime minister's appointment secretary. On the following day, Eastman met the Cheyenne River delegation and escorted them to the Radisson. At Lloyd George's arrival on October 15, he was honored at a ceremony in which the Cheyenne River Sioux, dressed in full regalia, adopted him into the tribe, presenting him with such gifts as a war bonnet, a peace pipe, and a tobacco pouch, and gave him the honorary name of Chief Two Eagles, a prominent Sioux leader of the past. Adding to the excitement, movie cameras captured the event on film.[7]

Eastman reported to the commissioner that Lloyd George was deeply impressed with the ceremony and the Cheyenne River Sioux. President Calvin Coolidge later praised Eastman's and Craige's participation in the affair and believed that it would be the most memorable event of Lloyd George's entire trip to North America.[8]

After the Lloyd George affair, Eastman traveled to several reservations in Minnesota and Wisconsin, settling disputes and reporting on agency conditions. None of these cases was particularly important.[9] On December 10, 1923, Eastman arrived in Washington, D.C., to attend meetings of the Committee of One Hundred Advisory Council, organized by Secretary of the Interior Hubert W. Work to study and make recommendations on federal Indian policy.

By the 1920s Indians of the United States were in desperate straits. The Dawes Act had failed to eradicate the "Indian problem" and to achieve assimilation, but it did succeed in divesting Indians of their land. The stimulus to a renewed interest in Indian reform was provided by the Bursum Bill, introduced in the Senate in 1922, which aimed at accelerating the alienation of title to Pueblo Indian lands. It aroused protests from Indians and Whites that inevitably led to the abandonment during the New Deal of assimilationist policies sponsored by the federal government that dated from the Dawes Act of 1887. So great were the protests that when Work became Secretary of the Interior in 1923, he ordered the Board of Indian Commissioners to investigate the Bursum Bill and organized a National Advisory Committee of one hundred prominent Americans, Indians included, to study the question. Eastman, as the most famous Indian, was naturally included.

The august body contained many prominent Indian figures interested in Indian reform: Father Phillip B. Gordon, Arthur C. Parker, Thomas L. Sloan, Sherman Coolidge, and Henry Roe Cloud, a full blood Winnebago educated at Yale University. Non-Indian members included such well-known individuals as General John J. Pershing, Bernard M. Baruch, Mark Sullivan, and William Allen White. Leading Indian reformers and highly respected anthropologists also served on the committee: Herbert Welsh, Matthew K. Sniffen, John Collier, Roy Lyman Wilbur, Warren K. Moorehead, Fayette A. McKenzie, Frederick W. Hodge, Alfred L. Kroeber, Clark Wissler, and Charles F. Lummis.[10] Many were advocates of Indian assimilation, but for the first time cultural pluralists, such as John Collier, were included in significant numbers.

The Committee of One Hundred held their formal meeting on December 12–13, 1923, discussing several controversial issues affecting Indian and White relations and resolving major and petty differences which earlier had divided many of them. Although not much is known about Eastman's contribution, many of the final resolutions included positions which he had previously supported. For example, the Committee of One Hundred called for the development of a comprehensive Indian educational program, including government scholarships for Indians to attend public high schools and colleges, and the improvement of health and sanitary conditions among Indians. The committee also recognized all Native American dances and ceremonies as long as they were not dangerous or inhumane. Addressing the peyote issue, they recommended a thorough study of its effects by a National Research Council. They failed, however, to draft a resolution on Indian citizenship because many of the members believed immediate citizenship for Indians might create complications which would threaten their status and special protection by the federal government. The Committee of One Hundred's recommendations laid the groundwork for additional studies, most notably the exhaustive Meriam Report on the administration of Indian affairs, published in 1928, which recognized the failure of the Dawes Act and recommended such important measures as curtailing land allotments in severalty, providing protection of Indian lands, increasing appropriations for health and education programs, and training tribal leaders in political and business affairs.[11]

Eastman resumed his duties as inspector, pleased with most of the resolutions drafted by the committee. On December 20, 1923, Commissioner Burke directed him to conduct a general inspection of seventeen reservations in the West, including ones in the states of Washington and Oregon, advising him to pay "particular attention to the conditions among Indians, their prospects of coming through the winter without material assistance, and their opportunities for employment or engaging in some industry upon the reservation during appropriate seasons" and ordering him to investigate several charges made against Indian service employees.[12]

He left Washington, D.C., on December 24 to begin his inspection tour on the west coast, stopping first at Caldwell, Idaho, to visit Ohiyesa II, who was completing his final year of studies at the College of Idaho.[13] From there he proceeded to the Umatilla Reservation in Oregon and conducted an inspection, reporting that the Indians enjoyed good health and should make it through the winter months without any major complications. Unbeknown to Eastman at the time, he had gone to a reservation not on the list. When Burke demanded an explanation, Eastman apologized, explaining that his instructions had been packed in a trunk which had not arrived, and he had honestly believed that Umatilla was one of the reservations assigned.[14]

For the next two months, Eastman inspected conditions and investigated complaints at Klamath Reservation in Oregon and Tulalip Reservation in Washington. In his annual report, Eastman observed that of the three tribes which lived at Klamath, the Modocs and Klamaths were far more "advanced in the knowledge of the general American life" than the Paiutes, who needed "more closer supervision and care." Indians at Tulalip, noted Eastman, "are much more adapted to work and take more kindly to it than any of the plains Indians, and on the whole are very peaceful."[15]

Eastman began a general inspection of the Sioux agencies during the final week of February, 1924. He was happy to report that the diversified farming program among the Sioux appeared to be progressing well, yet he complained that too many Indians supported themselves by selling or leasing their land allotments.[16] He also investigated a number of complaints, most of which concerned minor or petty grievances. For example, at the Lower Brule Agency, an Episcopal missionary charged that the superintendent had not lowered the agency flag for thirty days in respect to President Wilson, who had died on February 3, 1924. The superintendent did not follow this time-honored custom, declared the irate missionary, because he had been pro-German during the war years. The superintendent explained that he had not received any orders from Washington to lower the flag, and he had had no intentions of dishonoring the late President. When Eastman questioned both parties, he concluded that the charges were unsubstantiated.[17]

Other cases, however, were not as routine or as easily resolved. One of the most interesting and controversial involved Frank C. Rogers, a special officer for suppression of liquor traffic at Rosebud Agency, South Dakota. While attending an Indian celebration in June, 1923, Rogers stopped a performance of an ancient ritual called Heyoka, a clown dance, believing it was a pagan ceremony, and arrested the Indian playing the clown. When others protested, Rogers drew his revolver and the crowd dispersed. Enemies of Rogers kept the issue alive, claiming that he had been guilty of excessive brutality and improper conduct. Eastman investigated the charges in April, 1924.

He reported to the commissioner that the ritual had no religious connotations. It was simply a ceremony in which a clown's gestures and movements were opposite their projected meaning. An outward sign of pleasure, for example, really meant internal pain. Eastman concluded that since the dance was not an important religious ceremony, Rogers should not have interfered out of deference to the tribe and its customs. He did, however, levy a more serious charge against Rogers: Eastman claimed that Rogers continually interfered in the investigation and even threatened him with bodily harm. Because of such behavior, Eastman suspended Rogers and ordered him to leave the reservation. Rogers, who was married to a Rosebud woman and had three children, charged that Eastman had been prejudicial in his questioning and sent an appeal to Commissioner Burke.[18] James H. McGregor, superintendent at Rosebud, also wrote to Burke, requesting that a new inspector be sent, adding, however, that "this is not meant to cast reflections upon Dr. Eastman's ability as an inspector but since the situation has grown so tense, I can see no other way of adjusting a very unfortunate situation."[19]

Burke responded by informing Eastman that his suspension of Rogers had been "unauthorized and beyond the authority of an Inspector." Rogers was reinstated. Burke also chastised Eastman for filing an improperly prepared report on the case and ordered a reinvestigation by another inspector.[20]

The new inspector, Samuel Blair, sent his report on the case to Washington on May 28, 1924. He believed that "Dr. Eastman endeavored to be just and fair in handling this investigation." However, Blair's findings indicated that Eastman had overstepped his authority and had been too friendly with certain witnesses who had made charges against Rogers. He also noted that Rogers had a "quick temper" and was "not always safe and sane in action." Because of all the turmoil created by this case, Blair recommended that Rogers be sent to another agency.[21] Rogers reluctantly accepted a transfer to Umatilla Agency in Oregon.[22]

Eastman later apologized to Burke and requested circulars on an inspector's authority and duties.[23] Even after receiving this information, Eastman found it extremely difficult to submit his reports on time. Indeed, Burke and others in the Indian service criticized Eastman for his tardiness in filing weekly reports and expense vouchers. Organizing materials had always been difficult for Eastman, though many people at the bureau considered his actions dilatory or explained the delays as "Indian time."[24]

Other assignments during his first year as an inspector included visitations to the Shoshoni Reservation in Wyoming, the Consolidated Chippewa Reservation in Minnesota, and the Mackinac Reservation in Michigan. His comprehensive report on conditions at Shoshoni contained information on agency facilities, employment opportunities, and problems Indians faced in their efforts to become successful farmers, like the fact that their cattle herds were small and frost had destroyed nearly 75 percent of their alfalfa crop.[25]

At the Chippewa Reservation, Eastman conducted a thorough investigation of a scheme to encourage Indians to relinquish their land allotments within the Minnesota National Forest in exchange for land to the south. Proponents of the plan argued that this would consolidate tribal land, but Eastman reported, that most of the Indians contacted did not want to move and suggested that nearby businessmen wanted control of the area for tourist trade.[26]

At Mackinac Reservation, Eastman investigated charges against the superintendent, complaints by several Indians that the superintendent had treated them unjustly, especially regarding allotments, and that he had illegally allowed a lumber company to enter the reservation and cut timber. After gathering information for three weeks, Eastman reported that all charges against the superintendent were unsubstantiated. Burke accepted Eastman's findings and dismissed the case.[27]

Eastman left Mackinac on August 7, 1924, and arrived in Washington, D.C., two days later, spending the next week writing his first annual report, which listed and briefly described conditions at all the reservations he had visited during the past year. He made some significant observations, for example, that most of the troubles and complaints at reservations "developed out of individual spite and animosity towards the Superintendent by one or a group of Indians. Of course, these are not unusual, but in most instances I found they were not sustained."[28]

Eastman concluded his report by calling for better health programs among Indians and a more realistic doctor to patient ratio on reservations. Of equal significance, he wrote:

> One thing I was very much impressed [with] in all the jurisdictions that I have visited is that the North American Indians are wide awake on the current events and the general progress of the people all around them. This fact has awakened them to the necessity of making a greater effort to maintain themselves as a people and the effect of the educational system of the Bureau is plainly shown by the young Indians of today, which is very often discussed. I observe also that many of the graduate Indians are doing efficient work at all the agencies. Here again is brought a wrong impression that the Indians always go back to the blanket after he finishes the education given him by the Government. I found several of the Indian graduates as Superintendents of large jurisdictions.[29]

After a leave of absence from August 18 to September 1, he received orders to report to the Osage Reservation in Oklahoma, where Commissioner Burke instructed him to assist Special Supervisor Frank E. Brandon in conducting a survey of the present holdings and properties of the restricted Osage tribe. Because of oil discoveries on their land, the Osages had become one of the wealthiest, if not the wealthiest, tribe in the United States. Eastman spent four months among 130 families. His report revealed how unique and atypical the Osages were in comparison to other tribes he had visited.[30]

Eastman observed that the Osages took full advantage of their high standards of living, building "luxuriously furnished bungalows" on their homesteads, with separate quarters for servants, and almost all owned expensive automobiles driven by white chauffeurs. Their frequent trips throughout the country made it difficult for Eastman to complete his survey. He noted that "no restricted Osage has a business occupation," and because of their economic status "the Osage people have grown to be suspicious and snobbish." In concluding his report, Eastman cautioned, "If their oil should fail the Osage people would be in a hard predicament, more so than any other Indian Tribe because they have lived expensively and have become accustomed to it."[31]

After the Osage survey, Eastman embarked upon his final and perhaps most important investigation as an inspector, locating the burial place of Sacajawea, the Indian who had helped guide the Lewis and Clark expedition. The equal rights movement for women during the late nineteenth and early twentieth centuries and the ratification of the Nineteenth Amendment in 1920, granting full suffrage to women, help explain government interest in the Sacajawea investigation. She was a woman whom many suffragettes pointed to with pride, a woman who helped build America. In addition, by the 1920s two conflicting interpretations existed on when and where she died and how her name should be spelled. One school believed that she died in 1812 at Fort Manuel, located at the mouth of the Big Horn River, while the other declared she died in 1884 at Fort Washakie, Wyoming. Those supporting the 1812 interpretation used the Hidatsa spelling, Sakakawea, while the 1884 advocates favored the Shoshoni spelling, Sacajawea.[32] Since Eastman preferred the Shoshoni form, that spelling will be used.

Interest in Sacajawea peaked and the controversy intensified when Dr. Grace Raymond Hebard, professor of political economy at the University of Wyoming in Laramie and an active supporter of the Nineteenth Amendment, campaigned for federal legislation to erect an edifice honoring Sacajawea's death in 1884. A storm of protest ensued. Lending proponents of the 1812 school, notably Russell Reid, superintendent of the North Dakota Historical Society, Doane Robinson, director of the South Dakota Historical Society, and Stella Drumm, librarian at the Missouri Historical Society, declared that such a memorial would be a travesty.[33] Officials in Washington hoped that Eastman's investigation would settle the confusion. Eastman, aware of the different schools of thought and how important his findings would be, began his investigation on January 1, 1925, by acquainting himself with published materials on Sacajawea, and then for the next three months gathering testimony from Shoshonis in Wyoming, Gros Ventres in North Dakota, and Comanches in Oklahoma.[34]

Throughout Eastman's investigation, Dr. Hebard, who was writing a book-length study on Sacajawea, wrote to him regarding his findings and offering her assistance. She reminded Eastman that those who ascribed to the 1812 interpretation based their evidence on a vague entry in John Luttig's journal. Luttig, a clerk who worked for Manuel Lisa's fur trading operation, noted in 1812 that the Indian wife of Charbonneau, a Frenchman who accompanied Lewis and Clark and husband of Sacajawea, had died at the fort. Since Charbonneau had more than one Indian wife and the death of such a famous individual had not appeared in other accounts or journals, declared Hebard, the Indian woman who died was not Sacajawea.[35] Hebard contended that Sacajawea left Charbonneau by 1812 because of his excessive brutality and other wives. Until her death in 1884, continued Hebard, Sacajawea regretted having led white men into Shoshoni country and wished to remain anonymous. Hebard based her evidence on Indian and white informants who had known and spoken with Sacajawea years after her alleged demise in 1812.[36]

Eastman never personally interviewed Hebard, but he wrote and thanked her for the information and requested additional material, which she gladly supplied. After interviewing Robinson, Drumm, and others who repudiated Hebard's interpretation, Eastman hurried to complete his investigation because his superiors in Washington wanted the report before Congress adjourned.[37] On March 2, 1925, Eastman submitted to the commissioner his findings, which fully endorsed Hebard's interpretation and contained a list of sources, both written and oral, employed in his investigation. Eastman concluded that Sacajawea lived to be nearly 100 years old and died on April 9, 1884, at Fort Washakie.[38]

On the very same day that Eastman sent his report to Washington, he wrote to Hebard, thanking her for the materials she had loaned him. Eastman also included his personal observations on Sacajawea, a woman who he romantically believed was the "Ben Hur" of Indians. Hebard, who was delighted that Eastman's findings supported her views, asked Eastman if he would write an introduction to her forthcoming book on Sacajawea, but he never answered her request, perhaps because he also planned to write an account of her life.[39]

Eastman's report on Sacajawea did not settle the controversy. Robinson and others still contended that she died in 1812, and even today, historians continue to address the question, although most support the 1812 death date because of evidence discovered after Eastman's investigation.[40] Nevertheless, Eastman expended a great deal of time and energy in attempting to resolve the matter. In fact, this was his last assignment as an inspector. Because the excessive travel had begun to affect his health, Eastman tendered his resignation on March 20, 1925.[41]

Eastman's life as an inspector was not an easy one, especially for a man in his mid-sixties. At times, he received criticism for late and incomplete reports. He had improperly handled and overstepped his authority in the Rogers investigation. Aside from these shortcomings, Eastman tried to be fair and honest. In his annual report Eastman observed that in most instances he dismissed charges made by Indians against superintendents because such complaints were usually based on personal grudges. He seemed to prefer special assignments, such as the Lloyd George ceremony and the Osage survey, which reinforced his proffered status as Indian elder statesman.

Working as an employee of the Indian bureau, an organization which he had frequently criticized, must have been difficult for Eastman. Perhaps he reconciled this apparent incongruity by believing that he could help improve the system, while at the same time improve his finances. Indeed, in his reports Eastman had brought attention to many of the problems Indians had on reservations, particularly the need for better medical programs. Although his performance as an inspector was marred by certain flaws, according to his white superiors, it was an experience which again placed him in direct contact with Indians and their efforts to adjust to a new type of existence. He sided most frequently with the bureau officials embroiled in controversy. Perhaps he had grown too fond of his paycheck if not his job; perhaps he had grown weary of the struggle. Though Indian reformers came and went and government policies were changing, the Bureau of Indian Affairs continued to administer.

NOTES

1. See Chapter 6, pp. 166–69.
2. Eastman to Burke, Jan. 16, 1923, BIA, RG 75, CF, NA. Eastman to CIA, Sept. 22, 1923, BIA, RG 75, Charles A. Eastman Special Agent File, NA; Dr. Charles A. Eastman Status Records, National Personnel Records Center, St. Louis, Mo.; James McLaughlin, *My Friend the Indian* (Boston: Houghton Mifflin, 1926), pp. iv–v.

3. Eastman Status Records, St. Louis, Mo.
4. Hertzberg, *The Search for an American Indian Identity*, pp. 197–98; Eastman to CIA, Oct. 9, 1923, BIA, RG 75, CF, NA.
5. Eastman to CIA, Oct. 9, 1923, BIA, RG 75, CF, NA.
6. Burke to Roscoe C. Craige, Sept. 15, 1923, ibid.; Meritt to Craige, Oct. 2, 1923, ibid.
7. Eastman to CIA, Oct. 16, 1923, BIA, RG 75, Eastman Special Agent File, NA; Craige to CIA, Nov. 5, 1923, BIA, RG 75, CF, NA.
8. Eastman to CIA, Oct. 16, 1923, BIA, RG 75, Eastman Special Agent File, NA; President Calvin Coolidge to Burke, Oct. 17, 1923, BIA, RG 75, CF, NA. See also Eastman to CIA, Oct. 22, 1923, BIA, RG 75, Eastman Special Agent File, NA.
9. For examples of some of the cases Eastman investigated during the fall months of 1923, see his weekly reports in Eastman Special Agent File, BIA, RG 75, NA.
10. Eastman to CIA, Dec. 18, 1923, BIA, RG 75, Eastman Special Agent File, NA; Hubert W. Work, *Indian Policies: Comments on the Resolutions of the Advisory Council on Indian Affairs* (Washington: Government Printing Office, 1924), pp. iv–v; Hertzberg, *The Search for an American Indian Identity*, p. 202.
11. Hertzberg, *The Search for an American Indian Identity*, pp. 203–4.
12. Burke to Eastman, Dec. 20, 1923, BIA, RG 75, Eastman Special Agent File, NA. The reservations were Klamath, Tulalip, Colville, Spokane, Fort Lapwai, Coeur d'Alene, Flathead, Crow, Tongue River, Blackfeet, Shoshoni, Pine Ridge, Rosebud, Lower Brule, Crow Creek, Cheyenne River, and Standing Rock.
13. Eastman to CIA, Jan. 2, 1924, BIA, RG 75, Eastman Special Agent File, NA; William E. Wallace, Registrar at the College of Idaho, to author, Mar. 4, 1976.
14. Eastman to Burke, Jan. 8, 1924, BIA, RG 75, Eastman Special Agent File, NA; Burke to Eastman, Jan. 14, 1924, ibid.; Eastman to Burke, Jan. 28, 1924, ibid.
15. Eastman to CIA, Aug. 18, 1924, BIA, RG 75, CF, NA.
16. See Eastman to CIA, Mar. 27, 1924, ibid.; Eastman to CIA, Apr. 26, 1924, ibid.
17. Eastman to CIA, Apr. 26, 1924, ibid.
18. Eastman to CIA, Apr. 15, 1924, ibid.; Eastman to Burke, Apr. 24, 1924, ibid. For Rogers's version of what happened see Frank C. Rogers to CIA, Apr. 13, 1924, ibid.
19. James H. McGregor to Burke, Apr. 14, 1924, ibid.
20. Burke to Eastman, May 8, 1924, ibid.

21. Samuel Blair to Secretary of the Interior, May 28, 1924, ibid.
22. McGregor to CIA, Sept. 26, 1924, ibid.
23. Eastman to CIA, June 2, 1924, ibid.
24. See for example, F. M. Goodwin to Secretary of the Interior, June 2, 1924, BIA, RG 75, Eastman Special Agent File, NA; Eastman to CIA, July 5, 1924, ibid.
25. Eastman to CIA, May 21, 1924, BIA, RG 75, CF, NA.
26. Eastman to CIA, July 30, 1924, ibid.
27. Eastman to CIA, Aug. 6, 1924, ibid.; Burke to Daniel Curtis, Sept. 2, 1924, ibid.
28. Eastman to CIA, Aug. 18, 1924, ibid.
29. Ibid.
30. Burke to Eastman, Sept. 5, 1924, BIA, RG 75, CF, NA; Eastman to CIA, Dec. 26, 1924, ibid.
31. Eastman to CIA, Dec. 26, 1924, ibid.
32. For books and articles on the subject see Grace Raymond Hebard, *Sacajawea* (Glendale: Arthur Clark, 1933); Harold P. Howard, *Sacajawea* (Norman: University of Oklahoma Press, 1971); Helen Addison Howard, "The Mystery of Sacagawea's Death," *Pacific Northwest Quarterly* 58 (Jan., 1967): 1–6; Helen Crawford, "Sakakawea," *North Dakota Historical Quarterly* 1 (Apr., 1927), 5–15; Clifford M. Drury, "Sacajawea's Death—1812 or 1884?," *Oregon Historical Quarterly* 62 (Sept., 1961): 288–91; Ronald W. Taber, "Sacagawea and the Suffragettes: An Interpretation of a Myth," *Pacific Northwest Quarterly* 58 (Jan., 1967): 7–13; Irving W. Anderson, "Sacajawea, Sacagawea, Sakakawea," *South Dakota History* 8 (Fall, 1978): 303–11.
33. Taber, "Sacagawea and the Suffragettes," pp. 11–12; Howard, "The Mystery of Sacagawea's Death," pp. 3–5.
34. A copy of Eastman's 1925 report on Sacajawea is at the Department of the Interior Library in Washington. Fortunately, it has been reprinted. See "Charles A. Eastman's Report on Sacajawea," *Annals of Wyoming* 13 (July, 1941): 187–94.
35. Grace Raymond Hebard to Eastman, Jan. 26, 1925, Grace Raymond Hebard Papers, Box 17, Center for Western Studies, University of Wyoming, Laramie, Wyoming. Actually, Henry Brackenridge, who had traveled up the Missouri River in 1811 in search of furs, made an entry in his journal that Charbonneau's wife had been sick. See Drury, "Sacajawea's Death—1812 or 1884?," p. 289.
36. See for example, Hebard to Eastman, Jan. 26, 1925, Hebard Papers,

Box 17; Hebard to W. E. Connelley, Mar. 6, 1928, ibid.; Hebard to Connelley, Mar. 7, 1928, ibid.
37. Eastman to Hebard, Feb. 9, 1925, ibid.; Hebard to Eastman, Feb. 13, 1925, ibid.
38. See "Charles A. Eastman's Report on Sacajawea," pp. 187–94.
39. Eastman to Hebard, Mar. 2, 1925, Hebard Papers, Box 17; Hebard to Eastman, Mar. 7, 1925, ibid.; Eastman to Hebard, Oct. 21, 1925, ibid.
40. See Hebard to Eastman, Oct. 9, 1925, ibid.; Eastman to Hebard, Oct. 21, 1925, ibid. For examples of recent historians discussing the controversy see note 32.
41. Eastman to Hebard, Oct. 21, 1925, Hebard Papers, Box 17; Hebard to Eastman, Oct. 28, 1925, ibid.; Eastman Status Records, St. Louis, Mo.

CHAPTER 12

THE FINAL YEARS ....

A̲FTER RESIGNING his inspectorship in March, 1925, Eastman spent the next several months regaining his strength and health. Hebard continued to correspond with him, asking Eastman for additional information on his findings and keeping him informed on how her book was progressing. She seemed pleased that he was also planning to write an account of Sacajawea's life and offered her assistance. Hebard again hoped that Eastman would write an introduction for her study. Eastman promised to send the materials she had requested but failed to respond to her suggestion that he write some type of foreword.[1] Although Eastman never published his manuscript on Sacajawea, Elaine, who acquired most of her husband's papers after his death, did. In 1949, she sent the account to the *Great Falls Tribune* in Montana, and the newspaper serialized the story in five weekly installments.[2]

He had recovered by October, 1925. Resuming his lecture engagements, Eastman traveled to New York, Washington, D.C., and Chicago.[3] He also attended class reunions at his alma mater, Dartmouth College, during the 1920s. The class of '87 was extremely proud of Eastman. At the June, 1927, commencement exercises, he led the class procession. Two years later, his classmates honored Eastman by presenting to the college a beautiful oil painting of him done by Julius Katzieff, a New York artist. In the 1930s, two additional portraits of Eastman and his deceased daughter, Irene, painted by another artist, Wallace Bryant, were given to Dartmouth.[4]

Eastman also accepted an offer to become a director of the Brooks-Bryce Foundation, an organization founded by Mrs. Florence Brooks-Aten, a wealthy philanthropist in New York, to promote better relations between English-speaking people in America and Great Britain. Included among the other directors were the presidents of Yale University and the University of Virginia and Rear Admiral William S. Sims, U.S. Navy, retired.[5]

As part of the foundation's functions, Mrs. Brooks-Aten conducted essay contests in English and American schools. Eastman made speeches encouraging white and especially Indian students to compete. Mrs. Brooks-Aten, impressed with Eastman's dedication and speaking ability, asked him if he would like to represent the foundation on a two-month lecture tour in England. He eagerly accepted the offer and sailed for England a second time on January 21, 1928.[6]

He delivered speeches promoting Anglo-American friendship from a Native American's point of view before large audiences at schools and universities throughout England. He was also asked to present special lectures on Indian culture at such prestigious places as Oxford, Eton, and the Royal Colonial Institute. Dressed in full Sioux regalia, including an expensive war bonnet, Eastman, as usual, cast a striking figure. At social events he sat at the same table with such prominent Englishmen as the Earl of Dartmouth and former Prime Minister David Lloyd George. He even accepted an invitation "to ride to the hounds." Eastman wore formal English riding attire and displayed skillful equestrianism, an art he had learned as a young Sioux in Minnesota and in Canada. Before leaving England, Eastman met with representatives of the Unwin Publishing Company, who purchased the publishing rights of his books in Great Britain.[7]

When Eastman returned to the United States in 1928, he purchased a site on the north shore of Lake Huron, near Desbarats, Ontario, Canada, where he "built a bungalow"[8] which he called Matotee Lodge. According to Dr. Herbert B. Fowler, Eastman's grandson, the lodge overlooked the lakeshore front and had no indoor plumbing. Eastman enjoyed the solitude the cabin afforded him. He would stay with his son in Detroit during the cold winter months. Occasionally, Eastman would lend assistance to medical colleagues in the Sault Sainte Marie region, usually treating Indian patients and, on one instance, taking over an entire practice while the regular physician went on vacation.[9]

Eastman remained active throughout most of the 1930s. He continued to accept lecture engagements and to write. Besides working on the Sacajawea manuscript, he was also preparing a novel on Pontiac as well as manuscripts on the Sioux, emphasizing their history and legends.[10] In addition, he supplied valuable information on his genealogy to a Minneapolis newspaperman, H. M. Hitchcock, who was writing an article on Eastman's ancestors. When the article appeared in the *Minneapolis Journal* on September 28, 1930, Hitchcock included among the pictures a sketch of Eastman's mother which he and Eastman had earlier discovered at the Newberry Library in Chicago.[11]

During the 1930s Eastman accepted several speaking engagements. One of the most important events Eastman participated in was a celebration held at the Minneapolis auditorium on October 12, 1930, honoring the 250th anniversary of the discovery of the Falls of St. Anthony by Father Louis Hennepin, the Recollet missionary and explorer. Because Eastman's ancestors had captured and later adopted Hennepin into their tribe, Eastman's presence enhanced the festivities. On the following day, he presented a lecture on Indian folklore at the University of Minnesota and another that evening on the Sioux at the Minnesota Historical Society.[12]

Even before the celebration in honor of Hennepin's discovery, Eastman had expressed a profound interest in him as well as other Europeans who had direct contact with his ancestors. Eastman hoped eventually to publish an account which would correct several errors made by Hennepin and others regarding Siouan bands and spellings of Indian and white names. Although the manuscript was never published, Eastman appeared to have done a considerable amount of research on the subject.[13]

Eastman's failure to publish, however, had not diminished his popularity and achievements. Indeed, as part of the festivities of an American Indian Day celebration held on September 22, 1933, at the Century of Progress exposition at the Chicago World's Fair, a medal was presented by the Indian Council Fire, a national fraternal Pan-Indian organization founded in 1923, "for the most distinguished achievement by an American Indian." From among more than fifty people considered for the honor, Dr. Eastman had the distinction of being selected the winner. In announcing Eastman's selection, the donor of the bronze medal stated, "Dr. Eastman's achievement record covers a long career that has contributed much to his own race as well as to the paleface." Among the large audience listening to Eastman's impressive achievements were William J. Kershaw, a Menominee and assistant U.S. attorney-general for Wisconsin; Dr. W. Carson Ryan, Jr., director of Indian education for the U.S. Department of the Interior; Scott H. Peters, a Chippewa and president of the Indian Council Fire; and Arthur C. Parker, the Seneca ethnologist from New York.[14] In 1935, when the Indian Council Fire presented the award to Henry Roe Cloud, a Winnebago who had graduated from Yale University, Eastman served on the selection committee.[15]

Written source material on Eastman's life after 1933 is extremely scarce. This is indeed unfortunate, particularly because Eastman's views on the Indian New Deal are not fully known. When Franklin Delano Roosevelt won the presidency in the election of 1932, he promised the nation a New Deal to combat the deadly effects of the Great Depression and to restore America's faltering economy. The President appointed John Collier, a social worker among immigrants and later an Indian reformer advocating the repeal of the Dawes Act of 1887 and recognition of Indian traditions, Commissioner of Indian Affairs in April, 1933. The new commissioner promised an Indian New Deal. The policy of complete assimilation of Indians into the mainstream of the dominant society was ended in favor of a new type of cultural pluralism, whereby Indians could be Indians, be proud of their heritage and practice their customs, and still function in the dominant society. Collier convinced Congress to pass major pieces of legislation such as the Indian Reorganization Act of 1934, which included provisions ending land allotments in severalty, providing for a restoration of Indian lands and tribal ownership of lands, and aiding Indians in the formation of tribal governments and tribal businesses. Dr. Fowler, Eastman's grandson, stated that he believed that his grandfather supported the Indian New Deal. Elaine Goodale Eastman, on the other hand, was a staunch opponent and open critic of Collier.[16]

During the winter of 1934, Eastman contracted a severe cold which forced him to curtail his activities. He was unable, for example, to attend a ceremony paying tribute to missionary efforts in Minnesota. Eastman noted, however, in a letter to Hitchcock in January, 1935, that his health was improving, and he had almost completed a manuscript on the Sioux creation legend which he called the "Sioux Bible."[17]

Commenting on his grandfather's personal disposition towards life and towards his son, Dr. Fowler made several interesting observations. He stated that Eastman's last years were pleasant ones, with a great deal of time spent working on his manuscripts and delivering occasional lectures. His recreational time was devoted to fishing, hunting, swimming, and playing pool. Ohiyesa II had a difficult time convincing his father to restrict his activities because of his age. Even in 1938, one year before his death, Eastman visited old friends in the East and delivered a few lecturers.[18]

Fowler remarked that Eastman and his son were not very close. Ohiyesa hardly ever accompanied his father on fishing and hunting trips and did not really like the outdoors. Fowler called Ohiyesa a "mama's boy."[19] Although the father and son relationship was not as cordial as it might have been, Ohiyesa took care of his father and gave him refuge during the winter months. When death came to Ohiyesa II on January 16, 1940, a little over one year after his father died, he was buried next to him in an unmarked grave.

On January 7, 1939, Eastman entered Grace Hospital in Detroit. He had suffered a heart attack, for which his doctor, Leslie T. Colvin, a cardiology specialist, was unable to help him. Eastman became comatose and died on January 8, 1939, at the age of eighty. Funeral services were held at the William R. Hamilton Chapel on January 11, and Eastman was buried in an unmarked grave at Evergreen Cemetery in Detroit, Michigan.[20] To date, Eastman's gravesite in section 9, lot B, grave 1 has no tombstone. After his death, Elaine acquired most of her husband's personal effects, including his correspondence and manuscripts. She later revised and published several of the manuscripts posthumously. On December 22, 1953, Elaine Goodale Eastman, in her ninetieth year, died. She was buried in Northampton, Massachusetts, a physical as well as a symbolic reminder of their estrangement.[21]

In retrospect, Dr. Charles A. Eastman was considered by many influential Indian reformers of the late nineteenth and early twentieth centuries to be the best example of what an Indian could achieve.

Most reformers failed, however, to recognize that Eastman was an acculturated rather than an assimilated Indian. He had not ceased to be an Indian. His books and articles substantiate this fact. Even his wife, an ardent assimilationist, could not through her editorial revisions of his works conceal her husband's syncretism. Blending the two cultures was not an easy task, and the pressures on Eastman from both worlds must have been overwhelming. He seemed to manage, nevertheless, to adjust to an alien culture and at the same time to retain his Indian identity. Indeed, as Hazel Hertzberg observes in her fine study of Pan-Indianism, Eastman "had a foot solidly in both camps and felt genuinely at home among Indians and among whites."[22]

Although Eastman remained a part of both worlds, by the 1920s and 1930s he could look back on several unpleasant memories. The white world had not been the ideal Christian civilization professed by the many reformers Eastman had encountered throughout his life. Perhaps he was somewhat bitter towards a society which did not practice what it preached. He had earned a medical degree in an effort to serve his people, but the two experiences he had as a government physician resulted in major confrontations with white agents who either disliked him, distrusted him, or felt threatened by him. Attempts to establish a medical practice in white communities never really proved lucrative, perhaps because white patients did not feel comfortable with an Indian doctor, though Carlos Montezuma, the Yavapai doctor, worked at a major clinic in Chicago and apparently had few problems.

During his final years Eastman found solace at his cabin in Canada. He had always enjoyed the outdoors, and the cabin served as a retreat, a place to reminisce, to commune with nature, and to write. Although it appears that he had developed a sort of separate existence, apart from either the Indian or the white world, such an observation needs qualification. He did not forsake either the Indian world or the white world and still moved freely among both. Even though he was disillusioned with the white world, he continued to speak before white audiences, including Boy Scout and YMCA groups, and he had many white friends. Indian relatives and friends presently living in South Dakota have nothing but high praise for Eastman, some even idolize him. They admired his intellect and his good sense of humor, the latter trait never really apparent in his writings. Also, his nephew, Oliver Eastman, recalled how his Uncle Charles once financially helped his father, David Weston (who changed his name to David Eastman).[23]

When life became too hectic in the two worlds, Eastman headed for his wooded retreat in Canada, where he escaped the pressures of acculturation and had only to be himself.

As a government employee, working for a system he often condemned, Eastman attempted to correct many of the injustices he believed Indians faced living on reservations. He found himself, on more than one occasion, in trouble with his superiors and had either to resign or to apologize for improper actions. Because he wanted to be truly effective, he longed for the appointment as Commissioner of Indian Affairs. In nongovernment activities, on the other hand, Eastman was again a spokesman for his people. He traveled throughout the United States and abroad, working on behalf of the Young Men's Christian Association, the Boy Scouts of America, and the Society of American Indians, encouraging Indians and Whites to develop a deeper understanding of and appreciation for each other.

Eastman also addressed many of the complex issues affecting Indians. He supported the Dawes Act and like many other reformers he perhaps expected too much from it. Unfortunately, Whites and Indians took advantage of the allotment system and the effects were devastating instead of beneficial. He was an outspoken critic of peyote. He called for the abolition of the Bureau of Indian Affairs, and to replace it, recommended the formation of an independent commission with at least half of its members being Indians. He also campaigned for Indian citizenship. It is a tragedy that no written source material has been found regarding Eastman's views on Indian legislation passed during the Indian New Deal. He had always advocated, like others of the small group of educated Indians at the beginning of the twentieth century, the preservation of Indian culture but realized the urgent need for Indians to adopt the positive aspects of white civilization.

His books and lectures brought him national recognition as an authority on Native Americans, but Eastman was constantly plagued by financial difficulties. He had a large family to support and often worried about their welfare. The summer camp in New Hampshire temporarily solved some of his monetary problems. Frequent absences from his family also brought in needed revenue but contributed to the growing tensions between Eastman and his wife. Perhaps Elaine viewed her marriage to Charles as an assimilation experiment, while Charles went into the marriage because he had been overwhelmed by a New England woman who not only spoke the Sioux language but knew about their culture. As the years passed both became disillusioned when neither one lived up to the expectations of the other. Charles had not become totally assimilated, a commitment which Elaine dedicated herself to and espoused for all Indians. Also, the suspicions that Charles had strayed from the marriage bed may have proved too much for the strait-laced New England lady. To Charles, his wife apparently became an unpleasant person to be around, never quite pleased with him. Consequently, their separation in 1921 was a welcomed escape for both parties because it was better than living a life together filled with bitterness, recrimination, and alienation. After the estrangement, Eastman was unable to publish any of his manuscripts because he had relied too heavily on his wife's editorial revisions, which he nevertheless despised. Many of his works published before 1921 continued to be popular and were frequently cited and quoted. Their popularity continues to this day.

In the 1960s, a decade of rediscovery of Native Americans, Eastman's memory was revived. Two scholarships were established for Indian students enrolled in schools of medicine. One, the Dr. Charles Ohiyesa Eastman Scholarship, organized in Minneapolis, Minnesota, was short-lived due to lack of funds, but did aid a few Indian nursing students. The other, the Charles A. Eastman Fellowship, had a better financial foundation. The Association of American Indian Affairs and Mead Johnson and Company each pledged $4,500 to provide three $3,000 stipends for first-year American Indian medical students. In 1973, the program was extended for another year.[24]

Charles Eastman's career was long and varied. Too much emphasis can be placed on the personal problems he experienced as an Indian operating in an alien culture, but they also reveal poignantly the failures of a man whose youth was filled with promise. A man who could wear both a war bonnet and a high starched collar with equal aplomb

was also quite capable of messing up his finances, having encounters
with women, and generally failing to remain the symbolic figure so
many others wanted him to be.

It was never easy to be the most prominent Indian of one's day.
The white world of the reformers and their middle class respectabil-
ity, as well as the educated Indian world, demanded much from
Charles Eastman. To a remarkable degree Eastman internalized the
paradigms of his class, yet he always remained the Indian in mufti.
He must have known he was a symbolic figure and he struggled
mightily with the consequences of that realization. Just as "blanket
Indians" were paraded before audiences to entertain, Eastman was
paraded before more polite audiences to edify, a living vindication of
the reformers' dream. But Eastman, unlike many of his white contemporaries, was a romantic about the old Indian life, a romantic
about Christianity and the white world. The old Indian life he con-
jured up was more romantic than real, which other educated Indians
such as Arthur C. Parker knew very well. But Parker was an ethnologist and had not spent his youth in the deep woods, a world that had
its own integrity but was not the Eden Eastman pictured. Similarly,
the white world was not about to become the embodiment of universal brotherhood. Eastman had caught a glimmer of its potential
while a student at Dartmouth, but that world had never been, nor
would it ever be, a larger version of his years in the Ivy League, where
he had only been a visitor.

Eastman the romantic put himself time and time again under the
thumb of the Bureau of Indian Affairs. He wandered into situations
he could not control despite his idealism, wading into the troubled
waters of Indian administration and getting caught in the undertow.
Work in the bureau required a surfeit of political savvy, something
Eastman was in desperate need of.

Eastman wanted to be the winner, to win the race, and be judged
a champion, and to a great extent he was a winner, yet he kept casting
himself as a loser. And in the end he became the winner lost. The era
that created him and sustained him—the era of the Dawes Act and
the final defeat of the Plains tribes—was passing. His pen failed him.
His wife chose to fight for the old standard of assimilation where the
Indian would be destroyed but the man saved. The new reformers,
the John Colliers, spoke about "warriors without weapons" and

sought useful object lessons for the rest of modern technological society in the pleasures and simple living of the pastoral Indian people of the American Southwest. The Sioux were no longer important symbolically. At the end of his long life Eastman withdrew—a very Indian thing to do. He could no longer live the expectations of others in the white world; he could no longer return to the deep woods. He lived instead alone and on an island, his most symbolic act.

NOTES

1. See Hebard to Eastman, Oct. 9, 1925, Hebard Papers, Box 17; Eastman to Hebard, Oct. 21, 1925, ibid.; Hebard to Eastman, Oct. 28, 1925, ibid.; Hebard to Eastman, Dec. 19, 1925, ibid.; Hebard to Eastman, July 14, 1926, ibid.; Hebard to Eastman, Sept. 7, 1927, ibid.; Hebard to Eastman, May 14, 1928, ibid.; Eastman to Hebard, May 17, 1929, ibid.; Hebard to Eastman, May 29, 1929, ibid.

2. See *Great Falls Tribune*, Mar. 27, 1949; Apr. 3, 10, 17, 1949.

3. Eastman to Hebard, Oct. 21, 1925, Hebard Papers, Box 17.

4. Charles A. Eastman Folder, Baker Library; *Standard Times* (New Bedford), Feb. 6, 1949.

5. *New York Times*, Nov. 29, 1925.

6. Ibid.; *New York Times*, Jan. 30, 1927; *Christian Science Monitor*, Jan. 23, 1928. See also Charles A. Eastman Folder, Baker Library.

7. *New York Times*, Jan. 30, 1927; Charles A. Eastman Folder, Baker Library; Stanley Edwards Johnson, "The Indian Ohiyesa," *Dartmouth Alumni Magazine* (June, 1929): 521–23.

8. Eastman to Hebard, May 17, 1929, Hebard Papers, Box 17.

9. Dr. Herbert B. Fowler, interview, Portland, Ore., Oct. 21, 1976.

10. Charles A. Eastman Folder, Baker Library; *Christian Science Monitor*, Jan. 23, 1928; Eastman to Hitchcock, Jan. 14, 1935, Hitchcock Papers.

11. Eastman to Hitchcock, Sept. 8, 1927, Hitchcock Papers; Eastman to Hitchcock, Sept. 21, 1930, ibid.; Dr. Charles A. Eastman Biography, Minneapolis Collection, Minneapolis Public Library, Minneapolis, Minnesota.

12. Prince Albert De Ligne, "Father Louis Hennepin, Belgian," *Minnesota History* 11 (Dec., 1930): 348; "Minnesota Historical Society Notes," *Minnesota History* 11 (Dec., 1930): 438; Charles A. Eastman Folder, Baker Library.

13. Eastman to Hitchcock, Sept. 29, 1930, Hitchcock Papers.

14. *Christian Science Monitor*, Sept. 22, 1933; Hertzberg, *The Search for an American Indian Identity*, pp. 231–33.
15. U.S., Bureau of Indian Affairs, "Doctor Henry Roe Cloud, Winner of Indian Achievement Medal," *Indians at Work* 3 (Nov. 15, 1935): 31.
16. Dr. Herbert B. Fowler, interview, Portland, Ore., Dec. 26, 1976. See Mrs. Eastman's letters during the 1930s to the Indian Rights Association as examples of her hostility toward Collier and the Indian Reorganization Act.
17. Eastman to Hitchcock, Jan. 14, 1935, Hitchcock Papers.
18. Dr. Herbert B. Fowler, interview, Portland, Ore., Nov. 15, 1976.
19. Ibid.
20. Dr. F. W. Hyde, Jr., director of Grace Hospital, to author, Sept. 17, 1975. See also Charles A. Eastman Folder, Baker Library; U.S., Bureau of Indian Affairs, "Dr. Charles A. Eastman, Prominent Sioux, Dies," *Indians at Work* 6 (May, 1939): 44.
21. *New York Times*, Dec. 23, 1953. Besides the Sacajawea article, Mrs. Eastman published some of his other manuscripts in *Standard Times* (New Bedford), Jan. 27–Apr. 24, 1949, and in *The Rotarian*, Feb., 1950.
22. Hertzberg, *The Search for an American Indian Identity*, p. 42.
23. Oliver Eastman, interview, Sisseton, S.D., Apr. 23, 1979. See also the last two chapters of David R. Miller, "Charles Alexander Eastman: One Man's Journey in Two Worlds," (M.A. thesis, University of North Dakota, 1975). Primarily employing the several stages of revitalization espoused by Dr. Anthony F. C. Wallace, Miller attempts to apply these phases to Eastman's life. While some parallels can be drawn, others are forced. Nevertheless, Miller has written an interesting thesis.
24. Mrs. A. E. Newcom, Mead and Johnson and Company, to author, Apr. 3, 1979; Dr. Thomas W. Milroy, Aberdeen Area Indian Health Service, to author, Apr. 9, 1979; Thomas W. Milroy, "A Physician by the Name of Ohiyesa: Charles Alexander Eastman, M.D.," *Minnesota Medicine* 5 (July, 1971): 572.

BIBLIOGRAPHY

Archival Material

GOVERNMENT DEPOSITORIES

Kansas City, Mo. Federal Archives and Records Center.
  Records of the Bureau of Indian Affairs, Record Group 75, Standing
    Rock Agency, 1890.
  Records of the Bureau of Indian Affairs, Record Group 75, Pine Ridge
    Agency, 1890–93.
  Records of the Bureau of Indian Affairs, Record Group 75, Crow Creek
    Agency, 1900–1903.
St. Louis, Mo. National Personnel Records Center.
  Dr. Charles A. Eastman Status Records.
Washington, D.C. National Archives and Records Service.
  Records of the Bureau of Indian Affairs, Record Group 75, Letters Re-
    ceived, 1881–1907.
  Records of the Bureau of Indian Affairs, Record Group 75, Letters Sent,
    1870–1908.
  Records of the Bureau of Indian Affairs, Record Group 75, Central
    Files, 1907–39.
  Dr. Charles A. Eastman Special Agent File, 1923–25, Records of the
    Bureau of Indian Affairs, Record Group 75.
  Special Case Number 188, The Ghost Dance, 1890–98, Records of the
    Bureau of Indian Affairs, Record Group 75.

OTHER DEPOSITORIES

Albany, N.Y. New York State Museum. Arthur C. Parker Papers.
Albuquerque, N.M. History Department, University of New Mexico.
  Doris Duke Oral History Project.
Amherst, Mass. Jones Public Library. Charles A. Eastman Folder.

_____. Jones Public Library. Elaine Goodale Eastman Folder.

_____. Jones Public Library. Irene Taluta Eastman Folder.

Chicago, Ill. Ayer Collection, The Newberry Library. H. M. Hitchcock Papers.

Columbus, Oh. Ohio State Historical Society. Warren King Moorehead Papers.

Hanover, N.H. Baker Library, Dartmouth College. Class of 1887 Merit Roll Book.

_____. Baker Library, Dartmouth College. Charles A. Eastman Folder.

Haverford, Penn. Lake Mohonk Conferences, Quaker Collection, Haverford College. Smiley Family Papers.

Laramie, Wyo. Center for Western Studies, University of Wyoming. Grace Raymond Hebard Papers.

Lincoln, Nebr. Nebraska State Historical Society. Judge Eli S. Ricker Collection.

Los Angeles, Calif. University of Southern California Library. Hamlin Garland Collection.

Madison, Wisc. State Historical Society of Wisconsin. Carlos Montezuma Papers.

Minneapolis, Minn. Minneapolis Collection, Minneapolis Public Library. Dr. Charles A. Eastman Biography.

_____. Minneapolis Collection, Minneapolis Public Library. Mary Nancy Eastman Biography.

New Haven, Conn. Beinecke Rare Book and Manuscript Library, Yale University. Richard Henry Pratt Papers.

New York, N.Y. Young Men's Christian Associations Historical Library. Charles A. Eastman Materials.

Northampton, Mass. Sophia Smith Collection (Women's History Archive), Smith College Library. Eastman Collection.

Philadelphia, Penn. Historical Society of Pennsylvania. Indian Rights Association Papers, 1886–1901, Scholarly Resources.

_____. Historical Society of Pennsylvania. Indian Rights Association Papers, 1868–1968, Microfilming Corporation of America.

Richardton, N.D. Assumption Abbey Archives. James McLaughlin Papers.

Santa Fe, N.M. History Library and Archives, Museum of New Mexico. Eugenie F. Shonnard Collection.

Vermillion, S.D. History Department, University of South Dakota. Doris Duke Oral History Project.

Williamstown, Mass. Williams College Library. Samuel Chapman Armstrong Collection.

Unpublished Material

THESES AND DISSERTATIONS

D'Agostino, Fred. "Parenthetical Person." M.A. qualifying thesis. Princeton University, 1973.

Gilcreast, Everett Arthur. "Richard Henry Pratt and American Indian Policy, 1877–1906: A Study of the Assimilation Movement." Ph.D. dissertation. Yale University, 1967.

Mensel, Ernst Jerome. "John, Charles and Elaine Goodale Eastman—A Contribution to the American Indian." B.A. thesis. Dartmouth College, 1954.

Miller, David R. "Charles Alexander Eastman: One Man's Journey in Two Worlds." M.A. thesis. University of North Dakota, 1975.

Ryan, Carmelita S. "The Carlisle Indian Industrial School." Ph.D. dissertation. Georgetown University, 1962.

INTERVIEWS

Note:

Several informants who were interviewed wished to remain anonymous.

Eastman, Oliver. Sisseton, S.D. Apr. 23, 1979.

Fowler, Dr. Herbert B. Portland, Ore. Oct. 14 and 21, 1976; Nov. 15, 1976; Dec. 26, 1976.

Jones, Bessie. Flandreau, S.D. May 14, 1978.

Moore, Grace. Flandreau, S.D. May 14, 1978.

LETTERS TO AUTHOR

Ewing, James D. Keene, N.H. May 3, 1976.

Haring, Mrs. Philip S. Galesburg, Ill. Sept. 9, 1975.

Hertzberg, Hazel W. New York, N.Y. May 6, 1975.

Hyde, Dr. F. W., Jr. Detroit, Mich. Sept. 17, 1975.

Irrmann, Robert H. Beloit, Wisc. May 22, 1975.

Keefer, Dorothy C. Boston, Mass. June 24, 1976.

Lowell, Blake J. Parma, Idaho. Mar. 8 and 21, 1976.

Milroy, Dr. Thomas W. Aberdeen, S.D. Apr. 9, 1979.

Newcom, Mrs. A. E. Evansville, Ind. Apr. 3, 1979.

Turner, Frederick W. III. Shutesbury, Mass. Apr. 30, 1975.

Wallace, William C. Caldwell, Idaho. Mar. 4, 1976.

Published Material

PRINTED GOVERNMENT SOURCES

Medawakanton Indians et al. v. U.S. *Court of Claims, Cases Decided* 57, 1921–22.

Sisseton and Wahpeton Indians v. U.S. *Court of Claims, Cases Decided* 42, 1906–7.

U.S. Bureau of Indian Affairs. "Dr. Charles A. Eastman, Prominent Sioux, Dies," *Indians at Work* 6 (May, 1939): 44.

U.S. Bureau of Indian Affairs. "Doctor Henry Roe Cloud, Winner of Indian Achievement Medal," *Indians at Work* 3 (Nov. 15, 1935): 31.

U.S. Commissioner of Indian Affairs. *Annual Reports*, 1856, 1868, 1869, 1874, 1888, 1890, 1891, 1892, 1893, 1900, 1901, 1902, 1903.

U.S. Congress. House. *Indian Citizenship Bill.* House Executive Document No. 228, 43th Cong., 1st sess., Vol. 16, Apr. 24, 1874.

U.S. Congress. House. Subcommittee on Indian Affairs. *Peyote Hearings,* 65th Cong., 2d sess., 1918.

U.S. Congress. House. Subcommittee on Indian Affairs. *Restoration of Annuities to Medawakanton and Wahpakoota (Santee) Sioux Indians, Hearings,* 64th Cong., 1st sess., 1916.

U.S. *Congressional Record,* 67th Cong., 4th sess., Vol. 64, Pt. 4, 1923.

Mooney, James. "The Ghost Dance Religion and the Sioux Outbreak of 1890." *Fourteenth Annual Report of the Bureau of American Ethnology.* Washington: Government Printing Office, 1896.

Work, Hubert W. *Indian Policies: Comments on the Resolutions of the Advisory Council on Indian Affairs.* Washington: Government Printing Office, 1924.

PROCEEDINGS AND PAMPHLETS

The Fourteenth Annual Report of the Executive Committee of the Indian Rights Association. Philadelphia: Indian Rights Association, 1897.

Proceedings of the Annual Meetings of the Lake Mohonk Conference of Friends of the Indian, 1890–1916.

Record of the Proceedings of the First Universal Races Congress. London: A. S. King & Son, 1911.

Welsh, Herbert. *Civilization among the Sioux Indians.* Philadelphia: Indian Rights Association, 1893.

NEWSPAPERS

Christian Science Monitor
Great Falls Tribune
Guymon Herald (Oklahoma)
Holloway Herald (Minnesota)
New York Evening Post
New York Times
Minneapolis Journal
Niobrara Tribune
Omaha Daily Bee
Omaha World Herald
The Red Man
Sioux Falls Daily Press
Standard Times (New Bedford)
The Times (London)

MAGAZINES AND JOURNALS

ALA *Booklist*
American Indian Magazine
American Review of Reviews
Dartmouth Alumni Magazine
The Nation
Quarterly Journal of The Society of American Indians

BOOKS

Barton, Winifred W. *John P. Williamson: A Brother to the Sioux.* New York: Fleming H. Revell, 1919.

Copeland, Marion W. *Charles Alexander Eastman.* (Boise State University Western Writers Series). Caldwell: Caxton Printers, 1978.

Eastman, Charles Alexander (Ohiyesa). *From the Deep Woods to Civilization: Chapters in the Autobiography of an Indian.* Boston: Little, Brown, 1916.

———. *Indian Boyhood.* New York: Dover Publications, 1971 (originally published in 1902).

———. *Indian Child Life.* Boston: Little, Brown, 1913.

———. *Indian Heroes and Great Chieftains.* Boston: Little, Brown, 1918.

———. *Indian Scout Talks: A Guide for Boy Scouts and Camp Fire Girls.* Boston: Little, Brown, 1914.

————. *Old Indian Days*. New York: McClure, 1907.

————. *Red Hunters and the Animal People*. New York: Harper & Brothers, 1904.

————, and Eastman, Elaine Goodale. *Smoky Day's Wigwam Evenings: Indian Stories Retold*. Boston: Little, Brown, 1910.

————. *The Indian Today: The Past and Future of the First American*. Garden City: Doubleday, Page, 1915.

————. *The Soul of the Indian: An Interpretation*. New York: Johnson Reprint Corporation, 1971 (originally published in 1911).

————, and Eastman, Elaine Goodale. *Wigwam Evenings: Sioux Folk Tales Retold*. Boston: Little, Brown, 1909.

Eastman, Elaine Goodale. *Indian Legends Retold*. Boston: Little, Brown, 1919.

————. *Pratt, The Red Man Moses*. Norman: University of Oklahoma Press, 1935.

Eastman, Mary. *Dahcotah: Or, Life and Legends of the Sioux around Fort Snelling*. New York: n.p., 1849.

Ellis, Richard N., ed. *The Western American Indian: Case Studies in Tribal History*. Lincoln: University of Nebraska Press, 1972.

Faris, John T. *Men Who Conquered*. New York: Books for Libraries Press, 1968.

Folwell, William Watts. *A History of Minnesota*. 4 vols. St. Paul: Minnesota Historical Society, 1961.

Fritz, Henry E. *The Movement for Indian Assimilation, 1860–1890*. Philadelphia: University of Pennsylvania Press, 1963.

Garland, Hamlin. *Companions on the Trail*. New York: Macmillan, 1931.

————. *The Book of the American Indian*. New York: Harper & Brothers, 1923.

Gilman, S. C. *Christian Work among the Dakota Indians*. Indianapolis: Carlon & Hollenbeck, 1894.

————. *The Conquest of the Sioux*. Indianapolis: Carlon & Hollenbeck, 1897.

Goodale, Elaine, and Goodale, Dora A. *Apple Blossoms: Verses of Two Children*. New York: G. P. Putnam's Sons, 1878.

Graber, Kay, ed. *Sister to the Sioux: The Memoirs of Elaine Goodale Eastman, 1885–91*. Lincoln: University of Nebraska Press, 1978.

Gridley, Marion E., ed. *Indians of Today*. Chicago: Lakeside Press, 1936.

Hagan, William T. *American Indians*. Chicago: University of Chicago Press, 1961.

Hamilton, Charles, ed. *Cry of the Thunderbird: The American Indian's Own Story*. New York: Macmillan, 1935.

Hart, James D. *The Oxford Companion to American Literature*. New York: Oxford University Press, 1965.

Hassrick, Royal B. *The Sioux: Life and Customs of a Warrior Society*. Norman: University of Oklahoma Press, 1964.

Hebard, Grace Raymond. *Sacajawea*. Glendale: Arthur Clark, 1933.

Hertzberg, Hazel W. *The Search for an American Indian Identity: Modern Pan-Indian Movements*. Syracuse: Syracuse University Press, 1971.

Hetrick, Barbara, and Levitan, Sar A. *Big Brother's Indian Programs, with Reservations*. New York: McGraw-Hill, 1971.

Howard, Harold P. *Sacajawea*. Norman: University of Oklahoma Press, 1971.

Hughes, Thomas. *Indian Chiefs of Southern Minnesota*. Mankato: Free Press, 1927.

Hyde, George. *A Sioux Chronicle*. Norman: University of Oklahoma Press, 1956.

————. *Spotted Tail's Folk: A History of the Brule Sioux*. Norman: University of Oklahoma Press, 1961.

Johnson, Fletcher W. *The Red Record of the Sioux Sitting Bull and the History of the Indian War of 1890*. Philadelphia: Edgewood, 1891.

Kunitz, Stanley J., and Haycroft, Howard, eds. *The Junior Book of Authors*. New York: H. W. Wilson, 1951.

Leupp, Francis E. *The Indian and His Problem*. New York: Charles Scribner's Sons, 1910.

McDermott, John Francis. *Seth Eastman: Pictorial Historian of the Indian*. Norman: University of Oklahoma Press, 1961.

McLaughlin, James. *My Friend the Indian*. Boston: Houghton Mifflin, 1926.

Mardock, Robert Winston. *The Reformers and the American Indian*. Columbia: University of Missouri Press, 1971.

Marriott, Alice, and Rachlin, Carol K. *American Epic: The Story of the American Indian*. New York: G. P. Putnam's Sons, 1969.

Meyer, Roy W. *History of the Santee Sioux: United States Indian Policy on Trial*. Lincoln: University of Nebraska Press, 1967.

Momaday, Natachee Scott. *American Indian Authors*. Boston: Houghton Mifflin, 1972.

Mooney, James. *The Ghost-Dance Religion and the Sioux Outbreak of 1890*. Chicago: University of Chicago Press, 1965.

Moorehead, Warren K. *The American Indian in the United States*. Andover: Andover Press, 1914.

Morse, Robert C. *My Life with Young Men: Fifty Years in the Young*

Men's Christian Association. New York: Association Press, 1918.

Nash, Roderick. *Wilderness and the American Mind.* New Haven: Yale University Press, 1973.

Nurge, Ethel, ed. *The Modern Sioux: Social Systems and Reservation Culture.* Lincoln: University of Nebraska Press, 1965.

Olson, James C. *Red Cloud and the Sioux Problem.* Lincoln: University of Nebraska Press, 1965.

Patterson, Robert; Mebel, Mildred; and Hill, Lawrence. *On Our Way: Young Pages from American Autobiography.* New York: Holiday House, 1952.

Pizer, Donald, ed. *Hamlin Garland's Diaries.* San Marino: Huntington Library, 1968.

Priest, Loring Benson. *Uncle Sam's Stepchildren: The Reformation of United States Indian Policy, 1865–1887.* Lincoln: University of Nebraska Press, 1975.

Prucha, Francis Paul. *American Indian Policy in Crisis: Christian Reformers and the Indian, 1865–1900.* Norman: University of Oklahoma Press, 1976.

————, ed. *Americanizing the American Indians: Writings by the "Friends of the Indian," 1880–1900.* Cambridge: Harvard University Press, 1973.

Riggs, Stephen R. *Mary and I: Forty Years with the Sioux.* Chicago: W. G. Holmes, 1880.

Sheehan, Bernard W. *Seeds of Extinction: Jeffersonian Philanthropy and the American Indian.* New York: W. W. Norton, 1974.

Seton, Ernest Thompson. *The Book of Woodcraft.* New York: Doubleday, Page, 1922.

————. *The Gospel of the Red Man: An Indian Bible.* Garden City: Doubleday, Doran, 1936.

————. *Trail of an Artist-Naturalist.* London: Hodder and Stoughton, 1951.

Spiller, Gustav, ed. *Inter-Racial Problems: Papers from the First Universal Races Congress Held in London in 1911.* New York: Citadel Press, 1970.

Standing Bear, Luther. *Land of the Spotted Eagle.* Lincoln: University of Nebraska Press, 1978.

————. *My People the Sioux.* Lincoln: University of Nebraska Press, 1975.

Underhill, Lonnie E., and Littlefield, Daniel F., Jr., eds. *Hamlin Garland's Observations on the American Indian, 1895–1905.* Tucson: University of Arizona Press, 1976.

Utley, Robert M. *Frontier Regulars: The United States Army and the Indian, 1866–1891.* New York: Macmillan, 1973.

————. *The Last Days of the Sioux Nation.* New Haven: Yale University Press, 1963.

Vestal, Stanley. *Sitting Bull, Champion of the Sioux.* Norman: University of Oklahoma Press, 1957.

Washburn, Wilcomb E., ed. *The American Indian and the United States.* 4 vols. New York: Random House, 1973.

————. *The Assault on Indian Tribalism: The General Allotment Law (Dawes Act) of 1887.* Philadelphia: J. B. Lippincott, 1975.

Zitkala-Sa (Bonnin, Gertrude). *American Indian Stories.* Glorieta, N.M.: Rio Grande Press, 1976.

ARTICLES

Anderson, Irving W. "Sacajawea, Sacagawea, Sakakawea," *South Dakota History* 8 (Fall, 1978): 303–11.

Babcock, Willoughby M., Jr. "Major Lawrence Taliaferro, Indian Agent," *Mississippi Valley Historical Review* 11 (Dec., 1924): 358–75.

Blegen, Theodore C. "The Pond Brothers," *Minnesota History* 15 (Sept., 1934): 273–81.

Crawford, Helen. "Sakakawea," *North Dakota Historical Quarterly* 1 (Apr., 1927): 5–15.

Crissey, Forrest. "Renaming the Indians," *World Today* 10 (Jan., 1906): 84–90.

De Ligne, Prince Albert. "Father Louis Hennepin, Belgian," *Minnesota History* 11 (Dec., 1930): 343–51.

Drury, Clifford M. "Sacajawea's Death—1812 or 1884?" *Oregon Historical Quarterly* 62 (Sept., 1961): 288–91.

Eastman, Charles Alexander (Ohiyesa). "A Canoe Trip among the Northern Ojibways," *The Red Man* 3 (Feb., 1911): 236–44.

————. "A Half-Forgotten Lincoln Story." *The Rotarian* 76 (Feb., 1950): 34.

————. "A Review of the Indian Citizenship Bills," *American Indian Magazine* 6 (Winter, 1919): 181–83.

————. "Camping with Indians," *The Teepee Book* I (Sept., 1915): 223–30.

————. "Education without Books," *The Craftsman* 21 (Jan., 1912): 372–77.

————. "First Impressions of Civilization," *Harpers Magazine* 108 (Mar., 1904): 587–92.

———. "Great Spirit," *American Indian Teepee* 1 (1920): 3–4.

———. "Hakadah's First Offering," *Current Literature* 34 (Jan., 1903): 29–32.

———. "How To Make Wigwams and Shelters," *Boys' Life* (June, 1914): 18.

———. "Indian Handicrafts," *The Craftsman* 8 (Aug., 1905): 658–62.

———. "Justice for the Sioux," *American Indian Magazine* 7 (Summer, 1919): 79–81.

———. "My People: The Indian's Contribution to the Art of America," *The Craftsman* 27 (Nov., 1914): 179–86.

———. "My People: The Indian's Contribution to the Art of America," *The Red Man* 7 (Dec., 1914): 133–40.

———. "Rain-In-The-Face, The Story of a Sioux Warrior," *The Outlook* 84 (Oct. 27, 1906): 507–12.

———. "Rain-In-The-Face, The Story of a Sioux Warrior," *The Teepee Book* II (June, 1916): 577–78, 645–47.

———. "Recollections of the Wild Life," *St. Nicholas: An Illustrated Magazine for Young Folks* 21 (Dec., 1893–May, 1894): 129–31, 226–28, 306–8, 437–40, 513–15, 607–11.

———. "Report on Sacajawea," *Annals of Wyoming* 13 (July, 1941): 187–94.

———. "Stories Back of Indian Names," *Boys' Life* (Dec., 1914): 21.

———. "The American Eagle: An Indian Symbol," *American Indian Magazine* 7 (Summer, 1919): 89–92.

———. "The Gray Chieftain," *Harpers Magazine* 108 (May, 1904): 882–87.

———. "The Great Cat's Nursery," *Harpers Magazine* 107 (Nov., 1903): 939–46.

———. "The Indian and the Moral Code," *The Outlook* 97 (Jan. 7, 1911): 30–34.

———. "The Indian as a Citizen," *Lippincott's Magazine* 95 (Jan., 1915): 70–76.

———. "The Indian's Gift to the Nation," *Quarterly Journal of The Society of American Indians* 3 (Jan.–Mar., 1915): 17–23.

———. "The Indian's Health Problem," *Popular Science Monthly* 86 (Jan., 1915): 49–54.

———. "The Indian's Health Problem," *American Review of Reviews* 51 (Feb., 1915): 240–41.

———. "The Indian's Health Problem," *American Indian Magazine* 4 (Apr.–June, 1916): 139–45.

————. "The Indian's Plea for Freedom," *American Indian Magazine* 6 (Winter, 1919): 162–65.

————. "The Language of Footprints," *St. Nicholas* 44 (Jan., 1917): 267–69.

————. "The Mustering of the Herds," *Out West* 21 (Nov., 1904): 439–45.

————. "The School Days of an Indian," *The Outlook* 85 (Apr. 13 and 20, 1907): 851–55, 894–99.

————. "The Sioux Mythology," *Popular Science Monthly* 46 (Nov., 1894): 88–91.

————. "The Sioux of Yesterday and Today," *American Indian Magazine* 5 (Winter, 1917): 233–39.

————. "The Song of the Birch Canoe," *The Craftsman* 23 (Oct., 1912): 3–11.

————. "The Story of the Little Big Horn," *The Chautauquan* 31 (July, 1900): 353–58.

————. "The War Maiden of the Sioux," *Ladies' Home Journal* 23 (Aug., 1906): 14.

————. "What Can the Out-of-Doors Do for Our Children?" *Education* 41 (1920–21): 599–605.

Eastman, Elaine Goodale. "All the Days of My Life," *South Dakota Historical Review* 2 (July, 1937): 171–84.

————. "Tales of the Indian Life," *Nebraska History* 21 (Apr., 1940): 125–26.

————. "The Ghost Dance and Wounded Knee Massacre of 1890–91," *Nebraska History* 26 (Jan., 1945): 26–42.

Feraca, Stephen E., and Howard, James H. "The Identity and Demography of the Dakota or Sioux Tribe," *Plains Anthropologist* 8 (May, 1963): 80–84.

Fowler, Herbert B. "Ohiyesa, The First Sioux M.D.," *Association of American Indian Physicians Newsletter* 4 (Apr., 1976): 1, 6.

Guenther, Richard L. "The Santee Normal Training School," *Nebraska History* 51 (Fall, 1970): 359–78.

Hawthorne, Hildegarde. "Over the Border," *St. Nicholas* 39 (Jan., 1912): 283–85.

Hebard, Grace Raymond. "Pilot of First White Men to Cross the American Continent," *Journal of American History* 1 (1907): 467–84.

Howard, Helen Addison. "The Mystery of Sacagawea's Death," *Pacific Northwest Quarterly* 58 (Jan., 1967): 1–6.

Johnson, Stanley Edwards. "The Indian Ohiyesa," *Dartmouth Alumni Magazine* (June, 1929): 521–23.

Littlefield, Daniel F., Jr., and Underhill, Lonnie E. "Renaming the American Indian: 1890–1913," *American Studies* 12 (Fall, 1971): 33–45.

Milroy, Thomas W. "A Physician by the Name of Ohiyesa: Charles Alexander Eastman, M.D.," *Minnesota Medicine* 5 (July, 1971): 569–72.

"Minnesota Historical Society Notes," *Minnesota History* 11 (Dec., 1930): 438.

Moses, L. G. "James Mooney and Wovoka: An Ethnologist's Visit With the Ghost Dance Prophet," *Nevada Historical Society Quarterly* 23 (Summer, 1980): 71–86.

"News and Comment," *Minnesota Historical Society Bulletin* 3 (Nov., 1919): 230.

Taber, Ronald W. "Sacajawea and the Suffragettes: An Interpretation of a Myth," *Pacific Northwest Quarterly* 58 (Jan., 1967): 7–13.

Taliaferro, Lawrence. "Auto-biography of Major Lawrence Taliaferro, Written in 1864," *Collections of the Minnesota Historical Society* 6 (1887–94): 189–225.

Weatherford, John W. "Warren King Moorehead and His Papers," *Ohio Historical Quarterly* 65 (Apr., 1956): 179–90.

Wilson, Raymond. "The Writings of Ohiyesa—Charles Alexander Eastman, M.D., Santee Sioux," *South Dakota History* 6 (Winter, 1975): 55–73.

————. "Dr. Charles A. Eastman's Report on the Economic Conditions of the Osage Indians in Oklahoma, 1924," *Chronicles of Oklahoma* 55 (Fall, 1977): 343–45.

————. "Forty Years to Judgment: The Santee Sioux Claims Case," *Minnesota History* 47 (Fall, 1981): 284–91.

INDEX

A NOTE ON THE AUTHOR

Raymond Wilson, Assistant Professor of History at Fort Hays State University, is the author of numerous articles and papers on western history, especially Native American history. After receiving his Bachelor's degree from Fort Lewis College and his Master's degree from the University of Nebraska, Omaha, he earned his doctorate from the University of New Mexico in 1977.